THE LIFE AND WORK OF ANTE DABRO, AUSTRALIAN-CROATIAN SCULPTOR

THE LIFE AND WORK OF ANTE DABRO, AUSTRALIAN-CROATIAN SCULPTOR

THE MIDNIGHT SEA IN THE BLOOD

PETER READ

ANTHEM PRESS

Anthem Press
An imprint of Wimbledon Publishing Company
www.anthempress.com

This edition first published in UK and USA 2023
by ANTHEM PRESS
75–76 Blackfriars Road, London SE1 8HA, UK
or PO Box 9779, London SW19 7ZG, UK
and
244 Madison Ave #116, New York, NY 10016, USA

© 2023 Peter Read

The author asserts the moral right to be identified as the author of this work.

All rights reserved. Without limiting the rights under copyright reserved above, no
part of this publication may be reproduced, stored or introduced into a retrieval
system, or transmitted, in any form or by any means (electronic, mechanical,
photocopying, recording or otherwise), without the prior written permission of both
the copyright owner and the above publisher of this book.

British Library Cataloguing-in-Publication Data
A catalogue record for this book is available from the British Library.

Library of Congress Control Number: 2023941826
A catalog record for this book has been requested.

ISBN-13: 978-1-83998-992-6 (Hbk)
ISBN-10: 1-83998-992-0 (Hbk)

Cover Credit: Genesis, Canberra Airport

This title is also available as an e-book.

TO STILL THE MIDNIGHT SEA IN THE BLOOD

You did what you could
To make a mark on stone like a mark in time
That the desolation of the mind and the midnight sea in the blood
Should be less of a desolation for the men to come
And who can do more than you [...]?

Douglas Stewart, *Rock Carving*

CONTENTS

Author's Preface		xi
Photographer's Preface		xiii
Acknowledgements		xv
Introduction: Making a Mark in Stone		**1**
CHAPTER 1	**Making the Outsider**	**9**
CHAPTER 2	**Making the Artist**	**25**
CHAPTER 3	**Making the Australian**	**61**
CHAPTER 4	**Making the Human Form**	**101**
CHAPTER 5	**Making Bronze**	**109**
CHAPTER 6	**Making Sculptors**	**131**
CHAPTER 7	**Making Commissions**	**145**
CHAPTER 8	**Making Behemoths**	**161**
CHAPTER 9	**Making Way**	**187**
Notes		199
Works Consulted		207
Index		213

AUTHOR'S PREFACE

Sixty years ago, the Australian poet Judith Wright discussed what she called the dangerous division between ourselves and our own real nature. She wrote:

> We think of ourselves as prosaic and rational beings, and starve ourselves deliberately into being so – forgetting that, like our ancestors, we contain also the power of joy and creation, as well as the capacity for the sober evaluation of facts, and forgetting that we have an inherited right in the principle of poetry as well as the principle of prose.

'The ability to see what other people don't see is a real gift. It's like a star wheeling round the earth, fertilising the imagination as it goes'. These words were said to me, during one of our many interviews, by the sculptor Ante Dabro. Yet when writing historical academic articles I have often felt as though I've been imprisoned in that block of marble that Michelangelo frequently referred to, awaiting release as the sculptor carves away the outside material to give light to the spirit. So in this work, my frequent allusions to other forms of creative thought exemplify how artists and dancers, sculptors and composers, ceramicists and singers, novelists and playwrights, each follow and share their intuitive visions to release us and enlarge our humanity. So, too, can historians if they allow their imagination and emotions to soar before the work of the intellect redirects them to the footnotes.

My purpose here is to rejoice in the intuitive moment, not to celebrate Dabro's every sculpture but to magnify the creative act, that leap into the abyss, which sustains his vision and that of every artist who has shared the principle of poetry with us since humans first walked the earth.

This book is a hymn to the humanities.

March 2023

PHOTOGRAPHER'S PREFACE

I began this photography project casually imagining a bronze sculpture as being an immutable solid, which is separate from its immediate context – a kind of corporeal hologram which floats in neutral space.

In reality, the camera captures a moment of light that bounces off the patina. In the process, it flattens three dimensions into two dimensions.

In situ, most of Ante's sculptures receive highly variable daily, seasonal and artificial light. At times, intense light is reflected from adjacent surfaces. With oblique light sources, shadows become darker, and highlights are intensified. Altering the direction and intensity of the source alters the appearance of a sculpture.

The sculptures have physical public or domestic contexts: skyscrapers, parked cars, kids playing, construction cranes, suburban houses and even discarded rubbish. These pull at the eye and stretch a sculpture's look.

Rain, spider webs, bird droppings, graffiti and ageing patinas may add their measure.

Thus, for the camera's sensors, sculptures in their natural habitats are shape-shifters.

As with the bust of Hercules, which was raised recently after 2,000 years from the seabed, once a sculpture leaves the studio it begins an unpredictable journey through light, place and circumstances. It may become simultaneously three different objects: that which the sculptor created, that which people see and that which the camera records.

Given these complexities, I gave priority to Peter's needs as an author. We worked together to ensure that the photos best complemented the text.

I am grateful to Peter for giving me this opportunity.

Con Boekel
Canberra
14 March 2023

ACKNOWLEDGEMENTS

I must first thank the artist and subject of this biography, Ante Dabro, himself. To be able to write the life of a living artist is a special privilege, not least to consider the technique, style and the meaning of the works themselves with their actual creator. I have discussed the meanings and technicalities of his works, and of sculpture generally, with him for over thirty years. I have learnt so much. I owe him deep thanks for engaging so wholeheartedly and for our many cordial differences in interpreting everything from the direction the eye follows in a sculpture to the ideological tendencies of Australian governments.

Con Boekel willingly undertook the task of photographing all the works that were available to be photographed in Canberra. Often this involved five or six trips to the same work in changing conditions. I thank him warmly for these painstaking efforts, and for our many discussions about each work, the available light, the best angles and whatever was in the background – and whether Ante would be happy with each one. This work would be much poorer without his joyful participation.

Janda Gooding brought her specialised knowledge of art and sculpture to the work. Other readers of parts or all of the manuscript included Vicky Dabro, Nicholas Brown, Andy Greenslade, Susan Boden-Brown, Marivic Wyndham, Mark McKenna, Jessie Read, Chantal Jackson. Thank you for your careful, considered and well-informed advice.

I particularly thank Jay, so well-practised in the poetry of words as well as of graphic art, who has lived with the project from the beginning and never failed to bring her calm wisdom to it.

Hospitality in the Dabro household is legendary. No session with Ante ever began without coffee, grappa and a slice of cake.

INTRODUCTION:
MAKING A MARK IN STONE

Ante Dabro arrives each day at his studio a little after nine. He bids good morning to the dozens of members of his sculptural family who, from 20 centimetres in height to 2.5 metres, crowd every space and nestle between the gas bottles and welding equipment. Now they fill the air with music: Dvorak, Liszt, Brahms, Bach for logical certainty, Mozart for cerebral serenity, Beethoven for passion. Dabro picks up the broom and keeps sweeping, along and around, until something catches his eye. He takes up the little tomahawk to continue on a recent work, the ironic plaster sculpture of a dozen quarter-size heads listening in awed silence to Karl Marx at his tomb in Highgate Cemetery, London. Such are the newest members of this diverse humanity. If Dabro is unhappy with them, they may not survive the day. In a corner, a bust of Sir Robert Garran threatens St Matthew, Churchill's head peers into a bag of plaster. Dozens of tiny figures in a Lilliputian throng disport in myriad contorted positions. The dominating image of *Mother and Child,* commissioned to adorn a mansion on the southeastern coast of Australia, indicates the imaginative force that created it. Dabro says of the work: 'The figures are energetic, as they have to be, but every inch of the work also is activated. Every square centimetre must bubble with emotion'. Michelangelo's dictum might well be inscribed on the studio wall: *What spirit is so empty and blind that it cannot recognize the fact that the foot is more noble than the shoe, and skin more beautiful than the garment with which it is clothed?*

The life and work of the Croatian-born Australian sculptor Ante Dabro, four centuries and twenty thousand kilometres from Michelangelo who inspired and inspires him, is a story of fierce devotion to the principles and values of the Italian Renaissance. Michelangelo's influence on him is so profound that his tomb is always the first point of obeisance on Dabro's regular trips to Florence. Frequently, he converses with the ancient master. Confiding

2   THE LIFE AND WORK OF ANTE DABRO

these conversations to me, and at his request, I have suggested these imaginary exchanges at intervals in the text.

Dabro's ideal sculpture is one that speaks clearly to humanity. This principle drives both his work and that of Michelangelo, which is to say, that if a sculpture is to speak to humanity, then it must *be* an element of humanity. Every work, Dabro maintains, must trigger an emotion. It must touch the viewer in some way or the sculptor has failed. Even the very few Dabro sculptures that might be called non-figurative imply a human form struggling to escape.

Dabro's sculptures are more directed than merely human: they are female, mostly nude. It is the compulsion to forever re-imagine the female form that drives his art.

> My models have something in common, and of one of these many elements is a sense of mystery. Like most artists, perhaps, I'm not trying to reproduce *this* model, but rather an essence of humanity, not necessarily a figure of beauty but of female-ness. As I'm working she [the sculpture] will begin to talk to me and I'll talk to her. There's a tension that I can't put into words. Almost like a dream. When I start I'm taken into a world that's not real. And it's a necessary mystery.

A large Dabro sculpture in bronze will be recognisable from 30 metres, a palm-size work in plaster from three. Over six decades he has colonised half a dozen styles, all recognisable as his own, but most of which he dismisses as now imprisoned by the emotions that he felt at the time of creation. The carved wooden sculptures of his first years in Australia he dismisses as over-decorated. A number of experimental styles in the 1970s in resin, marble and plaster drew on wider influences stored in his visual memory, from ancient Egypt, through Henry Moore to Rodin. Of some of these he muses, 'I don't know why I did them'. The sculptures of his children in the late 1970s and early 1980s that the critics and the buying public loved, he thinks now as too sentimental. The first of the massive, commissioned works, the Naval Memorial of 1985, drew on the closest attention to masters of the Italian Renaissance, as well as a hint of Yugoslavian Social Realism. At about this point, Dabro began to distrust his elegant and refined female nudes to produce works less classically beautiful. These were in part derived from images of the Croatian peasantry, stocky, tough and energetic, sometimes without limbs or heads, but all recognisably human and neatly described by one of his models as Romantic Brutalist. The metamorphosis continued. Two of his most massive and recent works at the Canberra Airport, *Dancer* and *Genesis,* which he considers among

Introduction: Making a Mark in Stone 3

his greatest, seem to be fully worked syntheses of the traditions of rural Croatia and Renaissance Italy. Sixty years of artistic enquiry have been generated by a prodigious skill set of abilities that allowed the artist to re-create the human figure in any style he chose. None of which, except the last, now satisfy him.

These abilities have enabled him to produce works of the most astounding diversity, all intimately connected to the relations between men and women. They range from the loving kiss depicted at the rear of *Resilience* to the orgasmic arched forms of *Genesis*. A little like William Blake, the biographer can only ponder, 'Did you, who created the exquisite study of your daughter *Sarah* also make the extraordinarily brutal *Diagonal Direction?*' My response to the enigma is: Seek first the emotional environment in which these works were created.

What makes an artist stand against an international roar of uninterest in figurative sculpture?

Dabro's almost fanatical re-imagining of the human figure has provoked criticism for decades that his work is that of a dinosaur. The critique has come at a heavy cost. Though a director of the National Gallery of Australia, Brian Kennedy, remarked that he wished he had known of Dabro's work before he retired from the position; no work of one of Australia's most accomplished bronze sculptors is represented in the Gallery at all, nor in many other Australian galleries. Why?

The largest sculptures, as for all Australian artists who work in large-scale bronze, have been made through the public or private commissions that some critical circles hold to be, by their nature, inferior. Another is that the superb modelling skills that he possesses are not shared widely among many artists, who, as the portraitist Judy Cassab once archly observed, may confine themselves to abstract works because they lack the innate and learnt skills to attempt the human figure. The third reason, of course, is that the depiction of the human figure, especially the female nude, was decidedly out of fashion among practising artists for half a century and even now is not as recognised as it once was. Dabro's work, in subject and execution, stands decisively outside the contemporary canon. The art critic Martin Edmond observed:

> [T]he scaffolding of time in art historical studies does have consequences. One, pertinent here, is that the assumption of a central narrative's existence has an effect upon what is or is not included within it. Key artists will be privileged because they have always fitted in, while others, who never fitted, are consigned once more to obscurity. They represent by-ways, irrelevancies, alternative pathways – all leading to dead ends. The central

4 THE LIFE AND WORK OF ANTE DABRO

narrative thus becomes in some sense self-replicating. Those artists who have previously been adjudged eminent, whose works have been widely reproduced or exhibited or bought by major galleries, exert a kind of gravitational pull upon the construction of the chronology. You can leave out, say, Walter Withers or Arthur Loreiro; but you can't leave out Tom Roberts or Arthur Streeton.[1]

To pursue the ancient, highly skilled and illustrious praxis of carving or casting the human figure in bronze may be attractive but risky for anyone who wants critical acclaim in their own lifetime. It's an admirable calling, but Dabro's dedication is perhaps like that of a contemporary musician who devotes their life to composing string quartets.

Dabro might respond that he has sold more works and attracted more admirers in his lifetime than most modernist or post-modernist sculptors; or that a final judgement on any work of art may take decades, even centuries. He almost enjoys the dinosaur-tag. The infinite resource of the human figure that he has followed so unerringly all his life is one that, as the director of the Canberra Museum and Gallery observed, has inspired the best of the Western tradition since classical Greek times.[2] In fashion or out, sculptors have reproduced the human figure in bronze for five millennia and in graphic representation, for as long as we humans have been here.

In the biography that follows, I have ventured beyond a purely sculptural analysis into an interpretation of what the sculpture means. Here, I am following Sigmund Freud, who famously correlated the angles and contours of Michelangelo's *Moses* to the ambiguous mental condition of the subject:

> As our eyes travel down it, the figure exhibits three distinct emotional strata. The lines of the face reflect the feelings which have won the ascendancy; the middle of the figure shows the traces of suppressed movement; and the foot still retains the attitude of the projected action. It is as though the controlling influence had proceeded downwards from above.[3]

Dabro's work demands such a humanistic interpretation. It has been said that Rodin 'extends the work's meaning into a world which is no longer that of sculpture but rather one of poetry'.[4] So do Dabro's sculptures. All his major works are self-revelations of different phases of his life and thought that traverse an emotional spectrum from elation to the blackest despair. Indeed, his monumental *Resilience*, depicting the multi-generational experience of migration, is explicitly autobiographical. Of the sorrowing male figure in contemplation of an endless and painful process of migration, he exclaimed:

The standing man? That's me! That's my portrait! I was going into an unknown, always jumping into the abyss. I'm proud of being Croatian even though I left. I'm proud to be a peasant even though I never really accepted being one. That's why I'm an outsider. It was bloody hard when I came here. I wasn't glorifying anything. My language was non-existent.

Since Freud, critics have also used psychiatric tools to dissect sculptures as if the carvings or castings were drawn from a session on the couch. The art historian Anne Wagner's discussion of the British sculptor Barbara Hepworth focusses on a number of her works entitled *Mother and Child*. (Hepworth was the mother of triplets). One of the most striking is her *Figure (Mother and Child)* of 1933, which in grey alabaster depicts an undifferentiated human form with an enormous stone ball on her lap nearly half the size of the figure. The mother may be pregnant, or she may be caressing the child (the figure has no hands); or the child may be preventing the mother from standing up. There is no hint of resentment in Hepworth's carving, rather, to me, a somewhat sardonic acceptance of the fact that one cannot mother and carve simultaneously.[5] The exultant physicality of Dabro's *Mother and Child* that dominates the photograph of Dabro's studio above (Figure 0.1) and Hepworth's maternal resignation draw a

FIGURE 0.1

Ante Dabro's studio, 2021, Canberra Airport. Source: Con Boekel.
Ante Dabro (l), author (r).

It was an intimate space, surrounded as I was by my family. In the end, it got too small.

6 THE LIFE AND WORK OF ANTE DABRO

polarity between a male and female sculptor on precisely the same theme and indicate a justification, if one were needed, that I should view Dabro's work in terms of his own history and personality.

In discussing the works, sometimes Dabro bristled at any suggestion that he had borrowed ideas from other works. Of course, he did not do so directly; but, like most serious artists, he has visited most of the major Western galleries and sculptural sites and knows their collections well. He has absorbed into his visual memory a stupendous array of paintings, sculptures, woodcuts and prints which, once implanted, are never lost. Whenever an artist takes up a brush or chisel, this immense throng is ready to whisper advice on shape, design, colour or mass. The artist may not even be aware of its ghostly presence.

It happens like this. In 1837, William Turner painted *The Fighting Temeraire*. He showed the famous British warship being towed by a steam tug to be broken up, an inglorious yet, to Turner, a majestic end to something fine and valued. The significance of a quite everyday event is magnified by the absence of anything else on the vast, plain-like sea, just the reflection of the massive hulls at sunset and the coloured, sinister smoke issuing from the tug. The strong vertical lines of the funnel and the rigging of the *Temeraire* oppose the huge and horizontal sky.[6] In 1977, the Australian Indigenous artist Lin Onus painted *The Firing of the Humpy* in which he depicts two policemen, having set fire to a simple Aboriginal tin shack, nonchalantly watching their work of 'encouraging' an Aboriginal family to quit this part of Victoria. A heavy storm has passed; the tin hut, its chimney and the destructive flames are reflected on a soggy plain on which virtually nothing else is visible. The solid shape of the hut and the sinister coloured smoke following the contours of the limitless sky impose a solemnity on a sordid and shameful event. The strong vertical lines of the humpy and its chimney oppose the huge and horizontal sky on the vast, sea-like plain.[7] There is no reason to suppose that Onus had any painting especially in his mind when he composed this majestic scene. There is every reason to suppose that deep in the visual memory of the artist there resided some elements of *The Fighting Temeraire*.

Dabro's cooperation has given me an opportunity to track a lifetime's oeuvre with a close commentary by the artist himself. Dozens of recorded interviews over many years have helped me to frame a view of his life and work. Together, we discussed the impulses of the major public works and many more movable sculptures sold through galleries long ago. Frequently, I saw more in each work than the flat planes, visual cadences, negative spaces, lines of sight and endpoint resolutions with which he was preoccupied, but our discussions invariably provided a context that allowed me to roam more freely into his

Introduction: Making a Mark in Stone　　　7

emotional and psychic worldview that produced these remarkable creations. The excerpts of interviews with Dabro quoted here are all drawn from this collection unless indicated otherwise.

It was through these conversations over many years that I began to understand the qualities and beliefs that have driven him. First is the absolute value of art in its own right, a conviction formed by his postgraduate teacher, Antun Augustinčić, recognised after the death of Ivan Meštrović as the finest sculptor in Yugoslavia. Augustinčić traced his artistic descent through the Croatian master sculptors Radovan and Buvina of the Middle Ages, then through Rodin to Meštrović himself. From them, Dabro learned that the demands of high art are intellectual, spontaneous, intuitive, rewarding and excruciating, and that beginning a new work is to jump into an abyss without a compass. From the Dalmatian family farm in World War II, he knew life to be a hard, thankless, physical and mental struggle; from sheep-herding in the lonely hills, he grasped that each individual is ultimately alone in that struggle. Four years of wartime bombs made him terrified of violence; from the communist state, he took only its hatred of individual thought, subversive action and public commotion. From the loneliness of the immigrant without English, he knew that the past, once lost, as Brecht puts it, cannot be regained:

> If mastering the language is too hard,
> 　Only be patient;
> The telegram imploring your return
> 　Won't need translation.[8]

That the expression of an idealised human form is the highest pinnacle to which the artist can aim was Michelangelo's and his own. For all his boisterous and blokey bonhomie, Ante Dabro, the sculptor is a solitary observer, deeply distrustful of the crowd, standing forever between the culture of Croatia and Australia, adrift in a miasma of Western international art that, to him has lost its purpose as well as its technique.

Outside the Queensland Cultural Centre, Brisbane, stands Dabro's 1985 *Sisters*. It depicts two nude female figures, one standing, one sitting. At the time of my last visit to the work in 2022, I saw it first from a distance. Three young people clustered round it. One sat on the lap of the seated figure, another had an arm round her neck; their friend took a photo. By the time I reached it, they had gone, but now from close up, three elements of the work were apparent. The first was that the configuration of the figures, and the spatial relationship between them, were the creation of a classically trained master sculptor.

8   THE LIFE AND WORK OF ANTE DABRO

The second was that this artist, through the arrangement of the sculptures and the negative space between them, had taken inspiration from the artists of the sixteenth-century Italian Renaissance. The third, perhaps unexpectedly, was that this is a popular work. The toes, knees and shoulders of both figures are kept polished foundry-bright by hundreds of observers – one could almost call them participants – seeking a tactile connection with this re-creation of two human forms, nude and female though they are. *She is me, they are us.* How unfortunate, I reflected, that so many modern commissioned sculptures often require larger-than-life versions of famous men and women whose dimensions alone discourage this sort of intimacy.

The work of any artist can do far more than invite intimacy and popularity among adolescents. The 'Gloria' of Bach's *Mass in B Minor* can summon spiritual elation irrespective of one's beliefs. The 'Dies Irae' of Verdi's *Requiem* evokes for some listeners a terror of the unknown even if they don't understand the words. The guarded restraint of Anthonis Mor's portrait of Mary Tudor (c.1553) reveals her simultaneously to be regal but apprehensive, self-possessed and uncertain.[9] The so-called *Bulls of Guisando* can stun the viewer with the sheer presence of their granite mass.[10] Michelangelo's *Bandini Pietá* (1547–1555) ('The Deposition') can bring an observer to tears by the marble physicality of a sculpted corpse, his friends and his mother.[11]

That's the midnight sea in the blood that forms the epigraph to this book. The power of art to elate and uplift, its most common attribute, is also to comfort and sustain amidst grief and disaster. Dabro's Naval Memorial in Anzac Parade, Canberra is no simple act of collective mourning, but, through its representative crew of twelve sailors, can speak of the solitary trauma of active service that is more obvious now in the early 2020s than at the time of its creation. The dozen sailors of the sculpture are alone in their duties and in their thoughts.

Painters, dancers, composers, poets and playwrights may plumb those depths and share with us their emotions. Sculptors who choose to work with the figurative human form may touch us even more nearly. That is their gift to us. Our gift to them, though they may not know it, is our reaction to their work. That is the commingling of the humanities. We are the artists; they are us.

CHAPTER 1

MAKING THE OUTSIDER

January in the Croatian language is known as *Siječanj*, the 'time of timber cutting'.

It is the month of *Siječanj*, 1938. In the annual State of the Union address, President Roosevelt has announced that the world is in a state of 'high tension and disorder'. 127,000 Romanian Jews have just been stripped of their citizenship. The German Condor Legion is bombing Barcelona and Japanese planes are raiding the Chinese city of Hankou. Italy and the Soviet Union have foreshadowed a major expansion of their naval forces. In the creative arts, the International Exposition of Surrealism has opened in Paris.[1] Social Realist painting is gaining strength amidst the shaky world economies emerging from the Great Depression. In sculpture, the same style is winning admirers in the Soviet Union, but among the states that will form post-war Yugoslavia, it is a form almost unknown.

And in Croatia, in this time of timber-cutting in the deep mid-winter of this troubled year, a woman has toiled as usual up the hill that the people call Lačina that lowers over the family farm in what was once known as Yugoslavia. She is Maria, the mother of Croatian-Australian sculptor Ante Dabro.

Maria's purpose is to bring the winter fodder out of the stone storehouse for the sheep. Birth pangs assail her so urgently that she has no alternative but to give birth on the hard floor – the phrase which in the Spanish language translates as 'giving light' – to her baby. Cutting the cord with the fodder knife, Maria staggers down the track with the blue, lifeless form, back to Čavoglave, the little Dalmatian village, back to the family home. Her sister-in-law revives the tiny baby, places him in warm water, and returns him to his mother for his first feed. In the next few years, he is nurtured by women and grows up in their world. In the long years of wartime scarcity, more than one village woman acts as a wet nurse to the young child Ante, who by the age of five is known as *Djule* ('rosy'), thanks to his ruddy, human milk-sustained complexion. Of the many

10 THE LIFE AND WORK OF ANTE DABRO

hundreds of women, real or idealised, whom Ante Dabro has sculpted in wax, plaster, clay, resin, wood, bronze, marble and stone, none can be described as less than dignified, imposing and serious.

Animals are another part of his life. In the Dabro household, chooks wander in and out; even the pigs seem to house-train themselves. Ducks are not welcome though; they poop everywhere! He has a favourite horse, donkey and dog Ibar. The piglets, who make such lovely snuggly pillows and warm up the stone floor of the family home, are the revered companions that creep into young Ante's blanket and later his soul and refuse to leave. Outside the home, it's dangerous. Don't go out at night without a light or a gun; the wolves are hungry, roaming right into the village.

1939. The violence that is the everyday part of farm life becomes the bombs and guns that shape Ante's clearest childhood memories of World War II. How cataclysmic is the death of his poddy (bottle-fed) goat, which an Italian Fascist military officer, billeted in the family home, gives him to care for in 1943. That same day, a soldier cuts her throat in front of him and throws pieces of his closest companion into the massive cooking pot.

> They were billeted in our house. I was only five, and they had a great huge cooking pot cooking their meal. I had been given a little baby goat to look after and I was feeding it and whatever, and the soldier just cut its throat in front of me there in the kitchen. The officer put me on his knee and reprimanded the soldier, but I was devastated, I was crying like hell. But the kid was dead and that was the end of it.

This brutal and, to the five-year-old, senseless act of violence comes to symbolise the war that had invaded his home. A pig is slaughtered, Ante catches his screams; a useless dog is shot, the report resounds in the village.

The violence of the farm is matched by violence within the family. One uncle is a member of the anti-fascist communist Partisans, a second uncle is a member of the fascist-supporting Croatian militia Ustase, which supports the Nazis, and a cousin has joined the Croatian Home Guard. Ante watches another cousin, no more than fourteen, shoot Ante's sister with a gun, in one cheek and out the other. Bringing her home from hospital in Dirniš, they are strafed by a German fighter. The frequent shouting matches disturb and frighten him. Nearly all the men are away. Čavoglave has become the domain of women. Incomprehensible cruelty, the endless travail of farm work far beyond his years, brief but ecstatic reveries in spring and summer when alone on Lačina with the sheep in the high country above the village: these are the

Making the Outsider 11

elements that are framing the patrimony of this rural war-baby of Dalmatia, raised on the limestone country in the Croatian hamlet of Čavoglave.

After 1939, nobody trusted Mussolini's armies to remain in Italy. The Croatian national government offered to evacuate the coastal communities to the Middle East. Ante's father Marko Dabro, sharing with his brother a wide tract of farm and grazing country round the village, well understood that this would be the end of the farm and its animals. They refused to leave. Nor did they wait long for Axis soldiers to invade Yugoslavia in April 1941. Armed resistance collapsed within a fortnight. Mussolini was handed Istria and Dalmatia as a reward for supporting the Nazis, including the major deep-water city of Split, a day's donkey ride from Čavoglave. Within six months, Italian and German soldiers infested not only the city but the surrounding villages.

Ante Dabro, the Croatian war-baby, has become a war-toddler. He cannot remember a time when, as a young child, his home was not occupied by soldiers. A military billet will provide no labour; the village men are away fighting for one side or the other; yet, even in winter farm production cannot stop.

In *Veljača* ('Festival time', February) the spring equinox is still a month away. Icicles are hanging a metre long from the lintels as someone wakes the tiny lad to grope about in the pre-dawn darkness to feed the horses and donkeys. One special animal of warm flank and affectionate nuzzle is a moment's relief against the cold; back for a crust of bread and cheese, then out to the barnyard. Every hen must be caught to check if an egg is in her egg canal, if so, she is thrown into the laying pen. 'Don't make the mistake of putting your finger up the rooster's bum. He doesn't like it.' Now, Ante, untether your favourite donkey, tie on his twenty-litre panniers, lead him down to the creek to fill up the household water tank. While he's there, Ante collects some pieces of *mulika*, the white limestone-like stone so adaptable to carving.

Ožujak is the 'deceiving' month of March. It promises a sunshiny spring, but beware the thin white clouds gathering on the mountain tops. They portend the icy tumultuous blasts known as the *bura* from the north-east that can come roaring down from the snowy coastal ranges. Bura doesn't affect Čavoglave as much as the coast an hour's ride away, but the winds can catch a horse and cart on the way to market at Drniš unprepared. Towards evenings of the Deceiving Month it's cosy inside the family home. In the short hours before bed, Ante whittles the soft limestone, or if he can get away with it, a piece of his mother's traditional round 30 centimetre bread loaf. One creation he puts outside to dry, soon to be gobbled up by the birds. More tears. He carves a miniature pigeon squatting on her eggs. She rocks gently on the kitchen flagstones as if

12 THE LIFE AND WORK OF ANTE DABRO

on a breezy branch, so realistic that the cat pounces on her. The first stirrings of reputation: at the age of seven he's created the Virgin Mary in stone for an aunt in exchange for several pairs of trousers. Shortly after nightfall, bed, secure until the pre-dawn from the violence outside. In the insistent reassuring warmth of the family hearth he cuddles up to the piglets, for a moment loosedfrom the raging family rows, the hungry wolves, the freezing stables, the indignant rooster, the bullets and the bombs.

If the Axis forces in the early 1940s ruled the country by day, the nights belonged to Yugoslavia's Partisans. Many were guerrillas, living rough and in hiding, whose need for arms, animals and food swelled throughout 1943. They spoke for national independence. Who could not support such a cause in a country that for two millennia had been invaded by Romans, Venetians, Turks, French and Austro-Hungarians? Now the Fascists. The Partisans expected sympathisers like the landholder Marko to provide information and supplies for their forages at agreed nocturnal rendezvous. Soon the sallies became more regular and requests became demands: the partisans were hungry and their forces expanding. Before long, whatever Marko and the rest of the district sympathisers could provide was not enough. Like other landholders, Marko began to restrain his natural sympathy. First the Axis, now the Partisans! What seemed to him to be their unreasonable demands for produce and stock were, to the partisans, perhaps, merely their rightful levy on the country.

Marko, never one to be pushed around, was a well-read and thoughtful man who in 1917 had been inspired by the Russian Revolution. Drafted into the Austro-Hungarian navy in 1914, he had joined the failed Kotor (Cattaro) Mutiny against the Austrians in Montenegro and counted himself lucky not to have been among the Croatians executed for taking part. A brother was killed fighting unwillingly for the Austrians, another badly wounded. A hatred of the demanding, conscripting foreign empires grew to a contempt of all authority. His duty as landholder was to preserve first the flocks and grain for the coming winter and beyond. He resisted the levy, however justified it appeared to the guerrillas. Sheep, goats and chooks began to disappear overnight, then a couple of horses. By the end of 1943, Marko had become much less cooperative for the midnight visitations had become raids. He reacted by hiding the stock in a stone barn: five-year-old Ante was called out to help the women drive the sheep, goats and horses at evenfall to a different location, for the constant and ever-increasing deprivations of the Partisans seemed worse than anything demanded by the billeted soldiers. Reflecting on Tito's Partisan victory and its easy slide into Russian-dominated communism, Ante supposes that Marko

Making the Outsider

13

was becoming steadily less cooperative to those who during the war had been regional commanders but by 1945 were becoming the rural Administrators of the People. Marko's wartime uncompromising attitude towards those who had become masters of the country, was, no doubt, noted.

As the only literate person in the family, acting as the village notary, Marko forms a close emotional connection with his young son. The little boy, he surely realises, is different from the others. He explains the history of the Roman Empire, the endless occupations of Dalmatia, the political history of Europe. It is in these interactions that his son bears the most affectionate childhood moments, the sort that most of us seem to randomly retain for reasons we now cannot locate. One of Ante's is this: It is 1946. Unusually, Marko has gone to market to sell his crop of giant tomatoes, walking beside their toiling donkeys on the 90-minute trudge to the Drniš market. On this day, eight-year-old Ante is failing from fatigue and hunger. Having nothing to eat, Marko tries the usual places, but night is closing, no food is to be had. Up goes Ante, for the first time, into an empty tomato basket on the donkey's back. Towards the church of St Ilija, still with twenty minutes to go, Marko administers a first but long draught of his homemade brandy. In reaching home, 'Maria, get little Djule a feed'. Maria produces a huge Croatian version of a tortilla. Little Djule eats the lot.

Christmas Eve, 1945. It is the ritual of *Badnjak* (logs). Ante has bread-sculpted baby Jesus asleep in his manger by the fire. Cooking for tomorrow's feast starts in the late afternoon, and the women arrange a thick layer of straw on the stone floor. Marko, no churchgoer but a respecter of ritual, also throws straw in the floor, then arranges two huge logs positioned to take fire slowly on each side of the cauldron swinging from its chain over the hearth. As eleven o'clock approaches, the family dresses as warmly as they might for the trudge through the snow to St Elija for Midnight Mass. How insistent to the young mind is the sound of the icy water bubbling under the bridge. Returned home, each member of the extended family who has gathered here, by seniority, takes a stick to poke either of the logs. As the sparks fly upwards, each one recites the Croatian-language invocation of 'Kyrie Eleison Criste Eleison' (The Lord have mercy, Christ have mercy) followed by a spoken hope or wish for the year to come – but only as many as there are sparks ascending. The guests depart and the feast, drawn from the best of last autumn's produce, is served. Ritual dictates that it must be shared by only those who live in this house. Dabro reflects: 'I would love more rituals in our lives. They're not meaningless. I could not be a creative person without them. There is something magical and extraordinary that I can't explain. They draw me out.'

Rituals are an imaginative response to everyday life. So is sculpture.

FIGURE 1.1

The Dabro home, Čavoglave, Croatia, Maria Dabro seated far right.
Source: 1997 (Author).

I really don't know why I never was close to her.

Ante's mother Maria was not close to him, nor, in his memory, to any other of the children. In a 1997 photo taken outside the Dabro home at the end of a long day touring the local zone of the War of Croatian Independence, some people, including Dabro, are standing while some perch on a low stone wall. Three metres away sits Maria, her head bowed, dressed solely in the black of widowhood, taking no part.

To this day, Ante is unable to explain why his maternal relation never matured. He knew her life to be one of ceaseless struggle, made very much worse by the absence of men like himself. He conjectures that she may have been tired of having so many children close together, or particularly disillusioned in him as the last able-bodied male to leave the farm. Ante, the adult longed for a secure and stable family, and found it in Australia, but his worldview, shaped by his parents, the village and the culture, placed women ideally in the home. In the 1950s, he understands through observation that women should be free to follow a creative life, but their responsibilities as homemakers came first. In the late 1960s, he will find the desire for sexual female freedom subversive and disturbing. From the 1980s, elements of the sexual revolution,

Making the Outsider   15

such as the identification of all men as potential oppressors, struck him as puzzling and hurtful. By inclination, more observer than participant, a potential outsider rather than follower of new artistic directions, the turning world kept him an outsider all his life.

Travanj, April, in Croatian means 'the season of growing grass'. Up in the hills, on Lačina, it's colder and windier, but the soil is better, while the view from the summit extends over the plains forever. The snow is deeper than in the village, but the first shoots are flourishing in that bright shade of the springtime green that seems peculiar to central Europe. It's time to establish the Dabro summer camp. Heavily laden are the donkeys with pots, bedding, food, saltlick for the animals, vats for cheese, shears for the sheep, bottles for the new-born animals. Though the upward journey is not the epic event of the Swiss pastures, most of the extended family will take part. On Lačina, grazing the cattle is the work not of the strong, laconic cattlemen of Australian legend, for Ante's older brother Jole is disinclined to help, and Ivan and his other brothers are away in the army. Nor do his brothers, having 'seen Paree', hold any intention to return. Care of the stock and grain is the task of women – and young Ante. Often he resents it bitterly.

A week or two after the mighty progression, many of the Dabro family trudged back to the farm below. Sometimes young Ante was left quite alone among the hills in the gentle breeze of the Jugo that blows from the south, heated by the Sahara, cooled by the Adriatic sea. Outwardly gregarious but frequently lonely, he resented that his family below were content to leave him alone. His inclination towards a serious and solitary interior life was solidifying.

In mid–1942, the Italians and Germans, their forces already depleted by withdrawing troops to the Eastern Front, were holding tightly to their occupied ports along the Adriatic. For several months, the coast and its hinterland became a battleground as the Italian Air Force tried to intimidate the Partisans and the Allies harried the Germans. From afar, Maria watched in horror as a plane, its British decals clearly visible, bombed the neighbouring village where she knew her four younger children, Boško, Jole, Ante and baby Darinka, were visiting. A farmhouse that she supposed contained the children vanished in a huge cloud of smoke. Surely, they could not have survived; but Boško, hearing the plane, had called the other children and his aunt, who was preparing lunch, to come outside to look as it circled, then dropped its bombs. Fascinated, they gaped at what looked like eggs tumbling from the plane. Not for long! One scored a direct hit on the house, which dissolved in flame and dust and covered the kids in dust and stones. Maria arrived at a run,

16 THE LIFE AND WORK OF ANTE DABRO

to find the bull charging in terrified circles, the village half destroyed and the children dazed, bruised by rubble but unhurt. Dabro recalls the hands scrabbling through the rubble to rescue him. The plane circled, then levelled to treetop height to strafe the settlement with its machine guns. 'Like a mother hen', in Dabro's words, Maria gathered her children round to hide beside a stone wall. As the plane banked to return from the opposite direction, they scrambled to the other side while the bullets smacked into it. In the end, none of the family was hurt. The very next day, Čavoglave itself was attacked – now by the Italians firing mortar bombs from many kilometres away as a warning to the villagers to cease their supposed support for the Partisans. Crouching against the kitchen wall, Marko, from its sound, identified each projectile that the enemy was using, and where it would land. Again, the kids emerged to look for the ricochets, marvel at the new holes in the walls and to play with the shrapnel and live ammunition. It was decades before the little boy Ante could understand how sudden and inexplicable violence, whether caused by urban rioting, mass rallies or aggressive public speeches, would continue to seize and terrify him for more than eighty years.

Svibanj, May, 'the time of budding leaves and plants'. The lambs have arrived and will be suckling for two months. After separating the chooks, Ante's morning task is to milk the sheep and goats. Until the Partisans start raiding the flocks, the only predators of the animals are the wolves; but secure in the stone barn by night and grazing by day, the lambs can stay in the high country for weeks. In these crisp days of early summer, Ante is out of bed long before the early dawn. Don't forget to separate the chooks! With Ibar the dog and at first with a cousin, he ascends the hill. If it weren't such a rush, milking would be a dreamy experience as he leans into each warm woolly fleece. But there's a knack to it too: 'I wasn't very good at it because I let the sheep piss into the milk, but if you put them too far forward they poo into it.' Now release the ewes to graze in the paddock round the same hut where he was born. Dog, cheese, *slavin* (speck), watery wine, whittling knife. The lambs, hungry but safe in their own barn, are calling to their mothers. By ten when the ewes are dry, the two cousins let out the lambs to suck at the dry udders. Ante marvels at their gentle ways, the speed with which mother and lamb recognise each other. Cousin winds back to Čavoglave, he won't be needed till nightfall. Like Giotto (according to Vasari) Ante remains in sole charge of the sheep. Both artists find the long middays a time for the imagination to soar, but while Giotto scratched images of sheep with a pointed stone on a smooth clean piece of rock,[2] Ante's creations are little animals carved from *mulika*, mother and lamb, bird, dog and donkey.

Making the Outsider 17

As the late afternoon light thickens, cousin returns. They separate the sheep and drive them from their separate folds into the evening shelters, round defensive stones under wooden roofs. Settled on Lačina they will remain throughout summer, grazing by day, tethered by night. The evening shadows lengthen and just out of sight the wolves begin a nocturnal howl.

A horse and cart took the fruit and vegetables to the market towns and returned with the few necessities that the farm could not produce. The plodding two-hour journey was made no faster than the speed that the villagers could walk with their pack animals, and from 1942 the journey was risky while cruising warplane pilots sought something to shoot at. The road to the coast was so exposed; there were so few places to hide. Early in 1944, returning from Knin, the little party was spotted and strafed. Everyone dived for cover; nobody, miraculously, was hurt; the children scrambled out to pick up the shrapnel; and another memory of senseless violence was laid in the psyche of the young child.

Lipanj, June, is 'the time of linden blossom', big, medicinal, bushy, lime green. *Srpanj*, July, is 'harvest time'. Half a dozen head-scarfed aunts and cousins cut the wheat with sickles, tie the stalks in stooks, load them onto the donkeys. Cabbages, tomatoes and potatoes, some for the village, most for the market. Next to be processed are the ash saplings, cut just above the stony soil, stacked in the storehouse for the stock to feed on the leaves throughout winter. As if not busy enough, Ante constructs waist-high stone structures to take the load of the women's burdens as they rest to negotiate the slippery stony track.

By June 1944, the air-raids on the farm were fewer, but down in Drniš, the newly-formed Allied 'Balkan Air Force' continued its attacks on the Germans. One night, Ante and those among the family who had not been conscripted for war work climbed a rise to watch the attack on the German-held town of Knin as the concussions thundered up the valley. The Allies had made another raid on the port, but to the children, from this distance, the explosions seemed no more than fireworks.

In wild weather, or when warplanes were abroad, whoever remained on Lačina retreated to a huge cave formed in the unstable limestone. Here was stored some of the produce, and it was there also that Marko, sensing, in 1944, a Partisan victory, loaded up the donkeys to transport his extensive library. Well he knew that the Communists were as suspicious of independent thought as that 'opiate of the people', the Christian church that they claimed to have overthrown. The Bible, the Koran, *Das Kapital*, Engels, nineteenth-century literary classics and political theorists: Marko was fluent in three languages and his reading was eclectic. Somehow a neighbour in a house a few hundred

18 THE LIFE AND WORK OF ANTE DABRO

metres away learnt of the expedition – perhaps he spotted the donkeys wind-
ing up the stony track – and betrayed him. The secret library was confiscated. Was he a neighbour informing against a Dabro, a Muslim against a
Christian, a Serb against a Croatian, a Četnik against a Partisan – who knows
now? Marko suspected that it was a cousin with a private grievance but Ante
took a lesson about adherence to political causes, ancient or modern, and the
meaning of loyalty and betrayal. Don't get involved. Keep aloof. If in doubt,
hide. Marko Dabro well understood that this evidence of independent thought
would be used against him and that, sooner or later, they would be coming
for him.

In the daytime hills of high summer, Ante, not yet seven years old, finds
himself alone more often among his animals, whittling in the solitary life of
Lačina that he endures day after day as the howls of the hungry wolves grow
ever closer. At times he weeps for his mother out of loneliness, but sometimes,
especially as the first long shadows of dawn shorten over the hut, he marvels
at the magical Bergen, a type of lark. How gracefully she rises from the grass,
slowly up and up to hover so high against the sun as to become invisible, then
a sudden swoop to earth.

Dawn and dusk are the hours that have entered the souls of many young
people. The Romantic poet William Wordsworth wrote of his own childhood:

The leafless trees and every icy crag
    Tinkled like iron; while far-distant hills
    Into the tumult sent an alien sound
    Of melancholy, not unnoticed while the stars
Eastward, were sparkling clear, and in the west
    The orange sky of evening died away.[3]

Granville Crawford, the sheep farmer, alone with his flocks on the Brindabella
ranges of southeastern Australia, rendered the same experience in less majestic
but heartfelt words:

A bloke's not blabbing in the pub about what he could do, it's just something
that he experienced himself and you share the joy with yourself. There's
some very special spots, very personal special spots, and I guess that everybody [...] who lives in open spaces has some very special places where
they feel security. I don't wish to go into a great spiel about faith and all
that sort of thing, but there's [...] some very special places where you can
feel very near.[4]

FIGURE 1.2

The summer pastures of Lačina. Source: 1998, (Author).

It was from here that I stood and watched the world and told myself I must go there.

'In the tumult of daily life', Ante recalls, 'it was so beautiful, I'll never forget that. The wildflowers around me, and the sheep. The cheeky sparrows in the village'. Under his whittling knife, the little birds of Lačina emerge from their lumps of *mulika* into their graceful hovering forms. From the peak of Lačina, he gazes at the distant prospect of an enticing world.

August is *Kolobvoz*, the 'time of driving the harvest wagons'. Since ready cash is still a novelty in the villages, Marko trades his expert produce as barter, even labour for his crops on the river flat. What can't be bartered before 1945 goes to Drniš for sale. The people of Čavoglave can produce anything except salt.

To Marko, going to market is for women and children unless there are animals to be traded. He remains in his workshop by the watermill on the creek, down by the vineyard, the rye and corn crops. He is the district barrel-maker, taking commissions for every form of liquid container from little twenty-litre water kilderkins to 10,000-litre wine containers so big they need their own barn to protect them. Take the seasoned oak cut last summer, split each with wedges, cut the staves precisely with the two-handed saw. Later, Marko will forge the iron bands to fasten the staves. Here, intellect and hand fuse in a single task of skill, knowledge, instruction, tradition, intuition and native ability. It's like being a sculptor, though seven-year-old Ante doesn't know it yet. His clearest vision of Marko is his father in the cosy workshop that smells of sawdust, prosciutto, garlic and wine as he bends his long planks over a cauldron of boiling water. Warmth, skill, patience, an intense, solitary concentration, a space that is both comforting and secure. The lessons are not lost on his youngest son.

Rujan, September, is the season of animal mating as the leaves start to turn. As testosterone rises, the jacks (males) among the donkeys must be stopped from wandering off to mate. One gets away, and to the family's amusement, only returns after three weeks, exhausted, bedraggled, demanding food and salt. The best of the dozen donkeys on the farm must fertilise the mare. She's too tall to be mated naturally, so she's led to a pit so that the donkey can reach her. Somebody holds her bridle, an aunt holds her tail out of the way and the mating is enacted with the excited encouragement of the village children. The young mule is sold into the district. A cousin has her genitals stung by a bee. Screaming in pain, she demands milk to be thrown on the sting. Ante obliges and relates the tale in the village to general childish glee. He's the youngest among a dozen kids. When they're playing mothers and fathers, Ante's role is baby. He watches enviously as boys sit or lie on girls, re-enacting what they see among the animals. At twelve and a half, he has his first sexual experience with an older woman, there, out in the hills, in the long grass. Sexual relations are cemented as one of the driving forces of his physical and artistic life.

If farm work is never far from sex, it is never far from death either. One serene midday of Rujan, the sun is strong but the breeze carries a hint of the autumn chill to come. The harvesters have gone. Ante has driven the lambs down to the village, but the sheep remain in the high country, nightly locked against wolves and partisans and, after 1945, neighbours! It's solitary and lonely for the youthful shepherd. Today, the cousin who helps with the animals at the busy dawn and dusk is to stay all day, but midday they spend playing cards. The game comes up short with a ferocious growl. A wolf as long as Ante is tall has seized a terrified sheep by the neck as, crazed with fear, she rushes blindly towards the lindens, while three or four wolves circle and feint to get at their share. To the rescue! (Cousin hides inside). Ante pulls the animal clear, the furious wolf at length snarls off, but the sheep is beyond hope. Cousin emerges from the stone hut to find their charge broken and bleeding. When the ten-year-old brings home the news and the remains of the sheep, an auntie

Making the Outsider 21

sends him halfway across the room with a back-hander. 'Why didn't you look after them properly?'

Sheep and the wolf are gone, but the horror of sudden violence is worse than an air raid.

January ought to be the 'month of bitterly cold', but it is November, *Studeni*, that is awarded that dismal title. It's dark by four p.m. Everyone's inside who is able to be. After the early nightfall, Ante is crouching and carving by the fire. Gone are the reproductions of Greek and Roman sculptures, for those originals in Marko's library have been confiscated. Marshall Tito had been proclaimed Marshall of the Republic of Yugoslavia in 1945, and in consequence, Ante's hearthstone subjects had become the photographs of Heroes of the Soviet Union. Under his hands, even these grim two-dimensional human heads blossomed into three dimensions for, by his seventh November, the young sculptor was learning more control over his lumps of *mulika*. 'How do you know what they look like from the back?' asks someone. 'Use your intuition' replies the instinct of the sculptor. One Christmas Eve, he stares at the formulaic sculptures in the parish church of St Ilija where one or two of the angelic faces were filled with sinister personality. Carved in black stone worked into striking features, they carried a distant suggestion, decades later, in some of Dabro's mature faces. They were the first non-realistic depictions of a human face he had encountered.

Outside, wolves and Tito's soldiers circle, but the Italian billets have gone, the air-raids have ceased. Inside, it's again secure and warm. The big iron pot bubbles on its chain over the fire, and the smell of baking bread wanders through the dwelling.

On Germany's surrender, Tito united Bosnia and Herzegovina, Croatia, Macedonia, Montenegro, Serbia and Slovenia under a communist dictatorship. The Republic of Yugoslavia had begun its short life.

At about midnight late in 1945, two trucks rumbled into Čavoglave. An officer, flanked by two soldiers of the Communist Party, ordered everyone out of the Dabro home to assemble in the darkness. Burnt into Ante's memory are the four headlights playing on the frightened family and the weird shadows of the carbide lamps. Marko and his son Ivan were called out, denounced and escorted to the vehicle. Months later, Maria learned that while Ivan was to be released, Marko had been condemned to death, later reduced to life imprisonment. Eight years later, he was abruptly released, more defiant than ever, having lost his faith, he said, in humanity. Had not Tito broken with Stalin in 1949, Marko Dabro would almost certainly have died in a Siberian Gulag, but the train containing the political prisoners had halted at the Bulgarian border,

22   THE LIFE AND WORK OF ANTE DABRO

then reversed to return to Yugoslavia. Stalin considered a Hungarian-style invasion to punish deviationism from the Comintern, then, probably recalling the ferocious tenacity of the Partisans, thought better of it. Marko remained unrepentant. On his release, he assumed a Hitler-style moustache, well calculated to annoy everybody.

To this day, Ante does not know the cause of Marko's arrest, but the possibilities are many. Though well-read and reflective, he was irascible, outspoken and disinclined to accept anyone's authority. While his political principles were on the left, he was as intolerant of the arbitrary authority of the Socialist state as much as anyone. He no doubt hated the 'workers' councils', which by a 1945 decree had to be formed wherever more than five agricultural or industrial workers gathered together 'to protect the interests of the libertarian struggle'. Doubtless, in the first year of peace, he hated the destruction of the ancient stone dividing fences of the whole valley that had now to be collectivised in the name of the Socialist People's Republic of Yugoslavia. He may also have fallen victim of the sort of denunciation of 'false ideology' that the Soviet system never failed to encourage; perhaps he was accused by a cousin or neighbour of 'treason' for reasons far more relevant to village than national politics. He had become, in short, too bolshie for the Bolsheviks. Tito's apparatchiks of Šibernik and Drniš may have thought him subversive, even if, to his family, he had done nothing more than they expected in defending the honour of the home, the farm and the village. His independence of mind and word may well have been enough to goad the newly-formed dictatorship towards punishment of anyone straying beyond the prevailing ideology of workers' representative councils. From the year that Ante turned nine, newly-identified 'enemies of the state' were being jailed for 'advocating anti-revisionism', 'subversion of the Socialist system', 'separatism', 'verbal offences against the state', 'felonies against the people and the state', 'encouraging Muslim separatism', 'hostile activity and hostile propaganda', 'encouraging Proletarian internationalism', 'opposition to the regime' and even 'criticising the regime in poems'.[5] As he turned eleven, the country suffered an acute famine, not least through the foolish restructuring of the agricultural economy. What chance would a belligerent *kulak* hold in opposing such nonsense?

Apologists for the regime have claimed that Yugoslavian socialism was their country's gift to the world, the 'voluntary association of all local initiatives, the spontaneous and free swelling of all individual forces towards a mutual goal – the well-being, freedom and security of all'. Yet four years later, the whole programme was under close critical scrutiny by the Communist Party itself. In 1953, the Jugoslav Commission for the Village admitted to the National

Making the Outsider   23

Central Committee that Stalin's tenets of collectivisation by mandatory quotas and class struggle through the liquidation of the *kulaks* and small land-owners like Marko had failed. 'We have lost the peasantry', the Commission admitted, 'and now they will never trust us again'.[6]

Of these tumultuous events, Ante understood little, but he witnessed the raging rows that had nightly turned dinner conversations into shouting matches, splitting the family and the nation for all the years of his young life. He understood that every month since his birth had brought sudden, irrational, inexplicable, cruel and violent changes to his parents, his family, his village and his country. A slain poddy goat and a Soviet-style brutal arrest bookended the life of a child of war whose love of animals, a constant search for security, a fear of violence and a hatred of ideological Communism had entered his soul like shrapnel that remains in the body forever. And yet, in the brief years between the collapse of Italy in October 1943 and the delusion of forced collectivisation in 1946, the people of Čavoglave had begun to resume the cycle of rural life that they had followed for centuries. In this, the lad was deeply implicated. Though soon terminated by the communists, never to return in its old form, enough remained of the rituals of the seasonal, rural-based economy to give him a glimpse of an existence that was immensely hard but predictable, animal-centred, loyal, safe, tranquil and secure. And solitary. But it was also a society that was closed and potentially suffocating. The breathtaking view from Lačina on a midsummer day was the same vision that his grandma Ika had pointed to him in 1951: 'Get away from here, do something with your life or you'll end up like Ivanetina'. (Ivan was a local illiterate hermit who hardly ever left Lačina).

Deprived of formal education during the war, four humiliating years in the village primary school follow, in which Ante towers above the seven- and eight-year-olds. He learns, through Jole, that the director of the Split School of Applied Arts has received a little box of Ante's sculptured animals and has invited him to come to Split to see him. In 1952, Maria and the aunties (but not grandmother Ika) are furious to learn that the only young male in the household is planning to join brother Boško in Split in an attempt to enter the School of Applied Art. He will not be dissuaded. Since Marko is still in jail, who will manage and protect the farm? Too late. Ante solemnly buries his shoes, clothes, even his whittling knife under a pile of rocks in a lonely farewell that is more than symbolic. His lack of interest in farm work is matched by a firming desire to create objects in stone or *mulika*. Scarcely aware of what it means to be a sculptor, he understands his wish to create and wants to learn how to do it. He arranges that Šimun, his brother-in-law, will take him to Split,

FIGURE 1.3

Engraved rock, Čavoglave, carved 1950, revisited 2014. Source: Vicky Dabro.

This was one of my very first carvings. There it was, sixty-four years later.

but arriving at a farm stopover after dark, he falls into the camouflaged pit dug to hide produce from the Partisans and has to be rescued with a rope. It is an untimely moment of an untimely exit. In more than seventy years, he has never again spent a single night in the family home. The seeds of the man who is to be are already deeply rooted.

CHAPTER 2

MAKING THE ARTIST

It is in the month of *Rujan*, September 1953, that Ante Dabro is about to arrive at the birthplace of one of the most successful Roman Emperors.

Diocletian, who ruled 284–305 CE, was one of the very few Emperors not to be assassinated. He was born in the great city of Solin (Salina) now a series of ruins near the modern city of Split. By the age of forty, he had had enough of the decidedly perilous existence as supreme commander of most of the known world, and retired to his birthplace. Since Solin was too far from the sea to make the regular grand but convenient returns-home that befitted a retired emperor, he planned an enormous retirement villa as close as was possible to Solin: the natural harbour of Split, now the busiest port in Croatia.

Now Diocletian hadn't been a dashing cavalry commander for twenty years for nothing. He understood the vulnerability of every landfall on the Adriatic coast and was determined to make his retreat defensible from pirate or invading army. His design, following the four-square military encampment long familiar to him, was massively defensible: 30,000 square metres, walls 216 metres long and 175 wide, 16 solid watchtowers, three landward entrance gates. Its interior was to contain a palace in marble and white limestone, court-yards, pleasure gardens, a temple, a known-world collection of Hellenistic, Etruscan and Egyptian masterworks and a Mausoleum for this self-appointed living son of Jupiter, Diocletian himself. The fourth entrance gave directly to the formal landing jetty where an artist's impression depicts the arrival of a barge that, like Cleopatra's, 'like a burnished throne burned on the water'. Diocletian's magnificent palace was the wonder of the age and is now one of the most significant and best-preserved masterpieces of the ancient world. It was listed as a World Heritage Site in 1979.

The arrival of Ante Dabro at Split in 1953, in peasant's sandals and home-spun clothes rather than a royal barge, is rather less than magnificent. Working against his success as a student-sculptor will be just four years of primary

26   THE LIFE AND WORK OF ANTE DABRO

education, his forlorn poverty, a total urban naivete and his connection with the known troublemaker, Marko Dabro. He speaks an accent and vocabulary somewhat different from the city-dwellers even though Čavoglave is barely forty-five kilometres away. Such is the antiquity of the city, that the term used to describe him – *vlaj*, a person of the high country – is the term the ancient Romans used to describe the Illyrians whom they supplanted when they colonised the Dalmatian coast. To be a *vlaj*, male or female, is to be an outsider: a peasant, practical, strong, tough, but the term carries also a hint of the ill-educated, the uncouth. At this moment, Ante is all of these, and he will come to be proud of it. Working for the newly arrived *vlaj* will be his capacity for any kind of practical or skilled labour, a determination to put farmwork behind him forever, a self-promise to succeed or perish, a precocious artistic talent and an invitation from the director of the Split School of Applied Arts to present himself on his arrival.[1] Throughout his life, the strong, tough sculptures of the *vlaj*, the outsider, will compete under his chisel with another conception of the human figure, the sophisticated smooth resolutions of the Italian Renaissance led by the great Florentine Michelangelo Buonarroti. Each human form in every style that he will create is waiting for this uncouth young man's hands to give them light.

Šimun, the cousin given charge of him, takes Ante to one of the many bomb sites that have made the city a partial ruin. Tonight he will sleep in the rubble along with several others until in the early morning brother Boško arrives, aghast to find his little brother's disreputable appearance. Yet the bomb site is no drop-out centre. Most of the young men sleeping rough in the city are employed. In post-war Split, while the unskilled labour market is plentiful, accommodation is not. Though his clothes, rustic ways and odd accent mark him as different from the sophisticated students of Croatia and all the other Yugoslavian states, Split already seems in another hemisphere.

Dabro's career has, until now been determined by his family: 'Your father's still in prison, so as the last able-bodied male on the farm, just get your primary education, then come back to manage the farm for the rest of your life.' The family's expectations of the young man to return home, as old as the generations of the world, lie heavily on Ante, but he will have none of them. Equally ancient are the expectations of society itself that can crush the spirit of the young, suffocate enthusiasm and hope and which may demand much hardship to escape.

So too have the Croatian authorities a plan for their talented graduate-in-waiting: 'After your military training, and your education in the principles of State Socialism, you will become a teacher specialising in art to be sent to any part of the country that we choose.'

It is in this year of 1953 that Ante Dabro is presenting himself at the School of Applied Arts. The director, impressed with the collection of stone carvings that he received from Šimun, is further impressed with the account that this hungry and scruffy fifteen-year-old *vlaj* gives of himself. A teacher leads him to a drawing class, hands him a large sheet of white paper and points to a chair. 'Draw this'. The only drawing Ante has ever drawn previously is of his own shadow with a piece of charcoal on a rock. His first effort is the size of a matchbox. Someone signals to him to make it cover the whole sheet. His confidence and grasp of perspective are good enough to allow him instant entry even though he should have completed eight years of primary education, not four, before enroling. Without money, accommodation or clothes besides those he wears, he learns that he is to be admitted as a trainee teacher of art if he is prepared simultaneously to complete the final four years of junior matriculation, the Australian equivalent of primary grades five and six, and the secondary years seven and eight by the time he graduates. From that point, he will qualify to teach everything, including Applied Arts, to primary and secondary school students. Appearing to thank the director, he tells himself that standing in front of a bunch of chattering adolescents will not be for him; but he does not share such subversive thoughts with anyone, not even his siblings. There are many ideas that he is learning to keep private. The young *vlaj* is becoming a little alienated even from his family. Boško, a trainee draftsman, still embarrassed at Ante's uncouth appearance, buys him some new clothes. Sister Anna, who has been hoicked out of Čavoglave to join the Communist Pioneers en route to the manual work brigade of the Communist Youth League of Yugoslavia, has given him money to buy food. So does brother Jole, working on a building site. Ante works by night humping bags of wheat and sulphur down in the docks. By day, he can't get enough education. He recalls that learning about art was 'water on a dry sponge'. He meanders through the palace courtyards, gazes in wonder at the sculptures of two millennia in the city and the plaster casts in the school, burrows in the library, sketches marble busts in the cathedral. Frequently, he tells himself: 'I'll succeed or perish'. Succeed, yes – but in what?

The curriculum for future teachers is by no means wholly artistic, but includes military training and socialist theory on Tuesday mornings – Marx and Engels, of course. The study of literature, though highly propagandist, is rather more thorough than much Western education today. Students study Dickens intimately to reveal the irretrievable consequences of capitalism, Zola for the excesses of the bourgeoisie and the Magna Carta to demonstrate how the power of a tyrant king can be curbed. Split students know their Tolstoy, Chekhov and Dostoevsky, for the great Russian authors together demonstrate

28 THE LIFE AND WORK OF ANTE DABRO

that nothing can be said in favour of Tsarism. Nor, after 1949, can anything be said of Russian intellectuals of any kind. Tito's break with Stalin releases the nation artistically from dull Soviet brutalism, followed by an inevitable purge of Russian culture. The spoken language vanishes in months, texts in years; but the political shadow persists.

Thankfully, true artists willingly recognise no geographic or ideological frontiers. Ante's teachers are among them. Their higher education in the French and German languages following centuries of Venetian and Austro-Hungarian domination, respects Paris and Germany more than Moscow. In particular, their curriculum derives from the famous Munich Academy of Fine Art. Ante will have formidable antecedents, for the Munich School has guided Kandinsky, Klee and de Chirico. Its teaching method is the unchallenged authority of the Maestro who will hold a strong philosophical conception of artistic creation and expect the continued deference of his few students. The thoroughly Teutonic instruction includes the study of Lascaux paintings and Australian Aboriginal rock carvings, as well as Egyptian, Aegean, Etruscan, Graeco-Roman and Italian sculptural styles. Dabro absorbs the clear inference: 'Decadent though the west may be, students, its artistic traditions form part of your artistic heritage. Study its artists. Know its sculptures. Value them'.

Teaching begins, first in life-drawing classes where even the most basic instruction is a revelation: 'Where is your light source? Look carefully at the angle of the furthest extremity of your model's body to the left, then the right. They will be your starting points.' Think of your positioning: 'don't let your model float like an angel suspended in mid-air'. Though the teaching is mainly theoretical, there is much to consider. Carving: This is where your own work can't be easily imitated by anyone else. Each stroke of your hand or tool carries your own gestural handwriting. Modelling: 'Look at the differences in detail one can achieve by working in marble, plaster, wood or clay.' If you work with a small maquette and scale it up you're going to lose some of the detail. Creating tempera using egg or animal glue. Piece-moulding. Frescos. Working in marble and wood. The techniques – taught theoretically – of metal casting. Analyse the use of colour in the paintings of Van Gogh and Kandinsky. Look how Degas's dancers balance ambiguously: Has the artist caught them in mid-flight or have they themselves achieved their own miraculous poise? How do each artist's figures relate to each other pictorially? How does one achieve artistic balance?

Classes demand understanding of human anatomy. If Michelangelo was able to observe the dissection of human corpses, Split students learn musculature by examining that of a dead horse. Ante, out of his respect for animals, sits

Making the Artist 29

those classes out. Before serious teacher-training pushes specialisation in the curriculum towards pedagogical studies, he is set a new challenge: 'Comrade Dabro, you can't understand the human figure until you understand anatomy. In this examination you will draw a human skeleton in chalk, then clothe it with all its muscles naming each one. In Latin'. There's a point to it. Years later he learns that Michelangelo, in sculpting Moses for Pope Julius II, has minutely observed and sculpted the *extensor digiti minimi*, the tiny muscle in the forearm that allows Moses to raise the forefinger that is intertwined in his beard. The closest examination can release the artist to greater liberties. He is entranced by the paintings of Cezanne whose sculptural-like surfaces reveal a light source of many directions, almost every brush stroke a transition to the next. The French sculptor Rodin offers an entrancing departure from the realities of human anatomy. Certain muscles vanish and tendons expand. An exhibition catalogue exclaims:

> Rodin's audacity knew no bounds. The body was left free to express itself and the manner of doing so unrestricted. Everything became possible: perspectives, views from above, foreshortenings, contortions, sectional views, use of lines that an eraser would have previously effaced, diagonals, and asymmetries.[2]

Most fulfilling and demanding are the sculpture classes: 'No whacking, use the weight of the mallet, not muscle power, to refine the work. Use the coarse and punch chisels first before refining your work with the more precise tools. The drills are for eyeholes and drapery.' Ante watches fascinated as his teacher applies his chisel to a piece of marble, never once glancing down, never once hitting his hand – and uses this learnt ability decades later as a sort of party-trick to impress new sculpture students. But taking a chisel to a solid lump of marble is rather different from chipping bits from a piece of soft limestone. 'As you start work, you may or may not know what is trying to emerge but your task is to release it. Give it light.' Release what? Think of Michelangelo, who used to say, 'By sculpture I mean the work that is done by subtracting.' An eye for symmetry seems to be innate, yet it is a skill that can be, to a point, acquired. He has seen his father Marko in his workshop achieve perfect verticals without using a plumbline, horizontals by observing water levels in a tube. An advanced exercise: 'Dabro: With your mallets and a few of these chisels here, turn this 80 kilogram lump of marble to a perfect cube. No rulers, protractors or set squares'. He manages it almost perfectly when measured by instruments, but more significantly, it looks right to his eye. The principle that reality is never symmetrical is not lost upon him.

30 THE LIFE AND WORK OF ANTE DABRO

Something about the perfect cube that Dabro has created calls to mind the Roman-engineered city in which he lives and daily absorbs. Though hurt by sundry wars, Split in the 1950s is no mean city. The palace within its protecting walls follows an essential engineering logic that is rectangular, solid, imposing. Practical too: the seaward frontage takes its cue from the Venetian waterfront: the walls hold no windows on the two lower floors to repel the highest tides and storms. Dabro mentally calculates that the proportions of both the buildings and interior spaces, which, though under repair, still often follow the proportions of the Golden Mean (1:1:6). Why is it, he wonders, that these dimensions seem satisfying both to the mind and eye? He marvels at the antiquities. He examines the classical simplicity of the peristyle (central courtyard) designed as the forecourt of the emperor's private apartments. Later architects have added an extra storey to the original two, but instead of following the simplicity of the first design, they have overlain theirs with ornate decorations. Are these as satisfactory to the eye as the original design? Where does architecture end and decoration begin? Why did the architects adopt those slender and graceful Corinthian columns, but choose not to flute them in the manner he has admired in the books of Hellenistic architecture in the school library? That granite sphinx that rests so elegantly in its eye-level space, though he does not yet know it, will find itself suggested in his later work. Did the ancient designers plan such a graceful site to contain it, he wonders, or was it somehow fitted in later? The perfect flagstone and the cemented stonework of the great cathedral of St Boetius, similar to but much more precise than the drystone walls of the paddocks back home. He notices how the force within some of the arches is carried by the traditional triangular keystone: but some of them seem to have been constructed without one. How? He follows the current excavation of the magnificent cellars underneath the palace, graceful and beautiful yet in no disharmony with the practical and utilitarian.

Across the bay is the city of Trogir, whose cathedral carries the carved lunette (portal) of scenes in the life of Christ executed by the great medieval sculptor Radovan in 1240. Ante examines the figures – and copies them. Then the enormous nave and soaring ceiling of the Cathedral of St Domitius in Split, still quite overwhelming for anyone like Dabro who has not yet grasped the profundity of Christian symbolism. Its interior is as dazzling as its succession of architects and artists intended. He gazes in awe at the Romanesque artist Buvina's immense ceremonial doors, recognised as among the best-preserved wooden doors of Europe – and copies them. He stands in astonishment at the works expressed in gold and silver filigree, marble, wood, plaster, fresco and stone, the carvings of donkeys and horses, angels, cherubs, citizens, soldiers,

Making the Artist 31

saints and martyrs, in every form of paint, mosaic, fresco, relief, bas-relief and three dimensions, in every style available to the plastic artist for 2000 years, from Roman, early Christian, Romanesque, Gothic and Renaissance – and copies them all. Perhaps there is no better site in the whole of the Western world for a young artist to absorb the millennia of European artistic development. They remain in the visual memory, forever, seldom consciously drawn upon yet never forgotten.

Eerily attractive for the young artist are the ruins. Salona, now gobbled up by the expanding suburbs of Split, could not defend itself against the Slavic invaders who sacked the Western empire in the sixth and seventh centuries. Survivors and refugees from the destruction had to scramble seven kilometres back to the fortress-palace, which, as Diocletian and later rulers intended, continued to rebuff every variety of invader for centuries thereafter. But the deserted ruins of Salona remain as the former great city of the empire through its foundations, city walls, forum, baths, paved streets and amphitheatre. Foremost among the Salona ruins is the famed necropolis. Christian pilgrims came to pray at the elaborate Christian tomb of St Domitius, but to Ante the Roman tombs were much more striking: the sarcophagi of the necropolis follow a proportional logic of geometrical form and rhythm unsuspected in the mountains above Čavoglave. Among the many hundreds of ornate interments that crowd the necropolis today, these tombs of the early Roman Republic retain their understated dignity: each a solemn waist-high rectangular stone oblong with overhanging lid, utilitarian yet elegant, set in rows not exactly symmetrical, anything but straight. Nor did they need geometrical perfection to visually satisfy Dabro's eye and imagination. He gazes at them, sketches them, ponders their proportions. They were not unlike that geometrically flawed but artistically almost-perfect marble cube that he has created at the School of Applied Arts at the end of his first year. Another lesson is absorbed.

Besides the artistry that fills his heart and brain, so much in the city is new to the young adventurer. Dabro has never seen women dress in anything but peasant clothes. Extreme poverty means several months of sleeping in the bomb site and eating at the Red Cross relief kitchen, where nobody thinks it necessary to tell him that sheets are supposed to be washed, and which after six months are quite black. Before the end of his third year, the director finds him a stipend that allows him a bed and clothes at a hostel. Money! So this is Italian wine! This is coffee! He buys two shirts, long pants, shoes and socks and feels like the king of the universe. Handiness with tools and help from his teacher lands him a job with a theatre company constructing sets for the convenient and easily accessible backdrops of Italian 'old-time' film productions.

FIGURE 2.1

The Roman cemetery, Solin, Split. Source: 1998 (Author).

Whenever I go there I can hear the chariots and the life of the city.

In 1956, he spots Orson Wells harbourside taking coffee with his retinue. A talent scout grabs him for a part in a crowd of extras during the shoot. He spies Gina Lollobrigida and Sophia Loren, admired from afar by the young men of the city.

The palace, the cathedral, class visits and the school library offer every chance to grasp the achievements of two thousand years of architecture and sculpture. His teachers send the students off to learn the textbooks written and followed by the ancient artists. He learns that Polykleitos's *Kanon*, written in the fifth century BCE, found beauty 'in the proportions, not of the elements, but of the parts, that is to say, of finger to finger, and of all the fingers to the palm and the wrist, and of these to the forearm, and of the forearm to the upper arm, and of all the other parts to each other'. Using the many hundreds of examples within the city his teachers demonstrate how the classical sculptors' search for idealised perfection in the human body became too limiting for the Hellenistic artists. The facial expressions of the Roman Republic began to express a wider range of emotions and age in their subjects. Faces became recognisable. 'Look how the preoccupations of Romanesque Christianity enriched the older, too-perfect male bodies and faces of the Greeks, edging them towards depicting deeper emotions of joy and grief, quietness and serenity, the seven deadly sins and their consequences, didactic narratives, symbols understood by the viewer to carry the exterior meaning into the interior life. Look, comrade students, how even our wonderful post-Romanesque sculptors like Radovan could not, or at any rate, did not, venture into what seemed to them to be the dangerous universe of sculpture that was lyrical and passionate.' That step must await the art and philosophy of the Renaissance. Staring in awe, Dabro grasps the solidity and strength behind their lack of elegance and sophistication. 'Just like my mountains'. Just like a *vlaj*.

Over months the lessons expand: 'Can we detect an artistic progression?' 'Is art getting better and better? No. Don't look for progress, look for artistic integrity. Each great work of art of whatever period or culture will carry its own validity. Its universal values will transcend centuries and cultures and boundaries and ideologies'. That is a third lesson heard and absorbed. Thoughtful students like Dabro have no need to see 'progress'. He intuits, though he cannot yet articulate, the wisdom of Croatian scholar Vladimir Voss who in 2008 wrote about Radovan:

> We need not despair that he closes a period. In an art history free from evolutionary, natural science models, what counts is the valour and validity of the moment, which, if true, should translate into their own validity forever.[3]

Artistic development from one era to the next, then, can change into something better or worse. Changing styles, even the intellectual forces that once produced great works of art, can atrophy, draw in on themselves run out of inspiration.

Run out of inspiration? It is hard for the young student not to admire the daring and liberating artistic visions he sees all about him, even though they

34   THE LIFE AND WORK OF ANTE DABRO

were thought to be out of date by the generations who came after. He admires the 72 individualised sculpted heads, recognisable men and women, peasants, fishermen and teenagers, on the outer walls of the Renaissance-inspired cathedral at Šibernik by Yuraj Dalmatinac, and the Renaissance Venetian sculptor Galeazzo Alessi's barrel vaults of the Trogir Cathedral, and the sixteenth-century Renaissance Dalmatian artist Jakov Selembrije's sarcophagus at St John's Baptistry within Diocletian's Palace. 'Comrade Dabro, don't think of progress, think of validity and integrity. Look for alternatives'. Raphael's frequent depictions of the harmonious, beautiful and serene perhaps answer Dabro's memories of the brutal war that remain embedded in the soul. The library's collections reveal Corregio's depictions of the female nude as a legitimate subject of enquiry – and joy. They release a profound liberation in his own future work. Rodin's sculptures depict narrative without diorama, ignore the rules of human proportion to create works of immense emotional depth. Titian shows that artistic endeavour need be no preparation for the afterlife but a celebration of individuals and the diurnal life that is about us. Sharpest is Michelangelo, who asks what is more beautiful than the nude human form.

That far Ante's teachers can take him – though in fact few of them do. Where they cannot follow is into the dangerous world of speculation and doubt that awaits any serious and thoughtful student of 16 years of age. Just stay in that exciting section of the Library marked *Preporod*, 'Renaissance'. Read about how so many scholars of two or three generations debated, and disagreed after learned argument, such profound questions as the immortality of the soul, the Copernican universe, the trustworthiness of knowledge gained through reason alone, the best form of government, the powers of natural magic, the existence of free will. These thoughts were, and should be now, the very meat and drink of any undergraduate Liberal Arts education. Yet within an ideological dictatorship, such speculations are not for the cafeteria or the bar, certainly not for the tutorial – but buried. Youthful minds like Dabro's, confronted for the first time in his life with the serious thinking of many generations, learn to keep ultimate speculations to themselves.

Among most creative artists, perhaps it is the interior or solitary life that most invites speculation. William Wordsworth spent much of his youth alone in the contemplation of the natural world, and by his later teens, he was exploring his own mind at Cambridge University as he contemplated a marble bust of Isaac Newton:

With his prism and silent face,
The marble index of a mind forever
Voyaging through strange seas of thought, alone.[4]

Making the Artist 35

The interior journey may be both the gift and burden of any mind that voyages alone.

Even the not-very-radical idea that each work of art should be valued for its own integrity and not for its place in the long advance of humankind may be considered subversive because it implies that one cannot be certain that any nation-state has achieved the perfection it claims for itself. Indeed, at this very moment of the mid-1950s such thoughts are landing brave Croatian thinkers in jail for 'advocating anti-revisionism', 'subversion of the Socialist system' and 'verbal offences against the state'. Students learn in their compulsory History of Socialism classes that the communist state that Yugoslavians enjoy is the product of historical materialism, the inevitable processes that have led from primitive communism through feudalism to monarchy, capitalism, State Socialism and at last to the utopia of true Communism. Well then, if Radovan might be forgiven for ending his artistry where he did, and if such profundities as God's limitations upon human reason could be debated so openly during Renaissance Italy, surely it might be possible to challenge the wisdom of the Yugoslav bureaucracy bent on educating its young people into a joyful acceptance of the everlasting People's Republic. Within a few years, Ante will come to grief with the authorities over that same question.

In the city, any political action by the son of a landowning farmer, a *kulak*, would inevitably be recorded. Dabro had acquired the reputation of a minor troublemaker that was to worsen in the years to come in Zagreb. Marshall Tito claimed the 1945 election to be the 'most democratic Yugoslavia ever had', even though voters were presented with only the 'yes' or 'no' alternatives, and 'traitors' were denied the opportunity to vote at all. The 10 per cent of Yugoslavians wishing by 'secret' ballot to vote against the Socialist Alliance of Working Men and Women party were required to cast a rubber ball into a metal bowl of a certain timbre quite audible to listening officials. Dabro recalled the belligerent defence made for decades: 'This is how we Yugoslavians do it.' Yet he never could ever forget the young man he saw in Čavoglave cowering 'like a wounded animal' before a series of blows and kicks after betrayal by a neighbour for 'anti-socialist deviation'. At a 1946 rally at Petrovo Polje, he accidentally dropped a Yugoslav flag on the ground, bringing down an angry bawling-out on himself. These were harsh and never to be forgotten lessons, the first personal brushes against a sometimes brutal and ignorant bureaucracy.

Five years later his life, like that of many other young students over many centuries, was one of friendships and partying intersecting with studies. The life of this student was also working on the docks, girlfriends and midnight scrambles back to the second floor of the hostel via knotted sheets. The *vlaj*

THE LIFE AND WORK OF ANTE DABRO

cultural expectation of male entitlement to a promiscuity not vouchsafed to 'good' girls, taught by Marko, once learnt, was harder to forget or even reassess. News got back to Čavoglave that Marko's youngest son was not the single-minded student they had imagined, rather, something of a Lothario. 'We thought he had left us to become an artist.' On the farm, the simmering anger at his abandoning his responsibilities erupted.

Nor could the nightlife of downtown Split be considered serene. One evening in 1956, while walking with a group of young people on the waterfront, Dabro encountered some by-now unpopular Russian sailors. Through a similarity in the sound of the words, a cheeky 'Would you like me to light your cigarette?' was heard as the deadly 'Would you like me to light up your cunt?' A free fight ensued. The underweight Dabro tried to stay out of it, but finished with a few cuts and bruises duly noted by the school authorities. On another occasion, Boško and his friend, a boxer, were involved in another free-for-all. Dabro shinned up a palm tree to keep out of the way, but again the incident found its way back to the school. Skylarking about in the studio, he and his mate Bezjak, a trainee hammer thrower, were practising tossing it, of all places, in the courtyard in which stood some marble copies of Michelangelo's *Slaves*. The inevitable happened. 'There goes your holiday, Comrade Dabro'. The punishment was to carve another copy of the work in marble, a task that required most acute observation. Several months later, he and his mate Bezjak embarked on the kind of lark that art students often get up to. Surely that fig tree would look better if it were painted another colour in the style of the *pointillistes*. His mate painted the trunk, and Dabro covered the leaves in a thick tempera; the tree died of suffocation. The artists were deeply mortified. Clearly, the director had a soft spot for the troublemaker, who received no more than a wigging.

The years in Split brought a further discovery: the work of a contemporary sculptor born in 1883, another *vlaj* from Otavice, a little village not far from Čavoglave. His name was Ivan Meštrović.

At the beginning of the twentieth century, Meštrović met Rodin, the French sculptor who would in time occupy the small pantheon of imaginative heroes of Dabro himself. Rodin followed the younger man's work while Meštrović absorbed his liberties with human proportions, the subtlety of curved drapery and the profundity of expression that can be imparted even to cast bronze. Dabro reasoned: 'So Meštrović is of the same rural backwater as myself, raised not more than ten kilometres from my own birthplace, who rejected the life of the peasant and devoted his life to artistic creation! And now he is world famous!'

Making the Artist 37

By the 1950s, some of Meštrovic's greatest works were already installed in Split in the church of St John the Baptist and in the Meštrović Gallery dedicated solely to his own work. Most striking of all was his colossal bronze sculpture of Grgur Ninsky (Gregory of Nin), an eight-metre work of Bishop Gregory who in the ninth century opposed the Pope's insistence on a Latin liturgy rather than the old Croatian language, and whose big toe tourists still rub to bring themselves good luck. Today, Grgur towers over visitors yet stands in perfect proportion to his surroundings. His head tilts left as he glares over and beyond the holy Croatian texts. His right arm is raised in an ambiguous gesture that can be interpreted either as passionate teaching or denunciation. Dabro gazed at it thunderstruck. Meštrović's treatment of the fingers, the folds of the garment and the fierce facial expression are reminiscent of Rodin, and it is under the stern demeanour of Grgur that Dabro was making his first practical studies. In 1959, Ivan Meštrović met the young Dabro, embraced his work as that of another *vlaj* and considered him a successor to his own work.

Without entering into formal discussion with his teachers, Dabro's mind is beginning to wheel around the nature of the created object. Scarcely knowing how he got there, he has arrived at one of the first enigmas of Western sculpture: *What is this thing that I am creating*? Is there an essence inherent in each human body, a tree, rock or bird? If so, does it depend on the age, culture, environment, point of view and angle of vision of the observer? St Augustine asks whether an object gives delight because it is beautiful or whether it is beautiful because it gives delight. Dabro, though he has heard of Augustine only in religious classes, is certain on this point, intuitively drawn to the visually beautiful. So, every work of art, in its potential, is beautiful? If so, does its essence endure beyond the moment of viewing? Dabro understands Meštrović's Grgur to be overwhelming rather than exquisite, while his sculpture of the body of St John the Baptist in the Baptistry is so distorted that the work could be called grotesque. He prefers Grgur, for if not beautiful, then certainly it is powerful. Yet somehow the artist has succeeded in making St John tall enough not to be crushed beneath the Baptistry's high ceiling while not dominating the chapel itself. No massive Grgur-style work would be appropriate here; yet, undoubtedly, Meštrović has set the emotions of the viewer in both locations ablaze. His professors tell him that both are masterpieces. Can it be that Meštrović's best works are like the vases so perfectly formed that they continue, like T. S. Eliot's Chinese jar, to move perpetually in their stillness? He ponders how it is that the distorted features and human disproportions can convey a passion in the viewer stronger than reproducing an exact physical reality – should that even

FIGURE 2.2

Ante Dabro stands before Meštrović's sculpture of Grgur Ninsky, (Gregory of Nin). Source: 1998, (Author).

I like to think that my work measures up to his.

be possible. Like the artists of the Renaissance, he is drawn to the Platonic conception of a perfect form that exists beyond the beauty of *this* created woman and to which the artist should forever strive. He intuits an immanent femininity, an inner flame of humanity that exists beyond the facial expression or the curves of the torso. 'Do your sculptures have souls?' 'Yes of course', Dabro

Making the Artist   39

answers. 'Sometimes they begin to talk to me as I'm carving them before I even know who or what they are'.

Dabro's mature works will for a decade or two sing as serenely as Meštrović's or Rodin's before his style after 2,000 veers towards a more uncompromising essence of humanity. His sculpted women will not always be beautiful, but they will be strong and dignified, generally untroubled and serene, with their own inner life, never ugly, grotesque or made as if to present themselves to the viewer. His sculpted men will carry determination, and when modelled on himself, resignation. Even those figures he will group together will remain voyaging in their own thoughts in a space in which speech is possible rather than necessary. That is how he sees himself as a student and sees himself now: the onlooker. 'I always talked to the animals and birds. I knew them all by name.' Nor will the people to be created in plaster and on paper relate closely to each other. Each, like their creator, will occupy a solitary universe. Here in Split, for all the bonding, the affairs and the relationships, in parallel to the camaraderie there sails a lonely voyager. The lonely days in the mountains have freed the young mind from the necessary interplay of conversation and rendered him more observer than participant. They were the same properties of the wilderness, of 'melancholy not unnoticed' that young William Wordsworth knew as he rowed his boat alone in the darkness of Lake Windermere. The dim perceptions of the burden of the artist will crystallise more precisely in Zagreb in a more equal discourse with his teachers.

This is the graduate schoolteacher-to-be leaving the Split College of Applied Art, steeped in Hellenistic perfection, Roman geometry, Romanesque humanism and the intellectual confidence and idealised bodies of the Renaissance, a young sculptor barely nineteen, uncertain of his future but firming his artistic values, whose creations sometimes begin to speak to him even before they are complete. The years in Split have given him a vision of what he will seek all his life, when the viewer for a moment shares the artist's passion or pain or memory or exultation, or the sorrow of the midnight sea in the blood.

In May 1958, the dynamic and emerging Yugoslavian sculptor, Dušan Džamonja, was passing through Split. A perceptive teacher introduced Dabro to him, whereupon, examining his student work, Džamonja recognised a significant potential. With a scribbled address, he invited him to come to his studio in Zagreb as soon as the young man arrived to enter the city's Academy of Fine Arts. The plan, formulated over a grappa or two, was that Dabro would stay with him while he sat the enrolment exams. Maybe he could assist Džamonja in the studio while awaiting the results of his application for entry. There was no time to lose; the two-week tests for the Academy would start soon in mid-October, and the results announced immediately. If he failed

40 THE LIFE AND WORK OF ANTE DABRO

admission, Dabro must either defer his military service for a year and be sent teaching to some remote location – bad – enrol in some other undergraduate course – worse – or report to the Drniš military barracks immediately as a conscripted soldier – worst of all. At the Split railway station, Boško gave his younger brother a bottle of wine in farewell. The young graduate-to-be, as penniless and almost as disreputable-looking as the day he arrived in Split five years earlier, caught the train to the great city of Zagreb to sit the entry exams that would take the form of life drawing and modelling the human head.

But arriving in Zagreb, Ante had lost Džamonja's address and had nowhere to stay! During the examination process, an Academy tutor offered him two weeks accommodation. The tutor got the wine, but the disastrous news arrived that Ante had not been accepted. Not good enough? Surely not. A *vlaj* connection with the temporarily unpopular Meštrovic? – possibly. Or did the long shadow of Marko still cloud his every action? Very probably. Immediately, the Army learnt of his failure to enrol and wanted him within a month.

Dabro can scarcely believe the catastrophe, but still not having found Džamonja, he must leave the kindly tutor. As he did five years before, he has to sleep rough under a bench near the Zagreb railway station, competing with other homeless men to carry the bags of travellers to find enough change for bread and milk. Each day he walks another kilometre of the city's major thoroughfare Ilica. All he knows is that the studio is here somewhere and that he should look for a 'courtyard within a courtyard'. He's so miserable that he doesn't even think to consult the phone book but slogs another kilometre up Ilica every day. In desperation, and with no intention of ever finishing the course, he enrols in Philosophy at the University of Zagreb. Rather unexpectedly, the department accepts him just before the last date that he must attend the barracks to begin compulsory military service. Do the authorities hope that a programme of 're-education' will reform Marko's son? While he continues to study, he will need to attend military training for one day a week, but he has escaped the army, for now. After weeks more searching: there is the studio, not more than 200 metres from the Academy of Fine Arts itself. Džamonja asks him where he's been all this time, gives him a meal and offers him the role neither of apprentice nor assistant but of salaried partner. He assures Ante that he won't need to take his philosophy studies too seriously.

Only ten years separated the births of the professional and acknowledged sculptor Džamonja and one who could hardly yet be described as his assistant, but while Dabro's childhood had been clouded with a violence no child could comprehend, in those same five years of savage cruelty, Džamonja had come of age. While the Croatian Dabro could only grasp the Axis occupation

Making the Artist 41

through the intuitive mind of a child, the Macedonian Džamonja understood the nation's suffering differently. He had grown up in Belgrade. He knew the meaning of treachery, occupation, reprisal, pitched battle, massacre and heroism. In 1945, he was old enough to comprehend state socialism, ideology, revolution, national unity and the teachings of the Communist Party. All had formed a deep part of his education. World War II and the Party were in his very being. Even Džamonja's thunderbolt of artistic enlightenment had struck him through the lens of the occupation. In 1943, as related in his biography, he was passing the former royal palace in Belgrade, then occupied by the Gestapo. The guard was momentarily absent.

> The great door of the palace was also open, so I crept in, finding myself all alone in the vast entrance hall. From here a broad flight of marble steps led to the upper floor. I went up, as if spellbound, until I came upon a sight that made me catch my breath; before me stood a forest of huge marble sculptures by Ivan Meštrović. I could hardly believe my eyes; my excitement was so intense that there could no longer be any doubt – I had to be a sculptor.[5]

United by their admiration for Meštrović, different though they were, this accelerating modernist was to become Dabro's only teacher with whom he could genuinely exchange ideas.

During the war, Yugoslavia lost more than a million soldiers, guerrillas and citizens. The decades following the defeat of Hitler and the rejection of Stalin were therefore years of intense national mourning and attempts at reforming a national unity. Into these had fallen the ambitious young gun Dušan Džamonja. He was not one to miss a professional opportunity: he spent half his artistic life creating huge monuments at dozens of sites of wartime national heroism or suffering. Artistically, he was the rising young Yugoslavian whose vast conceptions in concrete and rusty iron were unlike anything Dabro had seen in Split. The invitation to the lad from the bush had come when this master sculptor was barely thirty, already the designer of six vast public sculptures, including the Memorial to the Unknown Political Prisoner and to the Firing Squad Victims of Jajinci, Zagreb. Had Džamonja, by participating so enthusiastically in these national projects, diverted his creative potential, even his artistic integrity? Dabro could not bring himself to ask, but his biographer Giulio Argan remarked rather opaquely: 'Just as it is right that an artist should not be expected to put his work at the service of political authority and ideological propaganda, it would obviously be absurd to pretend that a culturally up to date country, such as Yugoslavia today, should not identify herself in

42   THE LIFE AND WORK OF ANTE DABRO

the work of one of her greatest artists.'[6] To Džamonja, creating abstract state memorials was a natural artistic response to the suffering and heroism that he had seen and, to a point, endured. Yet his promising young partner from Split knew only the nameless fear and irrational actions of grown-ups who had bombed his village and had planned to execute his resolute and loving father. Dabro hated violence in any form; it frightened him.

Thus, at several points, their minds did not meet. Dabro could interpret Džamonja's working drawings, produce his maquettes, fetch his supplies, pour his concrete and weld his chains and nails, but he never quite accepted either the technology or the national ideology. The personal coming of age that Dabro found in Zagreb in the early 1960s was a freedom from the monumental public sculpture and the rigid state socialism that Džamonja, of necessity, had embraced. For him, there remained a reassuring alternative. The treasures of Hellenistic and Renaissance artists that he had glimpsed in Split and in the college library intuitively offered him an artistic response to nails, chains and concrete: the power to create and re-create the human form amidst the serenity of the high country of Lačina, from which, ten years before, he had gazed into the distant horizon and longed for the greater world. The avant-garde of the sixteenth century and Džamonja's modernism presented stylistic choices that the apprentice easily resolved.

Little by little, Džamonja's confidence in Dabro increased. He might produce a maquette and ask him to enlarge it in full size. He might present Dabro with a sculptural blueprint, expecting it to be finished by the time he returned in six weeks. He taught him how to weld. Dabro absorbed Džamonja's recordings of Bach's music, which left him entranced. In 1959, Henry Moore, viewing photographs of some smaller works of the promising young Croatian, invited Dabro to visit his studio in Hertfordshire, England. The army, doubtless suspecting that the visit might end in a request for asylum, refused permission. In Zagreb, he should be considered part of the rising artistic elite of the country, but his refusal to join the Communist Party made for a dragging sea-anchor on his upward progress.

Amidst the bad news came better: his friend Tvrtko Meštrović, son of the sculptor, had arranged for Ante to meet the great man himself. 'My father wants to meet you in his home in Otavice. The local folk are planning a celebratory lunch for him. That'll be your opportunity.' It seemed that Meštrović had heard about and followed the uncertain career of Dabro not only for his abilities and potential but also as a fellow *vlaj*.

More than a little like the outspoken members of the Dabro family, Meštrović was an independent thinker. He had annoyed the Austro-Hungarians before

Making the Artist   43

World War I for advocating a union of independent southern Slavic states, then the Ustaše during World War II, who locked him up for three months, ostensibly because he was trying to leave the country. On release, he exiled himself to Rome and Switzerland, then the United States, before annoying Marshall Tito himself by refusing to return when invited. By 1959, he made his peace and returned, recipient of a prestigious United States award for sculpture and an invitation from President Eisenhower to become an American citizen. By now, he was something of a national hero. By bicycle and a lift, Ante arrived a little late at his home. 'My heart was beating.' Meštrović needed only a glance at Ante before remarking: 'Ah yes, I can see you're a Dabro.' They agreed to meet further in Split, where Dabro would show him some of his work.

Meanwhile, Dabro's career was beginning to accelerate despite the Yugoslav army and the party. Representing Yugoslavia in the 1960 Venice Biennale, Džamonja introduced him to a variety of internationally eminent artists and critics, including Herbert Read. Peggy Guggenheim, a principal sponsor, lavishly entertained her international coterie, among whom were Džamonja and his young studio partner; but Dabro was perplexed that her guests had to stand up in St Marks Square to take their coffee, because Guggenheim didn't want to pay the extra cost of her guests sitting down! Džamonja took his protege to several more Biennales. In 1962, it was the spidery figures of Giacometti that dominated discussion. In 1964, he could see the influence of Moore in the works of Andrea Cascella and Alberto Viani. He admired Arshile Gorky and Wassily Kandinsky, but it was in Florence in 1963, for the first time face to face with Michelangelo, Da Vinci, Donatello, Giotto and Brunelleschi that his convictions crystallised.

In his several visits to the works of Michelangelo in Florence and Rome, Dabro's life has met its great confluence. He stares, marvels, copies, makes small-hours visits when the crowds have passed, absorbs every limb into the visual memory where they will remain forever. These are figures with real emotional weight, capable of revealing not just the ancient past of the subject but the now-time of the viewer. He ponders Michelangelo's elusive ambiguity. Look how the weight falls in his *contrapposto* study of the drunken Bacchus. Is Bacchus trying to balance himself, about to lurch forward, or ready to fall over? How critical is the light source that illuminates his *Pietà* in St Peter's Basilica? Did Michelangelo mean to draw the viewer's eye to the face of the Virgin or the dead Christ; and why does she seem to look past his body? (The top lighting of the elevated sculpture today probably quite changes Michelangelo's intentions.) Is the face of David, viewed from below, fearful, apprehensive or watchful? How does it seem to change when viewed from the height of his face? Is the

44 THE LIFE AND WORK OF ANTE DABRO

lowered head of the figure supporting the dead Christ in his Florentine *Pietà* bowed in grief, or is he merely supporting most of the weight of the corpse? Dabro minutely examines Michelangelo's technique. How many of his most stunning body shapes do not carry a particularly memorable face: so much human emotion and psychology is invested in the twist of the head and the torso. Scholars believe it probable that Michelangelo modelled the tormented torsos of the Dying and Rebellious Slaves on the three figures of the *Laocoön and His Sons* (discovered only the year before, in 1507) but that the sculptor was less interested in their tortured expressions, more in the configuration of their bodies. Look how the *non-finito*, less-finished hair of Brutus diverts the eye towards the noble profile and patrician clothing. Doubt, mystery, enigma. Why is it only rarely that Michelangelo's sculptures return the gaze of the viewer? Are his sculpted figures experiencing an intimate moment or do they share them with us? Are they part of our world or theirs? That intangible space in which his figures float between wakefulness and sleep, silence and speech, stasis and movement, thought and contemplation. Almost none of his sculptures hold the shape of the human body as it actually is: the foreshortenings, lengthenings and distortions all serve their artistic purpose. The restraint: the angle of neck, hand, foot and torso have formed the deepest part of a lifetime's study of the human figure, which was very often young, male and nude. There's an artistic confidence in the self and its abilities that has no truck with post-Renaissance self-consciousness or the irresolute musings of the Mannerist Hamlet.

Like Dabro, Michelangelo does not appreciate criticism, but demands respect from those who commission him; he believes that, while artistic endeavour rightly belongs to all observers, it must be received and acknowledged at the very highest levels of society. Such is an appropriate sphere for the artist to inhabit.

Such an obsession with a long-dead master may seem bizarre unless we recall the many hundreds of artists of many centuries, from Keats and Byron to David Malouf, who have sought inspiration in Venice, Florence or Rome. One such Australian was the distinguished painter Jeffrey Smart, who travelled first to Rome in the 1960s before buying a house in Sansepulcro, Tuscany. This was the birthplace of Piero della Francesca, whom Smart regarded as his primary inspiration:

> Look, remember I came to live in this country to worship at the altars of the greatest painters in the history of art. To measure my standards against them and to maintain a grasp of reality. By that I mean to measure, not to equal or surpass them. Exemplars such as Piero or Giovanni Bellini and so

Making the Artist   45

on. The prospect of my coming anywhere near them would be absolutely absurd. In that way I always felt doomed to fail. Why do you think I rejoice when I find a single flaw in the paintings of the great ones? Such flaws remind me to be more forgiving of my own.[7]

In 2017, never one to be cowed by self-modesty, Dabro told a camera crew making a documentary about him:

[Florence] is my Mecca. This is my spiritual and artistic magnet. The city where art was born, where everything started. From the awakening of the humanities in the classical world it took about a thousand years to awaken again.

Strolling past *David,* he remarked:

This is my best friend Mr Michelangelo Buonarotti. I can do just as well as you.

At Cellini's sculpture of Perseus holding the head of Medusa, he added:

This is Cellini. Some of my work back in Australia is as good as his. If someone can take me back to the Renaissance it is Florence where I'd like to go back to, whether I am saying something politically incorrect or not.

Of all the artists of the Italian Renaissance, Michelangelo had entered Dabro's soul and would form the constant to which he would never cease to aspire. Every feature that he admired would be reflected, consciously or unconsciously, for all his artistic life. Early in his maturity, he began the most reassuring exchanges in his artistic life, the one-way, or in a sense, two-way conversations with the long-dead master. Each one of Dabro's many pilgrimages to Florence has begun with a visit to Michelangelo's tomb, where in his imagination this exchange began:

Michelangelo: So you're here again, young fellow. Where are you these days?
Dabro: Maestro, I live in Australia on the other side of the world, but my real home is where I can enjoy the beauty of art. I miss Split and my village, and I very much miss Florence, even though every summer I try to be here with you. Your star still guides me, but I feel like a lost soul born at the wrong place at the wrong time.

46   THE LIFE AND WORK OF ANTE DABRO

Michelangelo: You must be strong. You and I know that the greatest art is figurative and the greatest figurative art is the human form.[8]

Such a respectful admiration would come at a cost. From the early 1960s, Džamonja wondered if his star assistant was not a little old-fashioned in his choice of subject matter. An Australian gallery owner asked him to be more contemporary; the National Gallery of Australia failed to buy his work. Only public commissions, and later, a Medici-style patron, enabled him to make the mark on stone like a mark in time that his teachers were already beginning already to expect.

Back in Zagreb, master and assistant return to the conversations about practise and techniques that never happened at the Split School of Applied Art. Should one try as a first priority to achieve the greatest concision of form, and if so, how? What angles of vision does one need to consider in creating a spatial relationship between two objects? What light source? How best can negative space be utilised in an emotional work such as a national monument? What are the best techniques of fixing glass to iron? Can we fuse metal and cement? What are the advantages of working directly from a drawing to the finished work, without a maquette? They apply wet concrete to chicken wire – a failure. At the massive Memorial to the December Victims in Dubrava, Zagreb, Dabro wonders whether heavy concrete volumes placed in a mutual relationship really suggest the movement of the masses that is Džamonja's intention. Creating four identical sculptures in wood, aluminium, bronze and marble produces different results that confirm Džamonja's belief that the choice of materials affects not only the form but the emotional gravity of a work. Dabro, preferring the traditional contours of marble or wood, is less convinced. 'Large metal plates hammered in a circle', Džamonja conjectures, 'may convey the impression of multitudes on the move'. Dabro is not so sure. Džamonja has developed a technique of inserting nails into wood or clay before welding them together. Set the task of firekeeper, Dabro falls asleep to find the wood turned to charcoal. The accidental technique produces works that, when replicated become an international success.

In the workshop or in the bars, Dabro is much more intimately involved than the traditional apprentice with his master, creating or completing several works that he believes should have been at least partly attributed to him at exhibition. He is at work casting, observing, experimenting, discussing – and sometimes rejecting. Friendly but searching conversations may continue past midnight over a coffee laced with grappa:

Making the Artist 47

Duško, we're working with these three plaster objects, two upright and one flat. Now I know we think of the space between the volumes as a negative space, but in some ways it's positive space too, because it separates and creates a tension between the figures that has to be filled creatively, and from all directions. We arrange our shapes intuitively – but what works from this angle does not work well from the other side. Round the back here the forms relate to each other differently. How can we resolve that?

Probably there could not have been a better artist in the nation with whom Ante could begin his dialogic postgraduate awakening.

Despite reservations about the works in which his influence should have been acknowledged, Dabro is deeply grateful for this period of growth, discovery and education. Before one finds one's own voice, one has to understand what one is discarding. He concedes, 'I owe him a lot'. He was gratified to find Džamonja, on his advice, beginning to reject some of his spiky metal animal forms for which he had become well-known in the late 1950s, and was beginning at times to create works so much in the style of Dabro that Džamonja's brother could not tell them apart.

September again, the time for admittance examination at the Academy. Again, Dabro was still mysteriously rejected. He continued his studies in philosophy in courses that would keep him out of the army until the age of twenty-seven, but his progress satisfied neither student nor teacher. Everywhere on campus, there brooded resentment at the lack of free speech, the informers, the spying, the ever-present party, the complacent assumption that successful generals made good peacetime leaders. More than once, he was called to the Head of Department's office to explain himself for questioning the orthodoxies of the party. Here, the student must stand rigidly to attention, eyes fixed ahead, as his professor demanded,

Comrade Dabro, in your talk yesterday you challenged the axiom that under socialism everyone is equal. You stated that some individuals will emerge more equal than others. You will explain what you meant by that.

Or:

We have learned that in your History of Socialism class you wanted to know why does not everyone in western Europe embrace socialism. Did you learn that attitude from your father? Explain yourself.

48 THE LIFE AND WORK OF ANTE DABRO

Or:

> Comrade Dabro, you implied that if other empires of the world have crumbled, so may our Socialist Republic. Clearly you have not paid sufficient attention to the classes on Socialist Duty. Explain.

This was the point that marked the emergence of Dabro the dissenter and the outsider, the enemy of what he calls political correctness all his life. He knew enough to refuse several invitations to join the Communist Party. Membership was, of course, the way ahead for an ambitious artist, but he understood that the cost would be the surveillance of any political activity, a demand for sneaky reports about his friends and their conversations. 'They wanted you to report on your own brother.' He strongly suspected that Džamonja was a party member – how else could he have been successful in so many state commissions? – but he could not be sure.

Challenges to received wisdom did not end with philosophy classes but continued in the studio. He understood that Džamonja was ambitious, with an accelerating international reputation; but he still wondered privately if he might be sacrificing his artistic integrity to the state ideology. Sent to the ironmonger across the railway line to fetch back 200 kilograms of nails, he wondered to himself: 'Duško, you are becoming internationally known for those sculptures of nails welded into the wood before it's fired leaving only the fused metal. In fact I gave you a lot of help in creating it that time when I went to sleep and forgot to take them out of the fire! But I have heard that this idea is derived from certain African craftsmen, to whom every nail may represent a person, animal or idea. Surely something of that original artistic impulse may be now lost in your work?'

More often, after a grappa or two, the thoughts of the dissenter became explicit:

> Duško, why have you abandoned the teachings of the professors in the Academy here like Augustinčić who was taught by Meštrović who was taught by Rodin himself? You believe that abstract sculpture can represent the reality that humans know and experience through their work. Okay, so do I. And you say that you don't work in any material simply because of its inherent beauty. I love the old masters who were working in marble and wood. Your spiky signature animal, the deer, that you have created so many times and in so many forms, to me is really quite ugly. You've been inspired by those iron odd animal shapes of Lynn Chadwick that we saw

Making the Artist 49

at the Biennale. Well I prefer those rounded bronze forms of Henry Moore because they're beautiful and that is the reality of the model that Moore sees. And from what I've heard and read, I think Meštrović believes so too. To me there is so much beauty in natural curves and natural materials. Why turn your back on them? I'm not sure that either Moore or Meštrović would like what you're doing, and to tell you the truth, I don't like them much either.

Dabro had developed into the kind of *enfant terrible* that no teacher particularly wanted; but he was so hard-working, so dedicated and so obviously gifted that Džamonja tolerated these tiresome inquisitions until, in Dabro's view, he began to be influenced by his assistant's own techniques and ideas. The discussions, of course, were much more than the junior partner flapping his uncertain wings but a debate as old as artistic creation itself, those divisions that can endure for decades within a mutual respect. He acknowledged Džamonja as a major artist of his country, a brilliant draftsman and the only one of his teachers with whom he could seriously debate the passion for artistic creation that so gripped them both. Džamonja continued for decades with commissions for massive World War II memorials in rusted iron, bricks, chains and concrete, but after a brief period of experimentation in his thirties in a more abstract modernism, Dabro returned to the deepest convictions of his sculptural lifeblood, the beauty that is to be sought in both the subject and materials of the Renaissance, their potential finally released by the artist.

Rujan, September again. A month after his name is noticeably absent from the list of the chosen, he is at work in the studio at 11 p.m. when, most unexpectedly arrives the Academy porter.

We have been looking for you for a month. You are to come with me. Now.

Ten minutes later, he is standing in the office of the Head of the Academy, Franjo Kršinić.

There's a god behind you, Dabro.

Dabro looks mystified:

Meštrović says that it is unthinkable that such a talented young sculptor like you should not be admitted to the Academy. Don't explain anything to anyone, just come in tomorrow, sit down and begin the class.

50   THE LIFE AND WORK OF ANTE DABRO

In 1959, the national hero Meštrović could do no wrong. Dabro was now to work with the artists held in the 1970s to be among the greatest Croatian sculptors of the twentieth century, the Academy teachers Antun Augustinčić and Franjo Kršinić. The third, of course, was Ivan Meštrović himself. Džamonja, who had already broken with Kršinić and Augustinčić over the un-modernist direction of national sculpture generally and their work in particular, was furious. He feared, rightly, that he would lose his assistant, which, to an extent, he did.

Dabro finds other accommodation. The demands of the army for training for one day a week and the regular evening life classes draw him away so often that Džamonja is forced to seek other, though less able, assistants. By day, in civvies, he is the articulate and energetic sculptor who has sometimes in the past poured coffee for visiting senior officers and state officials in the studio. They have no idea that the passionate young man is none other than the Private Dabro who is due for training at 8 a.m. next Tuesday.

The postgraduate classes begin with study of the classical masters, the experience and instructions of generations that take the meditations that Dabro began in Split and continued through Džamonja, into formal sculptural theory. The students learn that in 1557 Benedetto Varchi advised the artist working with more than one standing figure to examine the work from eight separate but equal standpoints. He wrote to proceed to modify them without sacrificing or enlivening some at the expense of others. In the end, the sculptor might have to consider more than a hundred different viewpoints, which should reveal as few defects as possible.[9] Dabro reads and answers the set questions on the texts but thinks of them like the communist rantings that one has to appear to listen to politely – 'Yes, Comrade Professor' – but now follow your own philosophy and your own intuition.

Life is expanding in every direction. One evening he is threatened by a man accusing him of having relations with his wife. Dabro's genuine protests of false accusation do not prevent him from striking him. Dabro responds with a karate chop to the side of the neck which fells the self-persuaded cuckold. The onlookers think that he is dead; the police arrive. Dabro spends a night in the cells before the witnesses convince the police that he is the victim.

And in July 1960, at the age of 22, he marries the 17-year-old Zlatica Kuba. He relates that, though Zlatica was still at school, he found her drunk in a bar one night 'surrounded by circling human wolves'. He escorts her home safely. Next day Zlatica visits the studio to thank him; after which 'we couldn't get enough of each other'. He was seeking, he believes now, the security of a family circle. Unsurprisingly, the marriage is premature in every way. It barely lasts a week before the trust is broken. Late nights and evening classes do not improve the relationship until Zlatica departs to her aunt in West Germany, though the couple are still nominally together.[10] In 1962 he is allowed to visit West Germany to visit her but the authorities, wary of the truculent Castro lookalike from Communist Yugoslavia, follow him from time to time, and require him to report to the police once a week. 'These people are just like the Nazis.' He is offered further study in Cologne. Someone suggests Joseph Beuys in Dusseldorf, but Dabro knows that neither he nor Beuys himself would be in the least interested. 'I refused.'

FIGURE 2.3

An early Dabro work, postgraduate studio, Zagreb. Source: c. 1966 (unknown photographer).

Modelled from life, I think it's OK for a student.

52   THE LIFE AND WORK OF ANTE DABRO

Meanwhile, the intolerance of the young for the authoritarianism of the Warsaw Pact is affecting the students of Yugoslavia. A major cell of dissidence in Zagreb is, inevitably, the School of Philosophy, where by 1956 the failure of the anti-Soviet Hungarian revolution is urgently debated. Dabro's formidable appearance belies his approachable manner and rustic ways. Though he is much less politically radical than he appears, in 1959 he joins at the last minute a planning committee that meets in the cells below the student union, where, protected from eavesdropping by metre-thick walls, a dozen students plan a protest. But who can be sure that even down here they are safe from an informer?

The plan is that on a given signal the next day everyone in the refectory will slap their plates upside down in protest over the quality of the food before marching to the mayor's offices near the President of Croatia's palace to demand an improvement. March to the mayor just to demand better food? Clearly, he now reflects, the leaders held deeper agendas, but with his mind preoccupied with volumes, proportions and negative space, Dabro naively accepts the plan and agrees to march with the student leaders at the front.

Down go the plates and the students assemble to march to the mayor on a route that will take them past Džamonja's studio. Very soon it is obvious there has been an informer among the leadership. Dabro notices people waving encouragement from the balconies – but the pavements are empty. The trams have stopped. Where are the pedestrians? The marching feet echo hollowly from the city buildings. Sensing betrayal through the eerie quiet, he tells a mate in the front lines that he is heading towards the back. At the last traffic intersection before the Tuškanac Park, three police wagons appear from hiding to charge the demonstrators at full speed. From the other side emerge three troop carriers spraying tear gas and indelible dye on the front ranks. From the rear, but with two police in pursuit, Dabro scrambles inside a building, climbs to the roof, leaps to another one and descends into a different street where the shooting and screaming from round the corner show that the deadly reprisal continues. 'Like a guilty dog' he scurries back to college, where he tells his friend the porter to keep mum. He hides in an attic until well after midnight. The next day he confesses to Džamonja, who, afraid for his own reputation, is furious with him again.

The surviving leaders regroup to send a delegation that demands the release of the arrested students: 'Let them out or we will return and smash everything.' The wily mayor, probably after consulting Tito, orders their release but dozens are missing, including several friends whom Ante has never seen again. Were they killed in the demonstration or in the cells that night, or sent

Making the Artist 53

to 'Yugoslavia's Gulag', known as Naked Island. Who knows? 'Could that have happened to you if you had not made your way to the back of the march?' 'Shit yes. Typical Communists!'

A decade later, in 1968, locked-down factories and occupied universities brought France to a halt during the famous May 1968 demonstrations against consumerism, American imperialism and capitalism. Yugoslavian students believed that their country, despite the national reputation for 'enlightened socialism', was being betrayed by the 'commodifiers', that is, state officials looking after themselves to produce goods exceeding national demands and so turning the nation towards bourgeois capitalism. Less than a month later, in June, Yugoslav students rose in Belgrade, the nation's capital, with their own demands, much more nationally directed than those in western-European countries. Inadvertently, the protests revealed that the demonstrators retained the touching faith in the enlightened socialism that Tito's break with Stalin had seemed to offer. 'This is not the socialism that we have been promised.' The demonstrators demanded the suppression of inequalities, the establishment of 'real democracy', the release of arrested students, the convening of parliament to discuss their demands and 'brotherhood and equality'. A press report headlined 'Down with the Red Bourgeoisie of Yugoslavia' depicted an energetic debate between teachers, students and a reporter from a state-run newspaper. A sociology professor tells the journalist: 'We demand Marxist criticism of the [privileged managerial] class you represent. No, we don't want any more of this empty so-called socialist propaganda [...] What you happen to find opportunistically convenient you call "socialism". No, you are not socialist and you are not creating socialism.' Again, Tito mediated the tension, but the results of the negotiations were negligible. The bureaucracy never faltered; the dictatorship ground on; students continued to disappear. Far from Belgrade, as a decade earlier, these events left Dabro quite unmoved. 'I never believed in any of that communist stuff.' His intolerance of any kind of state-imposed sanctions, left wing or right, continued to harden. He distrusted, no, he hated violence of every sort.

In truth, throughout the difficult post-war decades, Dabro was drawn to neither the working-class struggle nor the student movement, but to art. In 1964, he graduated from the Academy, but he had become so personally and geographically remote from his family that no one was there to applaud him except for two sex-workers who arrived at the ceremony mysteriously carrying black roses. He returned to Čavagolave to visit Maria and Marko. Marko welcomed his son with tears, as the first graduate in the entire family as well as the village. He prepared to slaughter a bullock to feast the entire neighbourhood until Ante intervened. 'You must not kill him just for my sake.'

54 THE LIFE AND WORK OF ANTE DABRO

Immediately, not least in a ruse to stay out of the army for a bit longer, Dabro was welcomed into the postgraduate school for two years of further study under the conservative classicist Augustinčić. He was given permission to visit France for three weeks picking grapes for a Work Brigade, which allowed a week of artistic sight-seeing. Dabro used it to explore the museums and galleries where the French sculptor Aristide Maillol, popular during the 1930s for his smooth, beautiful female sculptures, less emotional and more classical than his own teachers' work, stirred his interest. Ultimately, he found Maillol, like the works of both Augustinčić and Krštinć, a little too elegant, too pretty or too close to Meštrović, or too Socialist Realist. Rodin and Michelangelo were and remain his gurus and masters, and, he asserts, they will always be.

1965 is the last year for the deferral of military service. Forgetting his undertaking to inform the army on his return from another trip to Paris, Dabro arrives in Zagreb to hear that the military police are looking for him. The message at last gets through to the reluctant soldier: 'Get yourself to the Drniš Barracks. Now'. Too late: on arrival he is classified as a deserter and locked up for the day with the expectation that he will be sent 'to the end of the world'. The same night he learns that instead he will be sent back to the barracks at Dugo Selo, only 20 kilometres from Zagreb. It seems that the politically powerful Professor Augustinčić, who wants his star student working with him rather than in Ultima Thule, has intervened. The professor, though, cannot save him from four months of full-time basic training beginning in Dugo Selo as a private soldier. At the barracks he hates the military trousers pressed to a knife edge, the rigid attention, the ironed shirt, the morning shave. He is bawled at by officers whom he considers to be no more than brainwashed Serbs. He learns to strip and reassemble the heavy machine gun in the dark and lug it about in midnight manoeuvres in which some of the blank ammunition is actually live. He attends the compulsory lectures in Marxist theory and the Glorious History of the Yugoslav Army during the War of the Partisans and thinks them rubbish. Thanks to his prolonged absences, he has lost his chance for officer training but is soon recognised as different from the other private soldiers. He is ordered to accompany his captain in locating land mines. 'Why me?' 'Because you're the only one with any brains'. Another officer sets a trap, telling the corporal to fetch Private Dabro immediately. Machine Gunner Dabro refuses. 'Go back and tell him to come now or he's on a charge'. 'No, I cannot leave my post until I have a replacement'. The officer rewards him with two weeks' leave. Private Dabro hates every moment – except when he's creating the snow-maidens that among officers and soldiers alike elevate him as a prince among sculptors. Constrictions, rules, ideologies, parades, drill, lectures, political correctness, informers. *This is not my country.*

Making the Artist 55

There follows, under Augustinčić's tuition, a more agreeable further five months in Zagreb itself. Released from the army, he suffers long and hostile interrogations whenever he applies for an exit visa for a state-sponsored Work Brigade. Without party membership, even obtaining a short-term passport signifies a bruising interview. *This is not my country.* Never does he identify personally with the artists and intellectuals of the working classes, which distances him further from a political Europe experimenting with 'Eurocommunism'. He remains unimpressed with Beuys's belief in 'social sculpture' or what passes as 'the power of art to transform society'. True art, he holds, must not carry social or political baggage. By 1967, almost thirty, he has acquired the confidence of a man and an artist that conceals the peace of Lačina and the terror of the bombs. Attending a sculpture symposium in Bihać, Bosnia, he wins the first prize for a sculpture to be placed in the city square. He creates two figures from a single block of stone that he names *Narikača* (Weeping Women).

Dabro has outgrown all his teachers and carries the arrogance of youth. For a memorial to the victims of Auschwitz, Džamonja adds vertical rods to horizontal welded chains to create deep shadows and hollows. Ante tells him the idea is a failure. In 1963, Augustinčić arranges for him an invitation to travel to Africa and carve a granite bust of the president of Guinea. 'I said I'd rather not. I don't know why, and now I regret it very much'. In the final confrontation between the Academy's top final-year postgraduate student and the country's greatest living sculptor after Meštrović, Dabro is in trouble finishing a work in relief. Rendering three-dimensional representation onto a two-dimensional surface is one of the most difficult arts that one can aspire to, requiring the most delicate touch and the most assured intuition. The *Encyclopaedia Britannica* notes that:

> [One] does this mainly by giving careful attention to the planes of the relief. In a carved relief the highest, or front, plane is defined by the surface of the slab of wood or stone in which the relief is carved; and the back plane is the surface from which the forms project. The space between these two planes can be thought of as divided into a series of planes, one behind the other. The relations of forms in depth can then be thought of as relations between forms lying in different planes.[11]

Dabro calls Augustinčić to help. After a few minutes of difficulty, the professor steps back exclaiming in exasperation, 'Oh only the old man [Meštrović] could finish that'. Then, out of shame, perhaps, his confidence returns. He steps forward and completes the most difficult part and returns to his office.

FIGURE 2.4

Narikače (Weeping Women), 1967, Bihacit (material) 1:1.5 life size, Bihać Sculpture Park, Bihać, Croatia. Source: Courtesy Dario Bajurin Opis film/Unimedia.

Looking at it again after sixty years, it seems to be a solid work, but I'd like the two women to be more liberated from the stone.

Ante, in feigned anger at the demonstration of a skill that he does not yet possess, hurls a lump of clay at the closing door. At the wrong moment, the door re-opens as Augustinčić re-appears, probably to offer some further advice. Splat! It is a case of 'My office. Now!' Dabro obeys the immediate summons, imagining that he is about to be expelled. Instead, Augustinčić invites him

Making the Artist

to sit down, then to have a drink. He asks Dabro about his postgraduation plans:

> I want to see the world. And I tell you that when the old man [Tito] dies, the whole thing will fall flat. I don't believe in Socialism.
> You know that if I reported you for what you just said, they would put you away for quite a while.
> I know that, Comrade Professor, but you won't.
> *This is not my country.*

Augustinčić implores him to stay at least until the sculpture competition at Bihać; Dabro agrees.

> Now Dabro, what do you think of my three-dimensional work that I'm just completing?
> Where will it be sited?
> Outside.
> Well, I'm sorry to say, Comrade Professor, that it is too small. It will seem lost outside. It might look better if you made it bigger.

The salon-trained academician Maestro Augustinčić is not amused.

Like the first generation of post-war migrants in Eastern Europe threatened by the Soviets, in 1967 Dabro was ready to leave a Europe that seemed devoid of promise. His experiences in the army had only stiffened his well-developed resentment of the party, the nationalistic art establishment, the uninteresting sculpture of the Academy, the weight of the violent past and what seemed to him to be the superficiality of the Venice Biennale itself. Even old Florence seemed not to be able to liberate him from new Florence. He felt nothing but contempt for 'so-called contemporary art movements'. He understood that the three sculptural giants now residing in the country would leave no room for him. More significantly, Dabro was beginning to catch in the wind the creeping distrust within the artistic establishment of the kind of sculpture in which, ironically, he excelled. A suspicion that self-aggrandising nationalism had contributed to the outbreak of World War II was circling in Europe, including a wariness of what seemed an unnecessary nationalism in the arts. Musically, avant-garde composers were beginning to avoid key structures, formal development and memorable melody to produce two generations of works that touched few outside the cognoscenti. The same impulse in Western art signalled two generations of less recognisable abstract forms in figure and landscape, and except in public commissions, the virtual abandonment of figurative sculpture.

58   THE LIFE AND WORK OF ANTE DABRO

No matter – yet. Dabro's training was complete. The touchstones of his artistic aesthetic were set.

What had made the man? On the farm he was proud to be raised a peasant but understood that rural work was a life of incessant toil rewarded only occasionally with glimpses of Arcady. He had inherited Marko's superb manual abilities, his father's penchant for taking the unpopular side in any argument (remember the Hitler moustache!) and his impatience with what he was to later define as political correctness. The violence of war also had made the man. Before he was four, his village had been occupied by invaders, from which experience he drew the instinctive reaction to any threat of frightening trauma. Somehow, it must be escaped or contained. The history of his family demonstrated the old human values of loyalty and a suspicion of anybody who did not first show their trustworthiness. From military conscription, he knew that rigid discipline was inimical to creative thought. From the Yugoslav bureaucrats, he derived the belief that all ideology was suspect and challengeable; for Marxist doctrine, he felt only contempt.

The mind and hand of the artist were also set firmly. In Split, he had rejoiced in the slippery feel of marble and how to work it, the measured understatement of the best of classical architecture; he marvelled at the bas-relief sculptures of the Croatian Romanesque. From the Academy of Fine Arts, he had learned advanced sculptural techniques, and from his postgraduate years, that the artist should be their own most fearless and persistent critic. The sculptors of the Italian Renaissance reassured him that the human body was the first and proper study of the artist. He held that beautiful materials, especially marble and wood, were among the most suitable materials in which to impart his vision. His thirty years of life had affirmed for him that artistic creation in literature, music or the arts was the highest pinnacle to which humans could aspire. Many long hours with Dušan Džamonja had revealed the act of artistic creation to be intellectual, spontaneous, intuitive, rewarding and above all, excruciating in its demands. Awakening in the pre-dawn with the lark on the solitary slopes of Lačina, he understood the distant horizon of artistic perfection to be unobtainable, as it was to Tennyson's Ulysses:

All experience is an arch wherethrough
Gleams that untravelled world
Whose margin fades for ever and for ever as I move.[12]

The Zagreb years had seen the almost-youth become the almost-man. The sculptor had slipped, unnoticed, across the shadow line of youth, the 'special

Making the Artist   59

intensity of existence which is the quintessence of youthful aspiration'.[13] Here lay the confidence drawn from the approbation of those whose opinion mattered, and his own innate ability. The artist was, or ought to be, free to voyage in those 'strange seas of thought' contemplated by Isaac Newton. He or she might have to be content with a solitary creative life, maybe poor, probably aloof from partisan politics. Art was to be pursued for its own sake; artists, if they were not to be the solitary heroes in the style of Beethoven or Liszt, should at least be treasured by their society. His driving passions were the beauty and dignity he saw in women, the strength and perseverance in men. Each work was a foray from the known to the unknown, a jump into the abyss, revealing to others the unfamiliar and the compelling that the artist saw in the everyday. The power of great art to distract the mind from the midnight sea was not, perhaps, within the imagination of anyone younger than thirty, but its power to evoke joy was unlimited. The creative impulse for this young man, (to invoke early Conrad rather than late), was to

> arrest, for the space of a breath, the hands busy about the work of the earth, and compel men entranced by the sight of distant goals to glance for a moment at the surrounding vision of form and colour, of sunshine and shadows, to make them pause for a look, for a sigh, for a smile – such is the aim, difficult and evanescent, and reserved only for a very few to achieve. But sometimes, by the deserving and the fortunate, even that task is accomplished. And when it is accomplished – behold! All the truth of life is there: a moment of vision, a sigh, a smile and the return to an eternal rest.[14]

To apprehend the midnight sea will be the task of later years. Dabro's first Australian decades, soon to unroll will be the time, like that of Mr Pickwick, when the brief sunshine of the world will blaze full upon him.

There arrives an invitation to teach sculpture in Quebec, but his French is shaky and his English non-existent. The British Consul, with the touch of condescension not unusual towards its former colonials, tells him that Canada will certainly be better than that 'cultural desert' Australia. Canada seems too near to the Europe that he is trying to escape – but Australia? Through years of schooling, he has been taught of the terrible plight of Aboriginal people and the Dickensian conditions under which some Australians are living. Yet Vera, a cousin of Zlatica living in the national capital, Canberra, has offered a bolthole from which he can at least emerge to learn English before any further journey. The voluntary exile joins several forced exiles on the plane bound for Sydney en route to Canberra, whose population amounts to scarcely 100,000 people.

60 THE LIFE AND WORK OF ANTE DABRO

Landing in Sydney in a late spring afternoon of 1967, he is unimpressed. Without the high-rise buildings of Europe, Australia's largest city looks more like a village. Wisely, his cousin does not respond to his disappointment with: 'If you think that's primitive, wait till you see Canberra.' After a meal, the family embarks on the long drive to the National Capital, interrupted by a thunderstorm such as he has never seen before, and arrives well after midnight. Tomorrow will bring the real glimpse of his new country.

CHAPTER 3

MAKING THE AUSTRALIAN

The first Canberra element that hits Dabro is – literally – the light. The tremendous storm of last night has become the dazzling blaze of a late spring Canberra morning. Not for nothing is Canberra known as the Garden City. 'Artists of Australia', Dabro tells himself, 'use your light. It's your finest asset'.

He finds himself in the new suburb of Chifley in Australia's newest city, founded only in 1911 and ruled since 1957 by the omnipotent National Capital Development Commission (NCDC). This agency of the national government has surrounded itself in rules that would cause no discomfort to the socialist bureaucracy that Dabro has abandoned. Buildings are restricted to six storeys only. Married arrivals may choose a dwelling from the government housing pool, old, new or in-between. They pay the government-fixed rental with an option to purchase a ninety-nine-year lease, for, unlike other Australian cities, no one owns their land but holds long leases from the state. Owners are obliged to mow the strip of lawn outside each dwelling known as the plantation, but may not erect a fence unless it is a privet hedge. Yet, planned cities carry advantages. Houses in new suburbs like Chifley are organised around shops no more than half an hour's pram-push away. They have quiet roads, a baby clinic, pre-school, primary school, parks and sporting fields. Though the influence of the United States is plain enough in the modernist faith in wide arterial roads, the default model is British. In 1970, the Austrian migrant Gus Petersilka tries to establish a European style of outdoors café. The Department of Interior, disapproving of the umbrellas and tables on the pavement, confiscates the lot. Public insistence eventually leads to their return. Why the opposition to what is now such a feature of every Australian streetscape? At base: because *British* cafes were not like that! An ungenerous assessment describes the planned city as the 'Eucalyptiana Kremlin in the middle of nowhere'. Yet for all the bureaucratic controls, there is a certain Australian raffishness even within the Canberra bureaucracy. Some facetious suggestions as to what the national capital should

62   THE LIFE AND WORK OF ANTE DABRO

be named include 'Gonebroke', 'Holy City' and 'Swindleville'. When the head of the NCDC asks the secretary of the Department of Interior for support in a particular project, the formal retort is 'Pig's arse'. The Commission produces a self-deprecating film that shows blindfolded bureaucrats advancing to stick words like 'school' and 'library', onto a map of the city, seemingly at random.[1]

Some 150 kilometres eastwards lies the Pacific Ocean, 300 kilometres north is Sydney, and to the northwest, the slopes and plains of sheep and wheat, the limitless bush and 1,500 kilometres westwards, the mysterious desert.

In 1967, though half the city's workforce was Anglo-Celtic and staffed the public service, the construction industry, the city's biggest employer, was dominated by European Displaced Persons, later refugees, migrants and former workers released from the completed Snowy Mountains Hydro Electric Scheme. Though the largest non-Anglo-Celtic population was Italian, a Croatian football team had played since the 1950s. Ante's countrymen subjected him to the usual gags. They smirked when he was told at the Civic Hotel that he was shouting (that is, it was his turn to buy the next round of beers) – laughed when he denies it, laughed again when he lowered his voice. They handed him a note to take to an ice-cream shop to read out: 'G'day. Give me six fucking ice-creams.'[2] Other cultural misunderstandings followed. His friend and fellow-teacher Lola del Mar recalled Dabro's arrival at a party with a full wineskin. 'This', she recalled, 'he proceeded to drink by himself the whole night'. Reminded of the story, Dabro replied: 'Yes, I offered it to everyone, but no-one went near it. They just thought it too strange'.[3]

Finding himself through sculpture continued to be the driving force in his life. Within a week, he bought plaster, tools and clay to set up in the garage of his cousin Vera and Nik Brusić and planned his first exhibition. It was here that he would find his first sense of belonging. Canberra itself he found exhilarating. Despite its modest population of 100,000, the people seemed charming and interested in his work. There were opportunities for exhibitions in several venues, including the newly opened Australian Sculpture Gallery. How wonderful to work in a free society where every opinion was tolerated! Dabro loved the openness of society, the belief in and success of democracy. As his English improved, he set out to understand the Australian national foundation document, the Constitution. He admired its division of functions and separation of powers, and naively expected them to be followed.

A national conviction that Australian art had entered a new and exciting phase since the 1950s was certainly shared in Canberra in the late 1960s. Gallery openings were 'Events' that embassy personnel attended with their chequebooks. *The Canberra Times* regularly reviewed new shows. Against his expectations, neither Canberra nor Australia itself was the often-portrayed cultural desert. Far from it: Ante was excited at the quality of Australian art.

Indeed, these were exciting decades to be an artist. Among the refugee painters who arrived from Europe between 1945 and 1955 were Stacha Hapern (Yugoslavia), Stanislaus Rapotek (Italy), Judy Cassab (Hungary), Desiderius Orban (Hungary) and Leonard Hessing (Austria), all of whom became well known in artistic circles and beyond. The Australian-born artists included Guy and Arthur Boyd, John Perceval, Sidney Nolan, Albert Tucker, Clifton Pugh, Russell Drysdale, Donald Friend, Margaret Olley, Margaret Preston, Grace Cossington Smith, Ian Fairweather, John Olsen, Brett Whiteley, John Brack and Jeffrey Smart, all well-established and accomplished painters. No cultural desert, this.

Sculpture offered a more dismal prospect. Of the twenty-odd sculptors who came to Australia as migrants or refugees soon after World War II, none is well-known today. Herbert Flugelman, Rosalie Gascoigne, Margel Hinder and Danila Vassilieff left an indelible mark, but they arrived before the end of World War II. Indeed, Vassilieff, from Russia, is regarded as a founder of Australian modernism, though this was hardly a recommendation to the Croatian new arrival of 1967. So while admiring the painters, Dabro did not think much of the sculpture. Neither did Ken Scarlett, critic and sculptor, who, introducing his 730-page appraisal of Australian sculpture to 1980, asked rather despondently whether sculpture had any relevance to twentieth-century Australian society. 'Gone are the days when 70,000 people witnessed the unveiling of a piece of sculpture, as for Thomas Woolner's Captain Cook monument in Sydney in 1879. Whether it is good or bad sculpture, whether the spectators looked at Captain Cook as sculpture or national celebration is uncertain, but [at least] nineteenth century sculptors were presenting ideas understandable by the public'.[4] In 1968, the figurative sculptor Guy Boyd was so disillusioned by the lack of critical interest in his and other sculptors' work that he left Australia for east-coast North America, which seemed to be steadily attracting the most avant-garde artistic thinking. Brenda Niall, considering Boyd's career in 2002, thought his departure understandable: 'Country towns have their unknown Soldiers, more often than not, the sculptor is too. [...] Even today if you ask for the names of two or three Australian sculptors you might be met with a very long silence'.[5] The critic Robert Hughes' history of Australian art, *The Art of Australia* (1966), did not mention sculpture at all.

Such miserable prognostications were not, of course, altogether bad news for a new arrival intending to make a distinctive mark. Although Dabro had been regarded as the decisive successor to Croatian sculpture, in the mid-1960s

64   THE LIFE AND WORK OF ANTE DABRO

Europe seemed too exhausted to him, drained of inspiration. In Australia, one could start afresh amidst what seemed to be something of a void. But start with what? Use the bright light of Australia, which sharpens sculptural edges and creates intriguing shadows. Even painters like Preston and Cossington Smith, well-known for their interiors, rejoiced in the full Australian light. Why imitate Venice and what he took to be the unexamined pursuit of abstract expressionism in New York, even as one of the real innovators, Arshile Gorky, was set aside. At least one Australian intellectual, the poet Alec Hope in 1939, anticipated Dabro's disillusionment with the old world, that of the

> [...] learned doubt, the chatter of cultured apes
> Which is called civilisation over there.[6]

So it was just one year after Boyd departed for Toronto that Dabro left the 'stale and tired' Europe for the fresh and the different in Australia.

What kind of artist should one be in a new and modernist culture? Figurative sculpture, in which Dabro excelled, was as old as Europe. But the avant-garde was not exactly new either. Dabro was only 12 when, in 1950, the first notices of abstract expressionism reached the Venice Biennale. Nine years later, just as he was meeting Meštrović to reaffirm his belief in the enduring value of figurative sculpture, Mark Rothko's refusal to base his work on natural forms was placing him at the peak of a formidable career. In 1964, midway through Dabro's postgraduate studies, Robert Rauschenberg won the Grand International Art Prize in Venice for a series of works including his famous (or notorious) *Bed*. While, in Croatia, abstract art was allowed, the excitement of the avant-garde had, to an extent by-passed his birth country, insulated as it was by the international fame of its figurative artists, the demand for massive post-war memorialisation and the strength of socialist realism. Yet even before he graduated Master of Arts, Dabro's work was being queried by some of Džamondja's semi-abstract practitioners as well as Džamonja himself, as unadventurous.

That was the question. Did formal sculpture have to represent something? Did it have to mean anything? Rauschenberg, for all his experimentation with materials, colour and subject, held that 'painting relates to both art and life', but many younger practitioners held that it didn't have to. Clearly, the avant-garde could not be simply swept aside as irrelevant even in a country blazing with light. The impulse to make an immediate artistic mark involved immediate decisions. It seemed that emerging artists like Dabro might soon be called upon to justify not just the quality of their work but their purpose and their intentions towards society.

Making the Australian 65

The controversy over art had bombshelled publicly in Australia in 1943 after a sensational attempt to overturn the prestigious Archibald prize for portraiture by denouncing the winning entrant as a grotesque caricature. A civil judge, knowing little about art, had to decide whether the work was a portrait or not. (The artist, William Dobell, won the case, but the subject, Joshua Smith, believed that he had been betrayed.) Fifteen years later, the influential art critic Bernard Smith stormed the parapet in proclaiming that figurative art, not the avant-garde, was 'the most vital movement in Australia today'. In 1957, he gathered together a number of prominent artists, John Perceval, Robert Dickerson, John Brack, David Boyd, Clifton Pugh and Charles Blackman, to prepare an Artists' Statement for their forthcoming (and only) exhibition of figurative sculpture and paintings. Under Smith's editorship, they prepared a manifesto of unusual belligerence in reaction to what seemed to them to be the suffocating dominance of modernist abstract art. Blackman, among the group, believed 'there is no real challenge in the non-figural art of the day'. Brack drew 'inspiration from our own life and the life we see about us'. David Boyd believed 'the artist to be a kind of moralist. [...] By moralist I mean the artist's function to continually remind the community of the need to adhere to human values'. Edited by Smith, the *Antipodean Manifesto* stood for the 'recognisable shape, the meaningful symbol [...] fashioned by the artist from his perceptions and imaginative existence'. Dabro, still a student in Croatia, would not have dissented from any of these positions, yet he too had come to realise that Džamonja could be seen not only as a young man trying to free himself from his masters but also as the challenger seeking new meanings for the sculptured object. If the art was abstract, was its meaning necessarily abstract? Smith in his collection of essays *The Death of the Artist as Hero*, rather spread himself:

> To me, neither painting nor sculpture are at their best when wholly abstract. My response to music and architecture is quite different. When I listen to Bach I perceive the music as a wholly abstract fabrication of sound possessing its own self-contained existence. I have no need to know what it possibly represents.

Abstract art, to Smith, had become the modern form of iconoclasm:

> It is not necessary to reject the human form in order to create great sculpture. [...] The fear of the image was the fear of the human. Yet to some, abstract expressionism was the one and only heir to the art of all the past.

66   THE LIFE AND WORK OF ANTE DABRO

He concluded the Manifesto with a significant question:

> When we think of all that happened to people like ourselves during the last
> fifty years we know that we do not fully understand them but we want to.
> How can they bear living? But they do. So we want to ask questions.[7]

In identifying a 'self-contained existence' in music Smith rather overlooked
how artists like Margel and Frank Hinder, Ian Fairweather and John Passmore
were among those who explored abstraction in a metaphysical, even mystical search for archetypal forms and systems.[8] Indeed Smith's contentious
Manifesto was later regretted by some of his fellow-travellers. A few friendships fractured, while the debate seemed at times to be rather between Sydney
and Melbourne artists rather than conflicting ideologies. Nor was the skirmish
over. A rival non-figurative group calling themselves, for an exhibition in 1961,
'the Sydney 9', outshone Smith's histrionics by persuading the young-gun icon-
oclast critic, Robert Hughes, to write its Manifesto and arrive at the exhibition opening in a helicopter. Yet Hughes, too, was advancing the position that
artistic endeavour was something that Australians should and did care about.
Art mattered. Indeed, the skirmish reinforced the conviction that Australian
artists mattered. The ground was set. Dabro did not need the Marxist Bernard
Smith to reassure him that depicting human values in a work of art should be
the artist's first concern. Yet twenty years later, after the somewhat artificial
dichotomy between 'realism' and 'modernism' had run its course, he still felt
the benefit of the view that the moral position taken by an artist in any work of
art was significant. That said, any sculpture or painting designated 'abstract
expressionist' or 'modernist' would continue to hold a handy lead for decades
over anything that seemed un-avant-garde. A 1970s assessment of an art piece
might be more aimed at an individual practice rather than its relevance to
humanity.[9] Smith's somewhat clumsy intervention had performed a service in
setting out the terms by which figurative art could be debated and defended.
Yet twenty years later, Dabro was to scream at some of his fellow teachers in the
Canberra School of Art: 'How blind you are. Can't you see how important this
kind of art is to humanity? The sculptures I create are not individuals nor even
idealised womanhood, but another step in the search for perfected humanity'.

This was the artistic culture that Dabro was to join in 1967, where anxiety
about the artist's obligation to society had already been wrangled for over a
decade.

Dabro's first needs in Canberra are money and proficiency in English.
He visits the pathetic row of huts called the Canberra Technical College

Making the Australian 67

– informally known as the School of Art, the precursor to the Canberra School of Art, which was so named in 1976 – hidden beside the bus depot in Kingston. On the first day, the Canberra sculptor Jan Brown invites him to introduce himself to the students and to examine the workshop. He sharpens the students' chisels. Bloodied fingers and yells of pain soon indicate that the tools have never been so professionally prepared. Brown cannot offer him a job, but she wants him to stay connected to the school. He accepts the position of Assistant Janitor, unaware that while janitors may be gatekeepers in England, in Australia they are cleaners. Ante's boss asks him to pick the papers up under the huts. Okay. Now, could you clean the toilets. Bucket, mop and broom hit the floor. 'I didn't come all the way to Australia to clean your bloody shit'.

He finds better work at a Queanbeyan stone-masons workshop, 15 kilometres away, creating moulds and carving tombstones. Of the twelve workers, none speak English save the Hungarian boss, Frank Satrapa and a grumpy Australian carpenter Ed whose vocabulary is limited to a single phrase, 'up to shit', with which he provides a comprehensive answer to any question. On Fridays, Satrapa often needs to go to Canberra for the day. Evidently, he recognises in Dabro the same qualities that the officers of the Yugoslav army detected in the conscripted soldier, 'Dabro, you're in charge. You're the only one with any brains'. Reviewing the worksheet, Ante carves a tombstone ready for the funeral. Somehow, the inscriptions on the tombstones are confused so that the names of the mourner and deceased are muddled. Ante returns on Monday to find an excited crowd in the workshop, gesticulating, crying, shouting, even a few laughing. 'Dabro you're sacked'. 'You can't sack me. I quit'. He agrees to work for another week for nothing, telling Satrapa that the mistake was in his instructions. In truth, Dabro is seeking a reason to leave anyway.

Sensing a new and exotic talent in Canberra, and on the basis of a portfolio of drawings, the director of the Australian Sculpture Gallery offers Dabro an exhibition just ten months after his arrival in Canberra. 'It was for a one-man show on the basis of my drawings and sculptures in plaster and wood. They seemed to think that if I was from overseas, I must be good'. Rather contemptuous of this sycophantic attitude and with scarcely a word of English, Dabro agrees to open on the 10th of August 1968. In May he gives up paid work to produce something to impress the new city. Interviewed in advance by *The Canberra Times* and in an uncharacteristic lurch from his innermost beliefs, Dabro declares himself an expressionist 'who considers realism in art to be unimportant'. In 2021, he was amazed that he ever had taken such a position and has never held to it again.

68   THE LIFE AND WORK OF ANTE DABRO

Among the crowd is the 18-year-old Vicky Butler, a highly talented student of the Technical College. She is overwhelmed by the work and hopes to meet the artist soon.

The artist and critic Robin Wallace-Crabbe in *The Canberra Times* does not quite share her enthusiasm. He likes the 'tough chiselled and rough surfaces' held in control by touches of 'crisp, abrupt geometry [...] Parallel chiselled grooves mark simple planes that constitute the, how should I say, post-Cubist fragmentation of the material and introduce secondary directional movements'. Except for the centrepiece, *Butterfly*, he is less impressed with the wooden pieces, which he judges to share a common language with other sculptors. Presciently, he remarked: 'What is required now is the difficult step from being good to being Dabro'.[10]

The director of the Sculpture Gallery is so impressed by the whole exhibition, especially the wooden carving of *Butterfly*, that she urges Dabro to enter it as an example of recent work in a closed competition to create a four-metre bas-relief sculpture in the entrance to a new Electricity Authority building (since demolished). Four sculptors are invited to submit. Six weeks after the opening of his first exhibition, Dabro is awarded the $14,000 contract. The assessors note the 'great strength symbolically contrasting the power and growth of Australian industry' of his entry. Large motifs depict water sources and electricity generation reflected in panels of illuminated cut glass. Refugees from communist Europe are perhaps a little uneasy on seeing the forearm and raised fist in the right-hand corner that symbolise, in Dabro's words, 'the part played by man in adapting natural resources into power through industry'.[11]

Who could resist such a talent? Tom Gleghorn, head of the School of Art in 1968, did not even wait until the end of the day of the opening of this first exhibition: 'Darling, come and work in my Art School'. Dabro, with his eight years of intense professional training, soon establish himself as a sculptor of the sensibility and promise that few Australians at the time possessed. In declaring himself an expressionist, it seems that he had set himself free from the mental manacles of the old world.

One could choose a style and stick to it, but how 'Australian' should a new artist be? And what did that mean? How readily could or should migrants mentally belong in the new country when the mental and physical journey was such a struggle? Should they try to? Was it possible that the intellectual currents of the new homeland might be so foreign to migrating artists as to seem incomprehensible? Jan Brown, en route to her status as a Canberra-based international artist, sculpted local animals and birds, but for these Dabro felt nothing in particular.

Making the Australian 69

The issues had become more acute in the years before his arrival. First among the Australian themes was the artists' discovery of the desert. Arthur Boyd, Fred Williams, Sidney Nolan and Russell Drysdale were among several who explored and painted desert landscapes and their inhabitants. The vast spaces were hot, dry and empty, their profound meaning immanent, apprehensible through the senses. While landscape painting of mountains and waterfalls had been a highly developed art form in Europe for centuries, these Australian painters frequently developed an intimately personal relationship with country far beyond the limits of the picturesque. The painter John Olsen wrote,

> One is compelled to inhabit the landscape [...] become part of it, stop, pause, run with it, twist around, walk straight, lie in it. One gets a feeling of landscape as a totality as opposed to the Renaissance ideal, 'here I stand, where I look is landscape' [...] it's basic flaw is that it does not inhabit the landscape.[12]

From the 1950s, artists read explorers' diaries, they visited their camps, they gazed in awe and silence in the immense spaces. They made their own forays into the desert itself, where some found a mystical union in the silence and peace difficult to imbibe in a more crowded and settled Europe, and where landscape painting had long passed out of fashion. One did not need, of course, to be touched by a desert spirit, but these Australian painters understood the mood and exhibited internationally. Les Murray, another poet somewhat at odds with his fellow intellectuals, was unimpressed, writing sarcastically in the poem 'Louvres':

> What to do in the crystalline dry? Well
> below in the struts of laundry is the four-wheel drive
>
> vehicle in which to make an expedition
> to the bush, or as we now say the Land
> the three quarters of our continent
> set aside for mystic poetry.[13]

Rosalie Gascoigne excepted, sculptors do not normally interest themselves in landscape as any kind of artistic platform – Mike Parr, Ken Unsworth and Imants Tillers were three who did not – but the larger point here is that these changing drivers of Australian intellectual thought were beginning to flower just as the European refugees and migrants were arriving. Many of them found it

70 THE LIFE AND WORK OF ANTE DABRO

hard to grasp its significance to the artistic community. Nowhere was there a place for the sculpted figure in this semi-mystical landscape. Dabro recalls that he was indeed aware of the changing fashion – how could he not be, prominent as it was in galleries and the words of critics: 'But that was not me!' Artistic creation, of course, has always followed fashions that can be at times constricting. The sculptor Donald Brook warned Dabro, in a friendly fashion, that every year the ambitious artist should invent or do something new. At times, he would wander with Rosalie Gascoigne in the hills of southern Canberra, helping her to gather timber for her popular creations. There, she confided in him her view that it was necessary that the contemporary artist wanting to get ahead needed to work in some way with landscape. Dabro was unimpressed. Even an informal artistic censorship, he recalled, reminded him too much of the Communist Party.

A second public preoccupation of the 1960s was the place of Australia's Indigenous people. Yugoslavian teaching, like that of non-communist western Europe, had presented Aboriginal people as somewhere far behind almost everyone else. Thus, in the long progression from Palaeolithic, through Mesolithic, Neolithic, Bronze Age to Iron Age, Aboriginal people seemed never to have progressed beyond the Stone Age. It was not until the 1960s that archaeologists belatedly realised that Aboriginal culture simply did not belong anywhere in this supposedly ever-advancing progression that, as it happened, triumphed in the flowering of modern Europe.

In portraying the iniquity of capitalist colonialism, the Yugoslavian curriculum had by-passed the capacity of white Australians to recognise their terrible history and to make amends. Social scientists and a few social realist artists were doing so, but educating their fellow Australians, let alone exiles and migrants, was another matter. In the 1940s, the painter and ceramicist Marguerite Mahood portrayed strong working men, Australian animals and birds, an Aboriginal woman within a desolate urban space, and three Aboriginal men held in police chains. Though the first artistic depictions of Aborigines were no more than victims, they were no longer to be ignored. In the post-war years, the movement to recognise Indigenous history and to make amends accelerated. The belated public discovery that some Aboriginal Australians could not vote in national elections created a campaign that accelerated in the middle 1960s. A typical encouragement in a referendum to allow the federal government to make polices and laws specifically for Indigenous people, ran:

> When you write Yes in the lower square of your ballot paper you are holding out the hand of friendship and wiping out nearly 200 years of injustice and inhumanity.

Making the Australian 71

A very large majority approved the change just four months before Dabro's arrival.

How difficult it was for recent European arrivals to understand Indigenous Australians differently from what they had learnt in school! Dabro had learnt that the British colonisers were cruel and non-caring, but now the best thing that could happen to a Stone-Age people seemed to be for them to move quietly out of the way of progress. He recalled: 'It came as a surprise to me. I had never before in my life experienced racism based solely on colour'. Already nervous at any form of public protest, he was suspicious of any apparent privilege given to any minority, especially when sponsored by what he was beginning to call the radical left. Naturally, all artists did not or should not have embraced desert landscapes or painted Aboriginal people in chains; but to fully participate in the Australian intellectual life of the 1960s and 1970s without comprehending these significant post-war intellectual currents might leave a migrating artist stranded in European concepts, never understanding what so concerned the native-born practitioners of their art form. Dabro never considered himself stranded; his attitude remained: 'I understand what they're saying but that's not me. It's the human form that matters'. He recognised the spiritual qualities expressed in Indigenous art but felt not sufficient affinity to work with Aboriginal subjects. The potential to associate oneself with Aboriginal artistic themes was more likely to be lost on one who was not native-born and who prided himself in pursuing universal rather than national values.

In the 1980s, Australian-born artists like Margaret Preston, the Social Realist Marguerite Mahood, and the South Australian Robert Hannaford, later commissioned to sculpt or paint a number of Aboriginal women, at times embraced the concerns of the native born. Rosemary Madigan, one of the most respected Australian female sculptors, discussed her late 1960s carving *Eigana*:

> Also at that time I was relating my own Western heritage to the Aboriginal, the fact that I was an Australian and lived here and loved and understood, I hoped, in the same way as a native Australian did. It was my land and yet I had this Western heritage, especially religiously. So I just combined those two things in the carving as a way of thinking myself at the time.[14]

What a powerful depiction of, say, the Stolen Generations Dabro might have made, but innate distrust of disturbing publicity and suspicion that the saga was being encouraged by left-wing agitators stayed his chisel. That, and his certainty that great art would emerge when the critics ceased to babble.

72 THE LIFE AND WORK OF ANTE DABRO

In truth, the Renaissance sculptors, whatever the political upheavals of their own day, had seen no need to neglect the longest and deepest artistic themes of the human figure. Now this outsider from a colourless Europe, who not so long ago had declared himself an expressionist, must hide his obsession with the human figures that peeped out in every corner of the studio. Now they were emerging. Some time in 1968, this abstract, or rather, this proto-human form, began to chirrup. Almost human! In Dabro's later analysis, the figure is groping towards a human shape. A suggestion of a head, still an outsized block in smooth planes, tilts left. Dabro alludes to an angled right arm, a single breast and genitals. No decoration here, this is precisely and unmistakably a human form emerging from its imprisoning substance. It was one of the last he produced in carved wood. From this point, he began modelling much more commonly in clay, cast in cement. Dabro was yearning for the sculpted human figures that were everywhere seeking the light. 'It took me three years in Australia before I broke free'.

Though virtually without English, his impressive qualifications landed him a job as art teacher at Deakin High School, where one of the students, Tony Stuart-Smith, still holds two clear memories of Mr Dabro. One afternoon, the Year 8 student Tony was in trouble from an unpopular headmaster who sought him in the classroom. Stuart-Smith quickly gabbled his dilemma. As the door opened, Dabro hustled the lad into the broom cupboard. 'Tony? No, headmaster, I haven't seen him'. Stuart-Smith holds another affectionate memory of Dabro's role in the Boy Scouts. To prepare for the 1969–1970 Jamboree (the biennial gathering of the nation's Scouts) at Jindalee, Queensland, Dabro helped him prepare a semi-diabolic head to adorn the camp entrance to the Canberra Scout contingent. 'It was large and frightening', he recalled. 'Mr Dabro helped me carve it, then we cast it in bronze'. In this small way, yet another human figure had been given light.[15]

Vicky Butler, brightest and best of the graduating class of the Canberra Technical College, is entranced by colour and form. To paraphrase Ethel Anderson's judgement on Grace Cossington Smith, she 'seem[ed] to paint for no other reason than to express her pleasure in painting', [life]. Vicky recalled of this time: 'The act of doing it was the most important thing. It was my reason to be'. It was obvious that her talent and dedication put her among Australia's most promising student painters. Now in her second year at the College, she very much wants to meet the author of the works that had so entranced her at Ante's first exhibition.

Sooner than she expected, one Friday in 1969, two weeks after the term began, she bumped into the besuited, handsome man of thirty who asked her

FIGURE 3.1

King and Queen, 1969, eucalyptus, 45 x 31 x 23 cm, from an unfinished chess set, the artist's home. Source: Con Boekel.

I don't like this now. It's overdecorated.

the way to class. 'I'm the sculpture lecturer'. 'Of course, I'll take you there'. Ante too was intrigued by the striking young woman 'wearing just 30 cm of mini-skirt, so talented, so enthusiastic, so innocent'. Later Ante met Vicky and her mother Doreen in Canberra's Civic Centre. 'Hello Mr Dabro, I've heard about you from Vicky. How are you?' 'Oh, up to shit' (stunned silence). Ante

FIGURE 3.2

Unnamed Figure, 1970, cherrywood, 32 x 10 x 14 cm, the artist's home.
Source: Con Boekel.

I can see the human figure locked inside waiting to be released.
I remember that I had the Venus de Willendorf in mind when I carved this.

Making the Australian 75

asked Vicky to come to Chifley to see his work but he had lost his car keys. They arranged to meet at another gallery opening where both, in Vicky's words, 'were beginning to feel some electricity'. Unlike her other boyfriends, Ante was older, he was worldly wise, he owned a car, he made Turkish coffee, he was exotic; above all, he created sculptures such as she had never seen before – 'He was a man! I was overwhelmed by how good he was, how accomplished, the passion for his work. This was a real artist'.

Yet she can sense in him, if not exactly a want of confidence, but a nervousness in the consequences of lawlessness. Walking in Sydney, the couple come across a soapbox orator denouncing the iniquities of government. Ante, in Vicky's memory, is terrified, flying into a nervous rage while looking around anxiously for the intervention of uniforms. He hustles Vicky away, and the evening is spoilt. This is the moment of reprimand for the seven-year-old dropping the Croatian flag in the mud, the thirteen-year-old watching a man being beaten like a whipped dog, the demonstrator running from the paddy wagons charging into the student demonstrators of Zagreb. Such is a common response of the non-believer to violent and arbitrary authority: Get away. Hide. Find somewhere safe.

Vicky Butler herself can go no farther to train as an artist in limited Canberra. In 1970, she enrols in the three-year painting course at that nursery of so many Australian artists, the East Sydney Technical College, there to resume, as she puts it, 'the struggle between eye, hand, brain, design and meaning'. Such are her abilities that she graduates in painting in two years. Yet, she reflects that in another life she might have been a sculptor: 'There is something complete about it, compared to painting, there's no pretence, this is the real thing'.

She and Dabro continue to see each other whenever possible until one evening in 1971 she steps off the train from Sydney to be greeted with a marriage proposal. At once, she agrees. But sadly, after his first exhibition, Dabro has become a social lion around the embassies and acquired something of a reputation. 'I was everybody's favourite boy. [...] But I'd rather not talk about that'. Stories of the favourite boy have rather preceded him. 'Oh God, not him', exclaims a Serbian friend of Vicky's parents, Peter and Doreen, much to their horror. By the time they formally meet Dabro, they are well aware of his apparent lack of financial prospects, his marriage to Zlatica and a second, proxy marriage unconsummated but still undissolved.[16] What they don't know, because nobody knows, is the outsider Dabro's hunger for the love and security seldom found outside a close family circle. For beyond the grappa, the

76 THE LIFE AND WORK OF ANTE DABRO

old-fashioned European courtesy, the affairs and the camaraderie, Dabro is more the onlooker on Australian society than ever before. Vicky recalls:

> Ante couldn't speak English very well, he was twelve years older, he came from a Communist country, his prospects were not good and he was a Catholic! He was not intimidated by my parents, in fact my father had to tell him sometimes to shut up and listen. They had imagined something very different for their little girl!

The couple persists and the parents inevitably assent. Peter Butler predicts: 'This is going to end in disaster'. By the time they marry in 1972, Dabro has been teaching art at the Canberra Technical College for some time. Vicky recalls, 'We weren't going to starve. It got better after that'.

While working somewhere in the style of Cezanne, Vicky recalls that she didn't have any particular ambition to be an artist, or even to sell her work. 'The act of doing it was the important thing, my reason to be'. Perhaps this was fortunate, since within a year or two of her marriage, Vicky, like Alma Mahler (wife of the composer Gustav) finds that there is room for only one creative artist in this relationship of two. Yet Peter Butler's gloomy predictions are not fulfilled. Five decades later, Vicky remains one of the greatest admirers of her husband whose driving passion was and is artistic creation.

Vicky returns from the East Sydney Tech, the best qualified school art teacher in Canberra, to hold classes for graduate Diploma of Education students at the Canberra College of Advanced Education. The arrival of the first child Sarah in 1976 reduces her own work to teaching on Saturday mornings.

> I didn't feel supported. I knew as soon as I had kids that my art was not going to dominate my life as it did his. I allowed him total artistic time, but the children were my priority. I don't resent it, and even though I had not come to see this as a conscious decision, I knew it was the deal.

Vicky planned picnics for the kids with her parents, never went to parties or the pictures. 'I always put the kids first, I didn't want to upset them, and I'm glad. I don't regret that decision at all'.

By late 1969, Dabro, still wearing a dark suit and in his words 'looking like a bloody wog', had left Deakin High School to teach part-time at the School of Art (Canberra Technical College). Trying to teach observational and perceptual skills, he presented the students with a plaster head to copy. Enter the Head Teacher Frank Lumb. 'No no no Mr Dabro. That won't do at all. You

Making the Australian 77

must teach them contemporary skills. No heads, please, no heads, that's so old fashioned'. The college's succeeding director, Brian Cowley, determined to keep him at the college, gave Dabro a full teaching load including, remarkably, English.[17]

Dabro exhibited some of the new and older Canberra pieces in his first Sydney exhibition at the Macquarie Galleries. Again, the critics were cautious. David Brook, one of whose examiners of his BA Honours thesis was Henry Moore, criticised his apparent lack of adventure in exploring new themes and forms. 'The territory [that is, the preoccupations and productions of the past] is only good for explorers in Pioneer Coaches'.[18] Writing in *The Sun,* the surrealist critic James Gleeson wrote: 'In his own way he is trying to do what Robert Klippel did much more successfully about twenty years ago. [...] *Embryo II* and *Reincarnation 1* and *11* are powerful and impressive works, but since Dabro commands only a rather limited command of form, he fails to invest even his best pieces with the richness and invention one finds in early Klippel'.[19] Klippel, too, had studied with Moore and his early works, like his 1948 *Scherzo,* showed it. It is obvious now that Dabro in these newer works was demonstrating the common source Moore rather than imitating Klippel, of whom he was entirely unaware. Other artists like Godfrey Miller, Oliffe Richmond and Rosemary Madigan were also simultaneously taking inspiration from Moore and the Italian-born sculptor Eduardo Paolozzi rather than Klippel.[20] Yet the point was not entirely misdirected. Robin Wallace-Crabbe had observed after his first Canberra exhibition, that Dabro was an accomplished sculptor but whose promise was still potential. Concluding his review of the Macquarie Gallery exhibition, James Gleeson added:

> In the age of kinetic art, and at a time when most sculptors prefer to work with less traditional media and techniques, Dabro's work looks rather anachronistic. This doesn't mean that it isn't good, but it is of a kind that no longer interests the avant garde sculptor.[21]

Dabro was inspired by Michelangelo; yet five centuries earlier, nobody had called Michelangelo old-fashioned. That was the rub. Whatever the critics' disappointment, the human form was urging a call that he could not deny.

Towards the end of the 1960s, Dabro had become impatient with the hardwood sculptures like *King and Queen* that had earlier impressed the critics. A figure, he reasoned, cannot easily emerge properly from a column of wood that already exists: the exterior surface is apt to become merely decorative. Sculpting from the outside inwards, as one must do with a lump of hardwood,

78   THE LIFE AND WORK OF ANTE DABRO

leads all too easily to abstraction and away from the human figure that carries – assuming the artist's understanding of psychology as well as anatomy – the truth of its humanity and its own cultural universe. Few of his hardwood sculptures have survived Dabro's periodic decimation.

As Dabro steadily turned from carving in wood and marble to bronze casting in the 1980s, his figures became, paradoxically, simultaneously more abstract and more human. By 2003, he had produced dozens of mostly headless, single or double but unmistakably human figures collected into a solo exhibition. It was almost as though, over twenty years, the base material that began as proto-human had taken physical form and then dissolved again to shapes that suggested human qualities rather than the actual bodies. The works, small enough to sit comfortably on a table, quivered in their static motion to pirouette, gesture, dance, dominate, explode with energy. The exhibition was advisedly named *Humanscapes*. Rightly, its curator noted the controlled tension and self-contained monumentality of the objects.[22] The style was a marked departure from the 'sentimental phase' of Dabro's sculptures of his children in the late 1970s, but in the end, *Humanscapes* foretold a road not taken further, for these dynamic explorations were in a sense shut down by the private and public commissions becoming more common as his reputation widened. Clients preferred that their works be produced in a more traditional and recognisably human style. We will not see a return to the powerful and enigmatic energy of *Humanscapes VIII* until the creation of *Genesis*, installed at Canberra Airport in 2009.

But at this point in the mid-1970s, Dabro had not yet become Dabro. He now reflects that many of his works of the time followed that trend that Smith had detected, in being too concerned with outward appearance. 'I was too decorative until I woke up.' He reflects now that these few years of the late 1960s pursuing abstract and decorative art were years wasted.

> The artist must go from inside out. Rodin disregarded muscles in portraying the human form: he knew the essence of what he wanted to create and needed to know more. It didn't matter whether the muscles followed reality or not. As soon as the artist thinks about what the final version will look like, it will be an artistic failure. The ability to see what other people don't see is a real gift. It's like a star wheeling round the earth, fertilising the imagination as it goes.

Other artists also have pondered how to induce observers of their work to apprehend something unnoticed until the moment of the artist's revelation.

FIGURE 3.3

Humanscape VIII, c. 2003, bronze, 24 x 21 x 16cm.
Source: Phillip Bacon catalogue, 2003.

These are my figures still trying to escape.
Where would I have gone next with them? I've no idea.

80 THE LIFE AND WORK OF ANTE DABRO

Paul Klee believed that 'we learn to see what flows beneath. We learn the pre-history of the visible. We learn to dig deep, and to lay bare'.[23]

It is also a mistake to over-stress the singularity of Dabro at this time. Lloyd Rees, John Olsen and Rosalie Gascoigne were among well-known Australian artists who followed their own inner calling. Some of Klippel's abstracted bronze and steel weldings of the 1960s achieved their own powerful negative spaces. His colleague Rosemary Madigan disposed of muscles in order to understand how the ribcage and pelvis acted together. She wrote: 'I like to have all my energy inside the space, it must come out of form, a Buddha sort of thing.'[24] Nevertheless, Dabro was different. While the British sculptor Anthony Gormley is famous for his lone and desolate human forms, Dabro's figures can be solitary even within their own company. In his largest works, the sculptor seems to hold no hope that the individuals will achieve intimacy with each other, nor reach their private goal. In these early years, he felt unrooted and unhappy. He had no interest in mystical unions with desert landscapes and believed that Aboriginal people should try harder to blend with other varieties of Australians rather than to make themselves different. 'Charny' (Charnwood), a new and working-class suburb remote from the city centre, he found remote, empty and unstimulating. 'It seemed like the end of the world'. He found security, support and love within his home and marriage but felt constrained by his surroundings. In 1974, he and Vicky visited Croatia to see his family to find them less interested in him than he had expected. He felt isolated from whatever was happening in the galleries.

In his first Australian decade, he had held an exhibition every year. Perhaps trying too hard to impress the Australians, he had called himself an expressionist, but had overdecorated, worked from the exterior towards a nothingness within and in this way ventured far from his own natural impulse to work from the essence of person or object towards an exterior that needed no decoration to reveal its own natural form.

Now, events in his own life as well as the larger forces of Australian society were shaping his work during the first, painful decade. His place in the Croatian community itself was a little equivocal. The Yugoslav embassy staff, recognising that Dabro moved in many circles, suggested that he cooperate in a little espionage within the refugee community. Within weeks of his arrival, he had scarcely taken a drink at an embassy soiree before a smart-suited executive took him aside to suggest a little regular information on the Croatian refugees that he met would not be unwelcome. Angrily, Dabro shoved him aside. 'There is no way that I will spy on my own people.' He pushed his way out, expecting never to be invited again; but he was too interesting, too exotic, to be allowed

Making the Australian

to escape from the diplomatic circuit. Invitations to events and parties flowed, and further clandestine invitations of espionage. Even ASIO, the Australian Security Intelligence Organisation, sent a feeler or two. Peremptorily, he rejected them all. Yet the Croatian community, many of whom were recent refugees from the communist state, regarded him with suspicion and kept away from his blunt and uncompromising political beliefs that did not always match their own. 'Why is he allowed to come and go as he pleases?' 'How did he get a passport so easily?' To this day, while Dabro feels close to Croatians, he believes they complain too much about Australia. 'I don't see myself as a post-war refugee and don't especially associate myself with those that are. I came as a migrant intending to live and work here.' 'I don't believe in multiculturalism. I don't believe in human groupings of any kind. I believe in humanity.' His sense of solidarity between himself and the multicultural community, never secure, was slipping.

Equally disillusioning in the journey towards a new sense of becoming Australian was the dismissal of Prime Minister Whitlam by Australia's Governor General. It was about 2.30 p.m. on September 1975 that the nation learnt that Sir John Kerr, the Queen's representative, had sensationally dismissed the Labour Prime Minister and asked the Leader of the Opposition, Malcolm Fraser, to form a new government until an election could be called. In the National Capital, enormous rallies began in favour of Whitlam. Dabro, always acutely distressed by civic violence, announced to his friend the journalist Paul Lyneham that he intended to challenge the strength of Australian democracy. Lyneham unwisely allowed him to fashion and wear a badge 'Shame Whitlam Shame' instead of the 'Shame Fraser Shame' badge that everyone else was wearing. In the furious crowd gathering at the Australian National University (ANU) someone noticed it. 'Take that off!' A threatening group formed around the two men. 'Within a couple of minutes I would have been bashed up'. Hurriedly Dabro removed the badge and the two men retreated. He not only felt angry and rebellious but also scared that worse would follow.

Dabro's later reflections took an unexpected turn. Prime Minister Whitlam, defined as a Socialist mainly by his critics, had been legally overthrown in less than an afternoon. Yet, rather than rejoicing that a controversial leader had been removed by unusual but constitutional means – an event quite impossible in any communist country – Dabro took the hostility shown towards him during the demonstration as evidence of Australian political immaturity. Here was an unfree country.

Dabro's somewhat perverse reaction to Whitlam's dismissal needs explanation. Did his existential unhappiness contribute to his extreme anxiety in

82   THE LIFE AND WORK OF ANTE DABRO

the face of the largest public demonstrations in the nation's history? Was it the migrant's trauma? Did the contra-suggestiveness, for which Marko Dabro was famous, propel his son to this rash act? Rather than a demonstration of Australian immaturity, surely the demonstrators' fury was closer to finding a supporter of the opposite team sitting in their stand at a football game! At root, the explanation is likely to be found in the little boy's terror in the face of extreme violence, leading him to blame the crowd's behaviour rather than the political act that impelled it. Sadly, this point marks Dabro's long disillusionment with Australian politics, which, except for the Hawke years, only deepened in coming decades. Claiming absurdly that he had more freedom to express his mind in Yugoslavia than in correct-speak Australia, he asserted:

> The Yugoslavs to their credit allowed new movements in art to continue, which the Soviets never did. On the other hand, the Yugoslav army never ceased to insist that change in society must come only through bloody revolution. I thought Australia was wonderful when I arrived. I didn't want any authority dictating to or influencing me. I was hungry for freedom and democracy. We had become complacent, I no longer believed in this failed minority democracy. The radical left had taken over just as it did with the Impressionists, and all the 'isms' came along.

As further indication of his deep spiritual malaise, it was in 1974, the same year that the Whitlam government began to fail, that Dabro created the disturbing *Diagonal Direction*, his response to the changing sexual mores that his *vlaj* sensibility labelled promiscuity.

After seven years of conservative government, on 5 March 1983 Bob Hawke was elected prime minister of Australia. Dabro felt an immediate rapport with the energetic and overtly masculine former unionist. The country was optimistic too. The reconciliator Hawke called a national conference of the traditional antagonists, business and labour. As the gloom of Ante's disillusionment brightened, he began work on two massive nude males.

> I wasn't as pessimistic as I am now. At that time I was pissed off with Whitlam and pissed off with Fraser and when Hawke came in I thought there was a light at the end of the tunnel. The return of Hawke was when I started believing again and started voting again, always for Hawke. The look I have here is a pensive look. I'm not happy-happy, but there is hope for the future. He's like the child crawling upwards in *Resilience*.

FIGURE 3.4

The Return of Homo Sapiens, 1984, plaster, 1:1.5 life size, the artist's studio, Canberra Airport. Source: Artist's collection.

I wasn't as pessimistic as I am now.

Dabro's faith in democracy that he had begun in 1969 by studying the Australian Constitution continued to flicker in the Hawke years and beyond. In 1999, he entered a competition to design a monument to the Magna Carta in Canberra. The design turned on the role of figurative sculpture to educate through an actual corporeal involvement by the observer. Its motif was

84 THE LIFE AND WORK OF ANTE DABRO

'A source of Inspiration rather than Memory'. The Statement of Design Intent began boldly with a defence of tradition and a swipe at contemporary preoccupations:

> In our opinion the form of the human figure transcends time and fashion, and timeless[ness] and lack of fashion is best achieved with a composition that includes human figurative pieces.

Revealingly, the figures were to be life size:

> Viewers are drawn to walk to and around the individual figures, to investigate their form and role (some are professional figures, some ordinary citizens) – almost to listen to their conversation. Deliberately, they are not raised on a pedestal, and are of varying heights and scale, to give a feeling of familiarity or intimacy.

The drama was to be enacted with an Agora-like enclosing frame. Seating on the inside perimeter was to invite 'viewers to take part in the sculpture'. Dabro continued:

> The figures themselves are King John ('looks somewhat indecisive and mistrustful') and Archbishop of Canterbury Langton '(looks determined'). Three authorities, a judge, an administrator and a (female) parliamentarian are to be dressed in clothing of three different periods to symbolise the passage of time since the signing. Two figures near the front converse, expressing our views of our political system without fear or hindrance.

A large androgenous figure at the rear of the composition was to represent 'humanity in its continuous search for justice and freedom of speech'. The figures were to 'move through the frame symbolising the transcending of time and the need for continuity in the protection of our system of justice and democracy'. Lastly, in a distinctive Dabro touch, an Observer was to stand outside the frame. This figure was 'our democratic conscience, watching the players on our democratic stage, to ensure that they maintain the traditions and values established by Magna Carta'.[25] As Dabro said about himself, 'What I'm really obsessed about, especially in my drawings, is that whatever is happening, there is an observer looking on. That's me. There is a drama and an innocence, it's a difference in my observation of the world, the innocence of my childhood confronting a world which is complex and corrupt'.

Making the Australian 85

It was a bold and intriguing concept that perhaps struck the judges as too quaintly literal. Of the 53 entries, the much more symbolic winning design was one in which

> the concept of the passage of time is explored at various levels within the monument – from the layered design of the wall cladding, evoking the sedimentation layers in a rock, to the careful selection of timeless materials (bluestone, granite, cast bronze and ironbark) and their hand-crafted finishes.[26]

Possibly Dabro's entry may not even have been taken very seriously.

As Dabro returned steadily to the figurative sculpture that would speak to humanity, the artists of the avant-garde remained uninterested. *Art in America*, with a little exaggeration, described the artistic preoccupations of the first decade of the twenty-first century as:

> The decade fostered a revisionist understanding of the modern legacy, driven by feminist artists and curators from around the world. [...] The early 2000s can at the same time look small and parochial. Escapism was rampant: psychedelia, microutopias, and hipsterism.[27]

The successful, rather predictable and forgettable Magna Carta sculpture, illustrates afresh an Australian lack of faith, at the century's turn, in figurative design as a tool of education. Ironically, the Magna Carta memorial in Runnymede, United Kingdom, is no more than twelve iron chairs, arranged as if in conference, standing in an otherwise empty, grassy field.

The Australian art critic Daniel Thomas remarked:

> I suspect that all the best art has always been highly individual. An artist's personal obsessions, in form or process, will be recognised as personally relevant to the spectator as well. And the greater the number of spectators who see themselves in the work of art, across the world and across time, the greater that work is judged to be.[28]

Thomas's observation is well taken by comparing three quite different sets of works completed by Dabro within the decade 1970–1980. They are quite different, each flowing from the intuition, volcanic passion, childhood trauma and ever-changing experiences of the sculptor, but all informed by the deepest European artistic traditions.

FIGURE 3.5

Observing the Masses, 1980s 90 x 64 cm, crayon on paper, the artist's home.
Source: Con Boekel.

That's me, always looking in, never taking part.

In 1976, Father Maloney of the Church of St Augustine in Farrer ACT, asked Dabro to sculpt a large crucifix to be placed behind the altar, and an image of St Augustine to occupy a prominent position to its left. To Dabro, as to Catholics generally, St Augustine of Hippo enjoyed a somewhat licentious existence before attaining the status of revered saint and author of the *Confessions*. (He is said to have coined the delicious invocation: 'God grant me chastity and continence – but not yet'.) Since St Augustine's earliest surviving portrait dates from a hundred years after his death, his physical features, even his skin colour, are unknown. Maloney did not specify which aspect of Augustine's life should be depicted.

Any pre-twentieth-century musician wishing to depict a sad event could utilise a toolbag of emotion-inducing devices that listeners would instantly recognise irrespective of the quality of the work. Thus the English seventeenth-century musician Henry Purcell, composing the lament to be sung in the

Making the Australian 87

musical drama *Dido and Aeneas* ('When I am dead and laid in earth', which Dido sings before she kills herself), chose a minor key, a descending scale and a halting rhythm to enhance what was already the sad melody in his mind. At the first slow chord, listeners knew what was to come. Sculptors have no such tools to guide the observer to an expected emotional response. Without such a trigger, and armed with no more than a native ability, a vast visual interior library and a lifetime of practice, Dabro had first to reflect on the available traditions, from the decidedly erotic *St Therese* by Bernini to Michelangelo's severe *Moses* and Botticelli's rather troubled *St Augustine*.

Dabro creates a youngish man, the newly converted intellectual, still a little uncertain of his reception by the listeners, distancing himself from, yet fondly remembering his lovers, perhaps yet to write in his Confessions: 'I tasted, and now I hunger and thirst. Thou didst touch me, and I burned for thy peace'. Dabro's St Augustine seems tired, apprehensive in the knowledge that his God-given task must be fulfilled. The anxious face suggests that Augustine wishes to share his teachings with others, but the upward-tilted, rather anxious expression of the protruding eyes and raised eyebrows suggest uncertainty and self-doubt. He is not catching – is he deliberately avoiding? – anyone's eye. On viewing the work for the first time in 40 years, Dabro exclaimed, 'God, it's Moses', but apart from the general position, and perhaps the fingers clasping the sacred texts, there is really not much resemblance. Michelangelo's *Moses* is more confident. He does not share the texts with anybody; rather, he holds them, albeit rather uncertainly, as a symbol of his authority.

Viewed from ground level at the entrance of the church, to where the sculpture has been moved, the figure's right hand looks too large, but may have been appropriate for the elevated position near the altar where it was intended. Approaching this work, the viewer's eye goes to the hand and face enclosed by their negative space. Today, Dabro consigns this work to 'my angry period' in the early to middle 1970s.

> I find my Augustine grotesque now. He's quite angry, a complaining scholar. What was in my mind was his objecting to the pope and his theology. He's not very Christian.

St Augustine's anxiety and the ambiguity of his offering exemplify the painful period of uncertainty in the life of the sculptor himself in the mid-1970s. *St Augustine* parallels the same disturbed emotions that he himself felt at the time of the work's creation, translated into a divine of the Church who had lived

FIGURE 3.6

Augustine, 1976, resin, 1:1.3 life size, Church of St Augustine, Farrer ACT. Source: Con Boekel.

I find him grotesque now. I did this in my angry period.

more than 1,500 years earlier and who reflected something of the same interior disturbance.

The enormous crucifix at the Church of St Augustine is just as striking. Cast in black resin, it hangs outside the entrance. As the priest had requested, Christ's expression is one of resignation rather than of unimaginable pain. As delighted with the work as he was with St Augustine, Maloney told *The Canberra Times*:

Making the Australian   89

The crucifix is that of Christ who is giving his life freely rather than having his life dragged from him by force: the Good Friday noon-day Christ rather than the 3 p.m. dead Christ.[29]

The figure's rather stylised face and body were evidently benevolent enough to please Maloney, but the arms, hands and feet are in agony. Searching for a starting point, the eye seizes on the outstretched arms and fingers whose contorted tendons and muscles call to mind Rodin's *Burghers of Calais*. This Christ possesses an ambiguity in which the body extremities shriek with a contrary message not of benevolence but of excruciating pain.

Placed above the altar as intended, the enormous work would have dominated, if not overwhelmed the worshippers. Even today, fixed to the outside wall, it lowers over the viewer like an enormous benevolent eagle. Together, the two works shout the uncertain exuberance and confidence of the young sculptor who has almost found his own voice in creating two powerful works of subjects that, among the avant-garde, had long passed out of fashion.

A second and more disturbing influence on Dabro's creative life occurred throughout Yugoslavia and the Western world in the 1960s. This was the period of the birth control pill (legalised in Australia in 1961), the sexual revolution, the time of 'free love'. Dabro was well-familiar with sexual liberation before he arrived in Canberra, for no frontier created by Tito or anyone else was able to hold back the revolution of young people that was sweeping western Europe. His first Canberra years found him in several situations that excited very mixed feelings that were reflected some years later in his sculptures. On one occasion in a university house, men and women unknown to each other were each allotted a room to make love in. Dabro found himself squashed into the toilet with a strange woman who found the situation as uninviting as he did. As they sat discussing what to do, the police raided the place, not because the activities were illegal but, it transpired, because someone had complained to the police. Dabro slunk out, wondering why he had ever gone there. On a second occasion, he was invited to a party near the university at which, on arrival, he was told to leave his clothes at the door and enter a darkened room. In the gloom, he could make out a plastic sheet on the floor covered in oil, a throbbing 'om' type of sound-track and several couples groping about on the plastic. He recounts that he stared incredulously through the door as a man loomed out of the darkness to proposition him. As angry as he was disgusted, this time he stormed rather than slunk out. 'It was never the sort of thing I would take my girlfriend to. I don't share with anyone'. To Dabro, it seemed

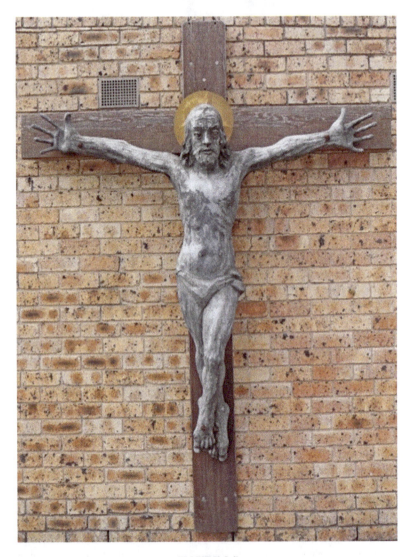

FIGURE 3.7

Good Friday Christ, 1976, resin, 1:1.5 life size, Church of St Augustine, Farrer, ACT. Source: Con Boekel.

I wished to portray Christ in agony. Father Maloney didn't want me to.

FIGURE 3.8

Good Friday Christ, detail. Source: Con Boekel.

It was only in Christ's extremities that I was able to show my emotions. The wrist and hand are in a spasm of agony.

that the holy Catholic ideal of wife-and-mother was being willingly prostituted by the women themselves. In giving men a sexual licence that he denied to women in this time of rapid social change, he found himself trapped in a conception of women's 'right behaviour' that was rapidly eroding.

Perhaps many of those old enough to remember what may seem now to be rather bizarre activities look back with mixed emotions. Virginia Ironside, a British journalist, however, does not. She outlined the heavy repression from which the young people of the 1960s were escaping: even a young woman bringing home a fatherless child might find herself rejected by her own parents. Ironside relates how writers in the journal *Woman* were barred from using the word 'bottom' (even 'bottom of the garden') while 'menstruation' might only be written in a sealed letter to the Agony Aunt. Yet the answer to heavy repression she found was very far from unfettered freedom. The sexually liberated era brought its own problems. Ironside wrote:

> Whenever I reveal I was young in the 1960s, people's eyes grow round with envy. 'Lucky you!' they say. Then they add, saucily: 'But of course they say that if you can remember the 60s you weren't there!' Well, I was there and I can, unfortunately, remember the 60s all too well. And although

92 THE LIFE AND WORK OF ANTE DABRO

I've no doubt it was a fantastic – or 'fab' as we used to say – time for men, for women (or young girls as we were then) it was absolutely grisly. [...] To be honest, I mainly remember the 60s as an endless round of miserable promiscuity, a time when often it seemed easier and, believe it or not, more polite, to sleep with a man than to chuck him out of your flat.[30]

Perhaps Ironside was mistaken in imagining it 'fab' for some male participants in group sex. How many men of conservative values who participated out of excitement have come to reflect in shame is unknown, but among these are some Catholic-raised men who had imbibed the church's traditional teaching on the role of women as devout mothers and homemakers. Dabro's negative reaction was one of horror that the pleasant everyday women of the university, the galleries and the embassies whom he knew well should thus, in his view, 'debase' themselves on a sheet of oily plastic. Marko Dabro had advised a wide sexual licence for his son that he would not have given his daughters. Ante Dabro sees no double standards in his judgements. 'I was angry with women', he reflects now. 'I love humanity but I'm deep down a conservative. I'm a very moral and religious person but belong to no creed.' Between the famous polarities of 'damned whores and god's police' drawn by the Australian feminist Anne Summers in 1975,[31] fell Ante's 'good' woman who was intelligent, a potential graduate and artist, but ideally holding these achievements *in addition* to her destiny as home maker, mother and passionate lover to her husband.

Several sculptures survive that flowed from this period of hate and, perhaps, of self-hate. One he called, quite misleadingly, *The Gynaecologist*, in which a male figure violently thrusts his fist into a woman's vagina. These semi-human creatures, cast in black resin, have only vague shapes for heads, and seem only partly human. Undoubtedly they represent Dabro's response at what seemed to him to be a profound debasement of the act of love. Peter Haynes, the curator of 'Ante Dabro Survey Exhibition 1968–1999' disingenuously labelled the work *Diagonal Direction* (though perhaps he did not recognise it for what it was), continuing: 'The figures are involved in a primeval struggle that is given sculptural expression by the simultaneous upward and downward thrusts of the two figures'.[32]

Another unnamed sculpture, also in resin, was a featureless woman. Her arms, no different from legs, wave upwards. She has no head, an indication, in Dabro's sculptural vocabulary, that she (or womankind) has lost her reason. She is in the act of giving birth to a sinister black mass. Is she giving light, or darkness? Is she participating in a misbegotten birth or has the ghastly matter flowed involuntarily from her? This is another deeply disturbing sculpture revealing the artist's serious trauma, a midnight sea in the blood of his own

FIGURE 3.9

Diagonal Direction, 1976, bronze, 58 x 32 x 35cm, the artist's studio.
Source: Con Boekel.

I don't know why I made these works.

experience, to escape from which hauntings artists paint, authors write and sculptors sculpt. The buying public was equally ambivalent. Someone bought *The Gynaecologist* from the gallery where it was first shown – then returned it. Another buyer did the same, then, on second thoughts (or those of family and friends), returned it, at which point Dabro withdrew it from sale. In this way,

94   THE LIFE AND WORK OF ANTE DABRO

Dabro produced a number of grotesque works that specifically related to these experiences. He now asks himself: 'Why did I make them? I can't explain it now.' Absorbed into the long tradition of Christian morality, he believed that the women were abusing God's precious gifts. They were now to be punished through his art. (He has since removed the black mass, rendering her no longer in the act of giving birth.)

On relations between a consenting couple, Dabro reflects:

> That's fine, it's natural to make love even if you don't know her name. Women want to make a nest, while men want to fertilise every woman in the world. Not five minutes goes past without my thinking about it. But group sex: no. I don't know what that black stuff is that's flowing from her, it's my wild imagination. My dreams even now are pretty wild. Sex has always been a driving force in my work, and always will be.

Analogous drawings in exhibitions equally did not impress the critics. One wrote:

> A major weakness is [that] the 12 drawings, unlike Kollvitz, Rodin, Barlach or Rodin [...] fail as drawings. It is a collection of highly mannered, erotic fantasies poorly drawn and lacking in subtlety.

Nigel-Murray Harvey wrote in 1970:

> One Portrait of a Bride is a hellish image, calculating and imperturbable, spawned by unpleasant experience, not yet conquered.[33]

Geoffrey de Gruen, reviewing another exhibition, wrote:

> There is nothing remote about the sculpture [...] It shows a copulating couple in a particularly aggressive and athletic position. The male is embedded in clear resin and although it is he who appears superior it is the woman who is free. Certainly the sexuality is overt, but whether you like Dabro's work or not, it can never be ignored.[34]

Or, as the critic Sasha Grishin wrote more positively following another exhibition in 1980:

> The two parts, male and female, are closely related suggesting an archetypal balance that is fundamental to this artist's thinking and which is probably his greatest strength.[35]

Making the Australian 95

Yet an even greater change was to soon follow.

Vicky's comforting and loving security and the birth of Ante's two daughters Sarah (1976) and Jessica (1977) brought a sensitivity and gentleness never seen before in his work. Some works portrayed the entire bodies of the two- and three-year-old girls, others, their heads alone. In all of these works, the heads are central to the viewer but dominated by the three or four protecting hands. The two-year-old looks down in a chubby-cheeked, half-smiling, contemplative gaze that will become more familiar in Dabro's later work. The soft, yielding hands reach over or through a straight-edged sheet of marble-like plaster. Round and straight, plane and curve, soft and hard are two polarities that will also grow stronger in his work.

In his dream, Dabro explained to Michelangelo:

Maestro, you have dedicated hundreds of sonnets to your beloved Vittoria Colonna. I have an inspiration too. I have dedicated all my work to my beloved Vicky, my guardian angel, my great love, my wife, my only real friend. She is the mother of these my children.

Like most artists, in discussion Dabro dislikes elaborating on the motivations for his work:

I am who I am, I'm a sculptor, I do what I do. Creativity is not a matter of two and two equals four, but in my work [after the birth of the children] had entered a contemplation, a gentleness. Everything seemed to change. My work became very caring with heads and hands, and I stopped doing abstracts altogether. The birth of Sarah accelerated that movement just when I was moving away from abstraction. The brutality was gone. All I could see were hands gently holding the heads of Sarah and Jessica. I didn't at first think of the hands as protecting them, but later it occurred to me that they *were* protecting them. Life is complex. Brutality can destroy life. And there's a brutality in love making. There's nothing gentle about that.

The critics loved these affectionate studies, perhaps unaware that the cradling hands might be interpreted as protecting the children from the wolves of the Russian forests, or from the brutality of his early life. They applauded the new and unsuspected gentleness:

Perhaps the single most striking innovation in this exhibition is Dabro's use of hands. While in earlier work hands were used to conceal faces or to heighten the general expressiveness of the form, now hands move into

FIGURE 3.10

Sarah, 1978, bronze, 1978, 60 x 40 x 35.6 cm, the artist's home.
Source: Con Boekel.

When they were born it seemed like I had gone to Graceland. As a sculpture it's very sentimental. Portraying one's own children is very tricky.

an expressive role all of their own. Hands now appear as a new force, which tries to hold back the emerging figure. In his bronze studies of hands with heads and the interflow of forms the conflict between the restraining hands and the emerging head achieves an effective dramatic expressiveness.

Making the Australian

FIGURE 3.11

Jessica, 1978, plaster, 50 x 48 x 33 cm, the artist's studio. Source: Con Boekel.

> *She's being protected by her father. My childhood was filled with Russian stories about wolves and animals and princesses that needed to be rescued. Who was there to protect my children?*

A critic at the Solander Gallery in 1977 wrote:

> [...] in the Michelangelo and Rodin tradition [...] Dabro appears at his best as a modeller; he has a wonderful sense of the tactileness of his material. In contrast, his work in marble has a laboured heaviness and [is] only occasionally rescued by the artist's natural compositional gifts. In marble, Dabro is unable to free himself from a certain 'classical' stiffness; the forms are clumsier and less convincing.[36]

98   THE LIFE AND WORK OF ANTE DABRO

Dabro reflects:

> I certainly strongly disagree with that last sentence. But it's true, I was con-
> stantly criticised for being old fashioned. Some of my exhibitions were a bit
> too romantic, but if I had to follow the latest fashion all the time, I would
> leave art. Fashion is art's greatest enemy. I would never do something I
> don't believe in. It has to be truthful to me. You have to be truthful to your-
> self, not just follow the blow-in critics. The National Gallery won't touch
> me, but I never had a problem selling. Rudy Komon in Sydney wanted
> me to be less old-fashioned. Even Phillip Bacon, [owner of one of the most
> influential galleries in Brisbane] whom I exhibited with in the early 'eight-
> ies, hinted that I might progress to be more avant-garde. But I tried and I
> was too decorative, and it took me a couple of years before I woke up. My
> abstracts had reached a dead end, they were just decorative and meaning-
> less. Good art will sail through the centuries.

Sasha Grishin wrote in 1980:

> The Exhibition is technically more polished and simpler and at the same
> time more resolved. The sense of expressiveness in the work is more
> explicit, less clouded in mysterious allusions. 'Jessica' achieves a lovely
> balance between a restful poise and a dramatic expressiveness that one
> also finds in Degas' sculptured figurines. [...] It is a bold and imagina-
> tive exhibition and one which further establishes the reputation of Ante
> Dabro as that of a significant Australian sculptor who has embarked
> on his own path of exploration, rather than simply imitating European
> and American imported models. [...] In a country so poor in sculptors
> as Australia, Dabro is quickly emerging as one of our most interesting
> and significant.[37]

Dabro had made a fair start in Australia, but most critics, who, through the
nature of their profession, seek something new, had certainly not been ecstatic.
He felt isolated in a remote and boring Canberra suburb. He was disappointed
in himself for having toyed with the avant-garde.

Critics, who love to detect influences in any work under review, understood
neither his personal history nor the depth of his artistic vocabulary. James
Gleeson had found traces of Klippel. One found *Scribe* (1971, figure 3.12) as
Rodinesque, but Dabro believes its inspiration was more Egyptian, of which
he had seen many examples in Split as a student. Just as possible was that he
drew from his artistic memory the ordered rectangles of the Roman cemetery

FIGURE 3.12

Scribe, 1971, cement, 54 x 45 x 30 cm. Source: Artist's collection, the artist's home.

It's clear that I was being influenced by Rodin with all the invented muscles, where the anatomy, though all wrong, can look right.
I had in mind some Egyptian art at this time of seeking a new reality.

at Solin. The hard surfaces characteristic of much of his later work, designed to throw the eye to the rounded curves of a figure, begin to strengthen.

Dabro had abandoned his position as heir-apparent to the most distinguished tradition of Croatian sculpture – for what? The first decade in Australia had made a complex Australian. He had lost his trust in the democratic process, yet

100 THE LIFE AND WORK OF ANTE DABRO

he remained distrusted by his fellow Croatians. His prodigious efforts to stage an exhibition every year won him a respect for both his talent and his potential. A new gentleness was balanced by works that invoked the unstoppable forces that unite and divide men and women. He had defied the avant-garde. Meštrović doubtless would have approved of his protégé's determination to hold true to his first principles. At the end of the decade, at the age of 42, Dabro was about to become 'Dabro'; but he was dissatisfied with the Australia that he had come to love. 'I'd take up arms to defend it tomorrow. My dilemma was that the country was being torn apart by multiculturalism and other minority groups that I don't believe in. We should be melting in together'.

And the works, of course, remain: the over-ornate decorative pieces of the late 1960s that work from outside in, and which he is later to disavow, *Butterflies* with its semi-abstract wood carving that bowls Vicky Butler off her feet, the lost Electricity House mural with its raised socialist-realist fist, the gentle caressing hands, the inky black sludge, the Egyptian figures of 1971 described as Rodinesque, the uncertain St Augustine, the agonised but benevolent Christ. All have found light, all have flowed from the sculptor's soul to find and fulfil their own independent existence.

Dabro's principal dealer Phillip Bacon featured his work in three exhibitions in 1983, 1988 and 2002. They were always popular, Bacon affirmed, though he had to work hard with the larger, costly pieces. *Now You See Me, Now You Don't* was tagged at $14,000 in 2002. The cheapest work for sale was $4,000, and the most expensive, *Introspection* (at the Judith Wright Court), $90,000, which was sold.[38] The art critic Peter Haynes, who curated Dabro's *Survey Exhibition 1968–1999*, at the preview in 2000, spoke of his fundamental Europeanness that embedded a stylistic cultural connection that could not be expunged, his serious and determined way of apprehending the world. He noted Dabro's hint of *chiaroscuro* that forced the viewer to examine the play of light, the touch of *non-finito* that intrigued, not closed off, the mind of the observer.[39]

In 1999, the Australian novelist David Malouf summoned for his readers the Roman poet Ovid, exiled to an obscure town in Romania. Malouf's Ovid grasped the creative process in this way:

> But the spirits have to be recognized to become real. They are not outside us, nor even entirely within, but flow back and forth between us and the objects we have made, the landscape we have shaped and move in. We have dreamed all these things in our deepest lives and they are ourselves.[40]

CHAPTER 4

MAKING THE HUMAN FORM

Sitting or standing before a sculptor or a life-drawing class of art students is much more exacting than it sounds. Among the professional artists and student classes alike, the model will traditionally be female and young. She will be protected by a set of rules as strict as they are unwritten. Generally, she will assume her own pose, but having taken it – no slumping! Nobody must ask her to change position or rearrange any material that she may be wearing, make comments or even move the radiator. No asking her to sit differently. Never ever touch her. Nothing must be done to upset her. *Don't disturb the model. She's working.*

Mounting the dais, the model assumes a challenging position that she will have to hold unmoving for anything from one minute to twenty. The atmosphere becomes intense. The model has transformed into a shape, an entity, a corporeal presence independent of the woman who mounted the stand. She feels a concentrated silence descend as she presents to the class that most demanding of all artistic challenges: to reproduce and understand whatever it is in the human body that each artist apprehends and responds to – the angle of the knee, the curve of the spine, how the head attaches to the neck, the neck to the shoulders, the tendons that raise an ankle, the muscles that manifest from each artist's viewpoint in a visual universe. The intense silence is broken only by the instructor moving about the classroom. After twenty minutes or longer, she resumes her everyday form and dismounts. She puts on a coat or gown, maybe moves about the room to see how she has been drawn, re-created or transformed.

The routine seems unproblematic, but the implications of the male artist's gaze on the female body will, in the 1970s, convulse the art world for two decades and sweep the uncomprehending sculptor Ante Dabro before it.

Imagine a day in 1978. Today a model is coming not to the Canberra School of Art but to Dabro's studio for whose arrival the sculptor may need only his

102 THE LIFE AND WORK OF ANTE DABRO

sketchpad. Or he may require wet plaster, a narrow-mesh wire frame, perhaps of full-size proportion, reinforced with a 25 by 60-centimetre frame. He'll add more netting later, even newspaper if the direction of the work requires it. Half an hour will set the plaster ready to be worked.

The model arrives. She has a coffee and chats. Dabro begins sketching.

> The head and face will come last. It can be almost ignored when I start. You have to see the whole body as one, you work as a whole. Ideally when the work is complete, the viewer will start at the toes, follow up the body to the head, then down again. I don't focus on the head as the pre-Hellenistic and Roman sculptors did, rather, I follow the lead of Michelangelo and the classical Greeks. The body is a rhythm, a golden mean so that's a sculptural issue. When viewers shut their eyes they see not the face first but the shape of the whole body. What I have to take in is the abstract, the essence of humanity, and that's conveyed through the body. Look at Rodin's figures. Like Michelangelo's, every square inch of Rodin's bodies are bubbling with emotion, not just the head.

Dabro begins the impossible struggle between form and meaning:

> I'm not exactly sculpting, I'm not modelling, I'm not copying. The presence of the model that I'm sketching is enough for me. It's almost an essence of humanity that I'm seeking, and what's inside that humanity. I'm not interested in formal issues, they will look after themselves. I'll warn her that I may not make much sense if I chat. If she asks me a question I may not answer. So I keep working and mumbling something that doesn't make any sense. Once she knows me well, between sessions she may wander around looking at my other work or start making coffee and even then I might sketch whatever activity she's doing.

Dabro's relationships with his models were never less than mutually respectful.

One of his favourite models was Susan Boden-Brown, a Fine Arts graduate, who in the 1980s modelled for the compulsory life-drawing classes at the Canberra School of Art. 'They liked me, not because I was particularly busty, but I was hippy. Art students always like a "hippy" model. I didn't mind being looked at, I thought of it more as me watching them'. She appreciated the strict protocol whereby the model was the focus, more significant than either student or staff. From the dais, she could hear Ante, the staff member, wandering among the students. 'That's going well'. 'No rubbing out'. 'Too chocolate boxy'; even, 'That's bullshit'.[1]

Making the Human Form 103

By the beginning of the 1980s, Susan had become one of Ante's most important models. She inspired him, she believes, through her intellect and conversation as well as her body. He found her widely read and informed. In return, she admired his physical abilities, his virility. 'He was so physically vigorous, so masculine.' She appreciated his many years of training, his extraordinary ability to work in clay, the man who, rather than taking a car, came trudging across from his home in Turner to the Canberra School of Art through Canberra's wintry weather in a heavy fur coat. She liked his flirtatiousness, his accent, his sense of himself as a European gentleman even though, in an Australian context, he knew this persona to be slightly ridiculous. She admired his humanity, his empathy, his accounts of outrageous Canberra adventures in the 1960s. She was tickled when, signing off on her modelling hours, he would write 'sex hours'. She understood that his flirtatiousness was strictly reserved for the periods between poses, and that when she resumed work, 'his art was incredibly serious'. 'There were two strands always at work, and that's what appealed to me [...] he was wild but underneath incredibly serious and solid.'

Sessions with Susan began in the School of Art on Sunday mornings. Susan recalls Dabro's very clear sense of what he wanted, never asking her to choose a pose beyond asking her to move a hand here or there. 'All you've got when you're a model is you. As I modelled I was most truly myself. That gave me a feeling that there was something unique about me as well as my generic qualities.' So began 'a real dialogue. [...] He was so steeped in tradition'. Putting a heavy coat round her shoulders with a flourish between sessions symbolised part of the extroverted but solitary transplanted European. Little by little, she came to feel that there was something in her that he especially valued. 'You have a lot of power in being a model in choosing your creative pose.' A concentrated stillness held during the modelling sessions. She was impressed by his sense of what was proper and correct in their relationship. Striking a pose, she enjoyed their exchanges, perhaps about politics, 'but never about nothing'. Over several sessions, she and Ante had, she believed, 'developed a really small "I" loving relationship. I was part of the process though we had different roles. It was like being the lead dog in a husky team. I was the lead dog. He really needed me and though I was not in charge, I had a lot of power to be creative'. Looking at her knee, he remarked, 'you have so much sadness, so much turbulence inside you'. In a relaxed but purposeful dialogue, often without words, Susan found that Ante had become not exactly a friend nor a fellow artist, but that together they made 'a wonderful ensemble, a rich and creative relationship'. Over thirty years, the relationship holds still. '[If] I had a glass of wine with him there wouldn't be all that much to say. But if he asked me to model for him again I'd jump at it. That was how it always was.' His work she described neatly as 'Brutalist Romantic'.

Dabro's best-known sculpture of Susan Boden-Brown is *Suzanne*, the life-size bronze sculpture in the Brindabella Business Park at Canberra Airport. Here, *Suzanne* sits with her feet dangling just above the surface of the ornamental pool. In a subtle display of *contrapunto*, the muscles of her stiff right arm swell with the weight of her upper body; her loose left arm suggests the curved angle of her spine. Her right hand is flattened rightward, while her left, at the specific request of the artist, rests on the sandstone seat. Her right leg mirrors the angle of her weight-bearing arm. From the front, just the right clavicle is prominent.

FIGURE 4.1

Suzanne, 1976, bronze, and *Susan Boden-Brown*, 2021, Canberra airport, life size.
Source: Con Boekel.

> Susan says, 'She is me at a time full of possibilities.
> [...] Ante made me so valued for being vivacious'.

Making the Human Form 105

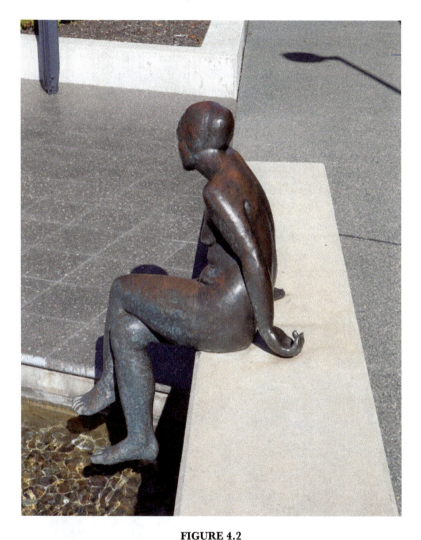

FIGURE 4.2

Suzanne, right side. Source: Con Boekel.

I find her a bit soft now.

Like Donatello's *David,* Dabro's sculpture follows an S curve, as pronounced when viewed from the right-hand side as it is from the front – except that Donatello used David's left arm on his hip and the sword on the right to carry the rhythm. *Suzanne*'s head, set unambiguously left, marks the decisive beginning of the curve. Did Dabro retain the lessons of Benedetto Varchi, who in 1557 advised the sculptor to examine the work from eight separate but equal standpoints? 'Proceed to modify each part', he instructed, 'without sacrificing or enlivening some at the expense of others'. More probably, his own intuition shaped the elegant curve of Susan's spine and the downward slope of her shoulders. Her widening upper body makes Susan seem rather more solid than she does when viewed from the front.

FIGURE 4.3

Suzanne in the Studio, 1975, plaster. Source: Artist's collection.

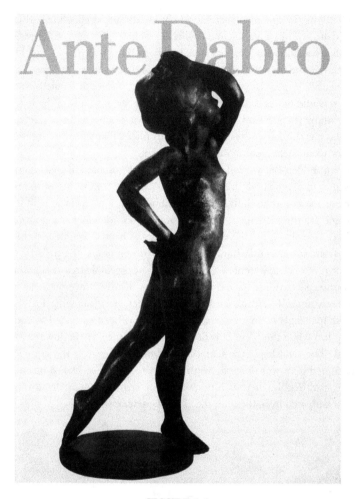

FIGURE 4.4

Dancer I, 1988, bronze, 1.78 x 82 x 50 cm. Source: 'Ante Dabro' (Phillip Bacon exhibition catalogue, 1988).

She is the first of my dancers. I'm always attracted by the moving figure. Creating a static figure like Suzanne brings different issues.

108 THE LIFE AND WORK OF ANTE DABRO

The figure's expression is certainly not Diana surprised while bathing but one of calm serenity on a warm day, like Susan herself in the Canberra School of Art live modelling classes, not shielding herself from anyone's gaze, but certainly not giving herself to the viewer. In shape, her head is a little reminiscent of Brancusi's *Sleeping Muse* (1910) yet *Suzanne* is in a state of serene contemplation and would not be outraged to be disturbed. She is totally of the moment.

For many years, Susan did not see the sculpture of herself, nor take visitors, but today she thinks of *Suzanne* as her sister, or herself at an earlier stage of life. She has taken friends and her children to see it.

Susan Boden-Brown reflects: 'She's a good companion who comes up sometimes in psychoanalysis sessions. I don't want a copy of her or to buy her, but she is me at a time of life full of possibilities. I don't want to own it; yet I do own it. It's the exchange. Ante made me feel so valued for being vivacious.'

Forty years later, Susan volunteered to model herself again beside *Suzanne*. Apart from the natural changes in weight distribution, the artistry of the sculptor is at once apparent. *Suzanne*'s neck is appreciably longer than her living counterpart. While *Suzanne* rests her eyes in misty reverie, Susan's eyes are merely shut. The distance between the feet, even allowing for changes in leg shape, suggests that *Suzanne*'s left thigh has been extended to complete the rhythm while the S curve is brought to a cadence by the inward-turning left foot. The right leg of the sculpture and model is exactly the same length. Preoccupied here with form more than precise anatomy, Dabro has allowed few physical details; there is little overt bone structure apart from the right clavicle and, seen from the rear, the elegant curving spine.

CHAPTER 5

MAKING BRONZE

The act of creation to me is no different to breathing.

Dabro (2019)

For several thousand years, sculptors have loved working in bronze. Bronze resists corrosion, it burnishes to a warm orangish colour, it absorbs the colours around it and protects itself with a natural patina. Copper mixed with about 3 per cent silicon and 2 per cent manganese will produce an alloy that will support a ton on the finger of a cast human figure. Other additives will create a wide variety of enchanting colours. Sculptors love the way that, if heated to a very precise temperature, bronze will pour into complex moulds. In the hands of a skilled artist, a bronze sculpture can be bewitching. The best bronze accepts a different patina determined by the ambient light, but in an exterior setting, the patina needs regular renewing.

Midway through 1553, Benvenuto Cellini, famous throughout Florence and Renaissance Italy for his superlative skill as a jeweller, began preparing for the most ambitious project of his life. He was beginning a huge sculpture of the Greek mythological figure Perseus moments after slaying and beheading Medusa, the monster who turns all who look on her to stone. He chose to work in bronze, not marble. Even though large-scale bronze casting had not been practised in Italy for many decades, he understood the principles and had absorbed the ancient Greek and Roman texts. He assured his patron, Cosimo de Medici, that his living bronze, not inert marble, would literally breathe life into a dead soul – just as well since bronze casting cost ten times as much as carved marble. He knew exactly what to do and had laboriously instructed his team of foundry assistants. What could possibly go wrong?

First, Cellini ordered ox carts of pinewood as fuel for his furnace. While waiting for them to arrive, he extracted the clay he had been preparing for several months to construct the larger-than-life wax model of Perseus standing atop of Medusa's body, looking down exhausted while holding aloft her severed head. The body he reinforced inside with iron rods; then, he encased it and its several limbs separately in the clay. Following the classical principles, he constructed a dozen vents for the hot gases to escape, the more the better. On a slow fire, he heated the clay containing his enormous model. Melting, the wax poured out as intended to create a hollow exact reverse-image of the work. The fire burnt for two days to thoroughly dry the clay.

Next, he set his team to construct a furnace. He ensured plenty of spaces between the bricks to achieve a good draught and made sure that the soil extracted from the pit was not piled too close to the top where it might obstruct the air flow or the earthenware vents and channels. Neglect of either precaution could mean a devastating explosion. Next, the delicate clay model, as fragile as it was heavy, was lowered to the bottom of the pit and pine logs heaped around it. Following the ancient formula, he filled the crucible itself with lumps of copper and some 8 per cent tin. The fire roared. More logs were thrown in as Cellini rushed from side to side keeping the temperature even. The sparks rose so high that the straw roof of the workshop caught fire, threatening to fall in over his team of master founders. Shortly afterwards, a tremendous storm blew over the workshop, extinguishing the burning straw but drenching the furnace and lowering the temperature of the crucible.

Pouring the bronze to fill the hollow space in the clay is the most skilful element in what is itself a lengthy and highly technical process. Often it will be supervised not only by the sculptor but the master-founder, who can gauge by its colour alone when the bronze comes to the warm golden red of 1150°C, liquid enough to pour into every crevice of the mould to fill up the last finger and toe. Cellini, immeasurably stressed, suffering from fever and probably not having slept for several days, retired to bed. Scarcely had he closed his eyes before his foreman entered: 'O Benvenuto! Your statue is spoiled and there is no hope whatever of saving it.' Rushing out, he knew instantly that the mix had cooled in the storm and begun to re-solidify in the cauldron. Yes, it might be saved by a rapid reheating. His team ran to fetch a pile of oak logs, which burn hotter than pine. The fire began to roar, which, the storm having passed, dried the roof and set what was left of it ablaze again. 'Suddenly an explosion took place, attended by a tremendous flash of flame as though a thunderbolt had formed and been discharged among us.' The furnace cap had blown off; the copper was now so hot that the tin alloy had burned away, making the mix flow too sluggishly. Clearly, it would not reach all the sculpture's extremities. Lumps of pewter, which has a much lower melting point than copper, went into the crucible, but the temperature was still rising so fast that it disappeared as fast as the team could throw it in. Cellini guessed that during the uncontrolled

Making Bronze

reheating too much of the pewter, like the tin, had burnt off: into the mix went 200 pieces of his household's pewter cutlery and dinner service, some for the crucible, the rest, in a last desperate measure, he fed into the channels leading directly into the hollows within. 'This expedient succeeded and everyone could now perceive that my bronze was in most perfect liquefaction, and my mould was filling.' After two days' cooling, Cellini broke apart the clay mould to find it very nearly perfect. Only half of Perseus's right foot was missing. What remained now was to connect the pieces, smooth the air holes, repair and remove small imperfections and several years of grinding, burnishing, polishing and applying a patina.

Cellini's sculpture of Perseus holding the head of Medusa is one of the glories of Western civilisation. He stands in the Piazza della Signoria in Florence in company with a copy of Michelangelo's *David* and Baccio Bandinelli's *Hercules and Cacus*.[1]

Fifty centuries of artistry. Fifty centuries of advanced technology. Fifty centuries of tradition.

Sculptors in bronze today need to consider several newer techniques. One is the large-scale process called sand casting, in which molten bronze of up to five tons is poured into a prepared mould filled with a substance like gelatin or vinyl that will burn off when the metal touches it; but the finished surface will not be as precise as other techniques and requires long and arduous post-casting processes. Another technique, developed in the 1950s, is known as ceramic shell casting, which is faster and allows very precise surface details in quite large objects while identical shapes can be reproduced more quickly. In the mid-1970s, it was a technique almost unknown in Australia.

Because the process of bronze casting is dangerous for all but the highly skilled, Dabro had received almost no practical experience as a student in Zagreb. The skills he mastered in Canberra had come through ten years at the Canberra School of Art and its predecessor, the Canberra Technical College, experimenting with his colleague Vlasa Nikoleski in casting ceramic shell techniques. By 1980, he had acquired almost all the necessary skill, artistry, strength and decisive thinking that would be needed and more as he began construction of one of the largest bronze sculptures ever attempted in Australia: the memorial to the Australian Navy in Anzac Parade, Canberra.

A Churchill Award with travel and living costs for four months provided an opportunity to visit Princeton to observe ceramic shell casting, and Berlin where sand casting (an expendable mould-casting process that uses resin covered in sand to form the mould) was practised. The Awards Chairperson, Vicky's uncle, the Hon James Muirhead, excused himself for the interview.

112   THE LIFE AND WORK OF ANTE DABRO

He remarked afterwards that the panel could hardly follow what Dabro was saying but decided that he deserved an award on the strength of his passionate conviction. In Princeton, he watched and learnt to cast in ceramic shells, while not omitting to remind the Americans that Jackson Pollock was not the fountainhead of abstract expressionism. 'Go and study the works of Arshile Gorky'. Eight weeks in Princeton, thence to the Hermann Noack foundry in Berlin, where Henry Moore, though living in England, had his major works produced. There, Dabro observed the techniques of massive sand mould casting, a process that uses covered sand to form the mould, five tons at a time, for pieces up to ten metres long. The feeders or 'risers', the reservoirs in which the molten bronze collects to counteract the shrinkage of the cooling metal, and the escape tubes for the superheated gases being driven out, are even more crucial to be of the right size and in the right place than in smaller works. 'Ante, when the metal is at the right heat – which will be between 1150 and 1200 depending on your alloy – you'll need to be quick. Too hot and it will burn the mould, too cold and it won't flow properly' The most skilled founders will judge the right moment by eye. When the mix reaches the subtle shade of orange-red – POUR! The founder has exactly 3 seconds to do it. 'Get this wrong', he was told, 'and it won't be just us that goes up, we'll take half of Berlin with us'. After cooling, there begins the 'chasing' (defining and refining) of the cast texture. Seamless welding, burnishing and polishing are laborious arts in themselves.

The splendid Anzac Parade, the most formal avenue in Canberra, was conceived by the city's first designer, Walter Burley Griffin. He foresaw a grand People's Avenue that would link the two most significant public buildings in the national capital, the Houses of Parliament and the People's Cultural Palace. The blistering wartime experiences of the nation in World War I caused the cultural palace to be replaced by the Australian War Memorial, but though the palace was never built anywhere, Burley Griffin's avenue remained. From that time, troops would march and parade on significant national days, especially Anzac Day. On each side were to be erected monuments to each of the Armed Services and to their individual campaigns. The memorial to the Australian Navy was chosen as the third to be created to coincide with the 75th anniversary of the birth of the national fleet.

In mid-1983 the government called for tenders to complete the work by March 1986 for an initial budget of $400,000, constructed within the appointed position and space halfway up the eastern side of Anzac Parade.

In August 1983, playing with Sarah and Jessica on Broulee Beach, Dabro formed a sandy model of a platform on which naval personnel could perform

Making Bronze 113

their tasks. If they worked on a platform, why not allude to a boat? The squarish shape became more rectangular. And if the platform had become a boat, why should not water be present? His thoughts turned to the torrent rushing past his father Marko's water mill on the creek, and the waterfall that burst violently from the rocky hillside at the Krka National Park near Split. On the beach, the sandy shape began to coalesce. Its size would demand bronze, not marble. His mind turned over images of the huge sculptures that he had long admired – Michelangelo's *David*, Cellini's *Perseus*, Veroccio's equestrian monument to Colleoni in Venice, the nearly five-metre-tall pre-Christian sculpture of the mounted Marcus Aurelius, Donatello's 1443 re-creation of the Venetian warrior *Gattamelata*, and fifty years later, Leonardo's never-fulfilled horse and rider that would have been nearly eight metres tall. All his training, his instincts and his very persona anchored him to the balanced forms of the Italian Renaissance; moreover, the human values manifest in his sculpture should be recognisable by the master sculptors of the Renaissance as one of their own. Modern but not modernist, its construction would deploy all the sculptural techniques he had mastered in Croatia, bronze casting in Canberra, ceramic shell casting in Princeton and sand casting in Berlin. It must not shout, like the Social Realist works he was supposed to admire in Zagreb. Nor should it imitate the vast symbolic abstractions he had once worked on with Džamonja. Unlike the Stations of the Cross of Split Cathedral that had surrounded the student, this work should not tell a story. Though the figures were sailors, the work must not be a simple narrative of the life of a warship. The face of each individual would speak of dignity, humanism, poise and dedication. If life was a struggle through difficulty, such would be this memorial, as King David's psalmist put it, to those who go down to the sea in ships and occupy their business in deep waters. This creation should do more than evoke pride in naval achievements, more than elate the emotions through Christian doctrine. It must stir the midnight sea of violence and grief to transfigure the profundity of wartime loss.

> Yea, and if some god shall wreck me in the wine-dark deep, even so I will endure with a heart within me patient of affliction. For already have I suffered full much, and much have I toiled in perils of waves and war. Let this be added to the tale of those.[2]

If, in the end, every human life is solitary, then this memorial must both celebrate interdependence yet salute the strange seas of thought into which every navigator sails alone.

114   THE LIFE AND WORK OF ANTE DABRO

Dabro turned to Vicky to exclaim: 'This is my Naval Memorial'.

Sixty-one expressions of interest followed the call for tender with detailed plans. In June 1984, fifteen sculptors were asked to provide a model to the assessment panel. A final five entrants were then invited to discuss the comments of the panel, and then to prepare a maquette for a final decision. On Dabro's first attempt, an escaping gas bubble ruptured the bronze scaled-down version, and the model was lost. He presented a second version, but it was not until 4 December 1984 that Prime Minister Hawke announced that he had been successful. Commenting on the maquette, *Navy News* reported:

> His proposed bronze sculpture was to be 7.5 metres in height, cast in geometric shapes with representational figures emerging from them. Dabro described his work and its symbolic reference as "Sailors and Ships: Interaction and Interdependence". He envisaged the members of the RAN as brave, highly trained and dedicated men and women operating well designed and well-constructed machines. The geometric shapes symbolised the machines, and the interaction of the more representational figures representing interdependence. The lack of horizontality in the planes of these forms recognise that ships at sea do not present their crews with horizontal surfaces upon which to carry out their duties. Also, from a sculptural point of view, a dynamic force is added.[3]

Dabro recollected:

> I didn't think how observable it might be until I'd finished. If something is big it's not just for its size alone, I have to remember what angle its's going to be looked at. For the Memorial I had often to go across the road and imagine it and ask – 'Is it working? Are the parts connected?' Then I had to think of it from the back. 'Are all the parts connected? What of the space between them?' There comes a point when the different parts start relating. And the more you squeeze them the more dramatic the work becomes. That becomes as critical as the work itself.

The Naval Memorial would be 7.5 metres in height, 16 tonnes in weight. Two specialist navy welders and an assistant were appointed at the government's expense.

The panel had taken almost a year to decide on a design, giving the winner only 16 clear months to construct a work of vast complexity by a sculptor whose first version of the bronze maquette had blown up, and whose experience in very large-scale bronze production was nil. The pieces would be cast

Making Bronze 115

by a team of aircraft manufacturers quite unfamiliar with the complex technologies and scale that Dabro had just learnt in Princeton. He himself would create the parts of the memorial that needed to be worked in *ciment fondu*.[4] The 84 separate bronze pieces would be cast in a city different from its assembly point by techniques that were not only highly skilled but highly dangerous, in a country that could not even produce the bronze sheets necessary for the work to begin without cracking. Nor could there be compromise on the date for completion, for on the 3rd of March 1986, at 10 a.m. precisely, Her Majesty the Queen would be driving from Government House to Anzac Parade to open [...] something. It had better be ready. Dabro asked himself – what could possibly go wrong?

Wisely, his liaison officer at the Department of Prime Minister and Cabinet gives him a direct line should he encounter difficulty. The first arises, as he anticipates, in less than a week. To maximise the available time, Dabro formally asks Udo Sellbach, Director of the Canberra School of Art, for 18 months' full-time leave to construct the monument. 'Sorry, Ante, but no, we need you to complete the summer teaching course that ends in March'. An urgent call on the hot line promptly brings him Prime Minister Hawke's Personal Assistant. Dabro recalls the conversation:

> Now what's the trouble Mr Dabro? Is there some kind of issue with getting Leave of Absence? Yeah? Don't worry, I'll fix it.

One can only guess at the conversation that ensues between the director and the Prime Minister's Office but less than half an hour later, Dabro is summoned to return. He is not invited to sit. The director signs an order of release for Dabro's eighteen-months absence from teaching duties and slaps it back to him without word or eye contact.

The most senior naval staff takes Dabro's education in naval matters seriously. His first destination is the guided missile Frigate *Adelaide*. He is flown to the Penguin Naval base at Balmoral in Sydney for early-morning war games the next day. Partying in the Officers' Mess leads to a sore head and a groan when a batman enters his cabin the next morning at six without even a cup of tea. Somehow he manages to struggle on deck and then to the bridge of the patrol boat HMAS *Wollongong* where a seat marked 'Mr Dabro' awaits him. Through the Heads, but the moderate sea that he has been promised he finds anything but calm. A HUUGE wave (his emphasis) causes him to be seasick, at which everyone laughs. 'Piss off the lot of you!' Next he is to transfer, via a rubber dinghy, then a rope ladder, to the much larger *Adelaide*, already at sea, to

116   THE LIFE AND WORK OF ANTE DABRO

observe the war games. In the five-metre swell, the *Adaide*'s deck seems to rapidly descend to him, then leap far above his head. 'Mr Dabro, jump!!' Several attempts nearly end in watery disaster. A helicopter appears with a harness and winch to transfer him. Thank you, but no. In desperation, the *Wollongong*'s skipper bellows from the bridge, 'Mr Dabro, I order you to go below!' This is the voice of the hated Yugoslavian army. 'I don't take orders from you or anyone else. Fuck you all!' The order seems, however, the best option. The sailor assigned to his care takes him below, whence he can hear the war games progressing noisily. Though his experience as a participant-observer so far has been less than successful, he forms a warm friendship with Commodore (later Admiral) Alan Beaumont. The Commodore sends a driver the next day as an escort and guide on the next leg of his naval adventure, but Dabro does not care much for life on submarines either. He refuses to fly to the Fleet Air Arm base in Nowra by helicopter, and a seat in a small Defence Department plane leaves him equally unimpressed. 'It was like flying in a milk bottle'. But the day is not wasted, for he learns that he must add an airman to the crew still assembling on the deck of his sculpture.

The schedule is first to construct a full-size mock-up to ensure that the existing proportions of the maquette will be effective outside. Dabro paces up and down the memorial site on Anzac Parade calculating the distance from other memorials, the height of the trees and from which point of view the houses in the domestic street behind will be visible. His ex-student assistant, George (Bratko) Zakaravic, helps to map out a floor plan to a scale of one to ten. Halfway up, he calls out that at his level, the platform is 70 centimetres wider than the model's specifications. 'That's OK, Bratko, it must always be done by eye, not ruler. As we get above the height of the viewer we have to start making allowances by making the work look correct when we're on the ground'.

Following the construction of a platform on which to build the deck, Bratko and Dabro began to construct the mock-up out of two-by-four pine laths supporting the 50-by-100-centimetre framework. To these, they attach plywood to represent the bronze sheets forming the base. The supporting pine frame enabled them to scramble up and down making adjustments. The welders began work cutting each sheet to Dabro's specifications, only to find that the Australian-made product was liable to crack when worked into the figurative elements of the sculpture. There was no time to waste experimenting to get the Australian-made sheets right. An order flew to Germany for an immediate and expensive shipping of the top-quality bronze sheets, enough for the whole structure plus another dozen.

Making Bronze 117

On the first of many visits to his studio – a huge shed in the Canberra suburb of Pialligo – an official from the National Capital Development Commission that shares supervision with the navy arrives unannounced, aghast to see nothing but a wooden skeleton that looks more like the framework of a bonfire than a sculpture. 'What is the next step, Mr Dabro?' asks a suit, little knowing that his commissioned artist is not exactly sure either. The official protests that he can't see much progress and reports, perhaps, to his superiors, 'I think he's lost it'. Meanwhile, the vertical shaft keeps lengthening till at last it visually relates to and balances the platform and its activity below. 'I really didn't have a clue how tall it would be, it was all intuitive'. The final measurements that seem satisfactory to his eye produce a full-scale structure 70 centimetres wider in the middle and a full 1.5 metres taller than the proportions of the maquette. Assistant Bratko sees a problem.

> Ante, the roof is going to be in the way when we lift it out.
> Well, the roof will need to come off.

Over coffee and a grappa, Dabro explains to his assistant that the taller the structure, the more it must be elongated for viewers at ground level. 'Bratko, that's what I learned from Mr Buonarotti'. Before mobile phones, it is Vicky at home who has to field the endless requests for modifications.

> Oh Mrs Dabro, this is the Navy Liaison office calling, I wonder if I could speak to Ante please.
> I'm sorry he's not here, he's at Pialligo.
> OK, could you pass on a message to him please. One of the crew members has to be a woman.

Urgent talks are meanwhile proceeding with the National Capital Authority about the positioning of the pump, the jets and the nozzles of the sources of cascading water. There will need to be three separate water sources, aft, forward and amidships, and the project will ideally involve the construction of an underground dry chamber that a mechanic can enter to make adjustments. 'No chance of that, Mr Dabro'; but still the estimated costs rocket. Another team from the Prime Minister's Protocol section worries about procedures on the day of unveiling. Will the work be finished on time? If so, will Dabro attend and meet the Queen? If so, can he be trusted to be polite? One midday, half a dozen suits enter unannounced to find Dabro perched five metres above their heads with two buckets of wet plaster balanced on the scaffolding platform.

THE LIFE AND WORK OF ANTE DABRO

Ante, Hello. How are you? We'd like to talk to you.
Okay.
When can you come down?
One thirty.
It's one p.m. now. We'll wait for you
I meant one thirty tomorrow morning.

The team withdrew to consult.

No, we need to see you now.

Two buckets of plaster hurtle down and explode messily on the floor. The group exits hurriedly. Dabro hears a voice exclaim,

I think he's gone mad.

Dabro explains now, 'I was under terrible stress at the time. It just seemed to be a needless interruption'.

Next day, Commodore Beaumont returns with a retinue of just one, a woman. 'In front was a beautiful young sailor girl. I could tell by hearing the click of her high heels'. The eminent Commodore comes out of hiding, Dabro climbs down the scaffolding, and in good humour, the working schedule is confirmed. Coffee and grappa all round.

Yet the foundry of the factory at Fishermans Bend, Melbourne, is in high tension. The plan is that Dabro will produce the figurative elements in Canberra, send them to Melbourne to be cast under his supervision, and then return them to him. A figure holding binoculars, for instance, will need to be cast in six different sections before the process of expert, seamless welding begins. But the heavily unionised factory workers discover that Dabro is not registered in the Australian Metalworkers Union and has no intention to become a member. 'I refused to join the Yugoslavian Communist Party and I'm certainly not going to join your Union.' The reaction is immediate. All out. 'No work to be done for this Dabro character. He can just send us the moulds for us to cast. We can do without him.' Dabro, indignant, flies back to Canberra, collects his family and disappears down the coast.

The wide skins of aircraft usually fabricated at Fishermens Bend need quite different techniques of production from the more delicate *ciment fondu*-based shells. The misplaced confidence of the factory-floor that it can manage

Making Bronze 119

without Dabro does not last, for it is not only the top of the crucible blowing off that can cause a Cellini-style explosion: the merest skerrick of moisture can also cause catastrophe. So can a trapped gas bubble. Trial and error learnt over a decade has taught Dabro how the pouring will be smoother if the mould is set upside down at about ten degrees from the vertical to allow the angled gas bubbles to escape through the 'gates' rather than straight upwards. He is unsure of the ability of the Melbourne team to set the risers and channels in the right number and place, preferring to make these himself in the knowledge of how the process will work. Like Cellini, he wonders if he can trust them. Sure enough, the Melbourne team gets it wrong. In his absence, the first three casts explode like cannons.

Events have moved fast, but now they move faster. The foreman calls Navy Liaison, who calls Project Manager Peter Butler, in Canberra.

Get hold of him whichever way you can. We need him here. Now.

Butler delivers the message that Dabro must present himself at ten on Monday morning, where he finds a packed and tense meeting of foundry workers, the foreman, union reps and the CEO of the Commonwealth Aircraft Corporation himself. The meeting, however, finds the foreman contrite. Dabro begins:

So your moulds exploded. How did you pour them?
By the direct method.
That was wrong. Especially in a big cast the gates have to be offset. It has to be an indirect pour.

A brief discussion.

Ok Mr Dabro, you're the boss now. We're weeks behind schedule and still nothing has been done. You can hire and fire anyone you like. If anyone asks, you're an honorary member of the Union.

Dabro and the team prepare the first pour of several tonnes from the huge cradle. The temperature rises past the lowest melting point of 1000°C and approaches the preferred copper–silicon mix at a pour temperature of 1150°. The colour shifts from dull red to a brighter, more golden yellow.

On my signal you have three seconds to do it.
Now!

120   THE LIFE AND WORK OF ANTE DABRO

The mix flows smoothly. The gases vent as designed. No explosion. Everyone applauds. 'To tell you the truth', Dabro confides later, 'I didn't really know what was going to happen either. If it had blown up it might have been the end of the project.' He chooses twelve of the best founders on the floor who, with him and the foreman, make up a team of fourteen. His welders wait in Canberra for the first castings to arrive. In these first few months, Dabro flies to Melbourne from Monday to Friday, adjourning before the return flight to Canberra to a Fishermans Bend Pub for a round or two and to apologise for shouting at the team all week. His temper is not improved by the students at Ormond College at the University of Melbourne, which has made him a Visiting Fellow in the Arts, who tease him by tapping at his door at 1 a.m. He sees a friend, a psychologist, regularly to debrief. 'I was impossible to live with. My marriage and everything else was in trouble'. Vicky is not exactly broken-hearted to find him away so often, not least because the mounting tension of the work makes him unbearable.

The 9th of December 1985, months late, is scheduled for the final pour. At the last knock-off sound, the send-off is enlivened by a jug of beer for each of the team, plus a couple of bottles of scotch.

Thanks for putting up with me.

The foreman responds:

Farewell Ante. We love you. We've loved working with you. We've learned a lot. But don't you ever, ever fucking come back!

The foundry workers have finished, but the welders in Canberra are labouring in twelve-hour shifts in their efforts to render each seam and join invisible, a task demanding fine judgement in estimating the differential expansion rates between the small and large pieces that have to be joined.[5] Dabro checks, approves and fills every join; he grinds, burnishes and polishes every square centimetre himself. Yet the position of the fountains and pumps cannot be finalised until the sculpture is in place. In anticipation of a crane lifting the work through the roof, off it comes, but an ill-timed strike by the Canberra crane operators adds a further complication. A fortnight before the unveiling, eight men from a Transport and Storage team flown from Melbourne push, pull and cajole the sculpture onto a low loader until, arrived at Anzac Parade, they winch and roll it into position. This is the most demanding moment of all: marble can shatter and be repaired, but once a large bronze sculpture starts

Making Bronze   121

bending, it cannot be saved. The accelerating weight of the vertical shaft acting on the lower sections could well reduce the whole work to a pile of scrap metal. 'The process provided plenty of diversion for Sunday afternoon dog walkers', writes the *Canberra Times*.[6] Dabro recalls, 'I was numb with fear that it would start bending'.

Urgent talks proceed about the water that is to flow around the sculpture, impeded, in Dabro's estimation, by the obstructiveness and lack of imagination of the National Capital Development Commission officials. Although not yet officially invited, in despair and in some Marko Dabro-style cussedness, he announces that he may not attend a formal dinner at Government House the night before the unveiling unless the position and flow of the unseen nozzles follow the specifications; and he may not even attend the unveiling either. A phone call to the studio. 'What's the trouble now, my boy' enquires the prime minister. Hawke promises that the fountains will be working properly by the third of March, but they are not, for the nozzle under the bow is not ready. Dabro, irritated at the excitement of his avowedly republican family and the elegant clothes that they are planning, still refuses to commit to the suggestion to attend dinner in honour of the Queen's visit. The last minute instructions begin: 'When you meet the Queen do please be polite. Don't offer your hand until she offers hers first. No kissing her hand, either. Be deferential. Don't disagree with anything she says'.

It is not often that the Queen stays long in Canberra, and protocol demands that the city make the most of it. Her procession arrives at the Memorial to a twenty-one gun salute. A navy escort clatters up the parade to come to attention before the memorial. Three F1 11 combat aircraft thunder overhead. The prime minister manages to whisper: 'Is everything OK my boy?' The speeches over, the Queen, the official party and Dabro inspect his work. He observes diplomatically that the skipper at the stern he has modelled on her sailor grandfather, King George V. Dabro finds her charming, well informed and genuinely interested in the Memorial.

From the other side of Anzac Parade, the National Memorial to the Royal Australian Navy first manifests as a huge triangular shape, a ship in the offing. Approach closer as the sound of rushing water grows insistent. Now two masses emerge, one perpendicular, one horizontal, that form two distinct axes. These two planes allude to a mast and a deck. Is the vertical column actually a ship's mast? It is too wide. Is the horizontal axis a ship? It is too short, half as tall as it is long, over-crowded and top-heavy. Each individual crew member is in motion or potentially so. The human forms are soft, but the disordered bronze trapezoids on which they work are tilted and formed by the smooth planes that

FIGURE 5.1

The Naval Memorial, 1985, 8.4 x 8 x 5m, Anzac Parade, Canberra.
Source: Con Boekel.

Don't think of it as a ship. Think of it as a sculpture.

Dabro had begun to use when sculpting the heads of his children in the late 1970s. These figures are different manifestations of the same substance that composes their vessel.

Up the vertical column, two sailors stretch towards something that seems to be unobtainable. Their elongated arms and hands accentuate the impossibility of their task, for they are at least a metre short of their goal.

Here is the first ambiguity. Have they completed their task and are now descending? Or perhaps the sailors no more than confirm that human life, and especially the life of the artist, is nothing but struggle towards something always unobtainable,

> yet all experience is an arch wherethrough gleams that untravelled world
> Whose margin fades forever and forever as I move [...][7]

However contorted the figures, the two planes together make sculptural sense. Much more dominant than even the mainmast of a clipper ship, the column

FIGURE 5.2

The Naval Memorial, detail. Source: Con Boekel.

They are trying to raise the flag. Metaphorically speaking, they will never succeed.

124   THE LIFE AND WORK OF ANTE DABRO

alone would be uninteresting, but the thrust of the distended bodies of the upward-straining sailors helps it to visually relate to the activities on the horizontal plane below. Through its size, it dominates them and is intended to: every sculpture will function differently in its different settings, and the height of the column in relation to the ship justifies the workshop correction of an extra 1.5 metres. That was a lesson well learnt by observing the works of Rodin and Michelangelo in the years as a student. *Well, I'm sorry to say, Comrade Professor, that your sculpture is too small. It will seem lost outside. It might look better if you made it bigger.* Taller now, it establishes the apex of an almost equilateral triangle that unites two dominant figures fore and aft.

Now the eye is drawn to the right, to the first commanding figure. Perhaps he is the Officer of the Watch, for he peers upward through binoculars at the horizon.

His upper body echoes the vertical central column. His right leg is absorbed into the structure of which he is metaphorically a part, but his left leg exactly follows the slope of the trilateral.

The left arm of the female diver perched beside him accentuates the same diagonal course as the officer's leg. Her elongated right arm hanging over her leg inexorably follows the direction of the unobtainable masthead.

In the stern, a second officer – could he be the skipper? – gives orders through a microphone while his line of vision hints at the left-hand diagonal. (During a playful moment in the construction, he held a beer can.)

Between the officers fore and aft, in the central void below the column, an odd group of heads emerges from the armour plating: at least one officer, and some ratings including a woman. They gaze upwards or to the horizontal. One stares directly towards the viewer. Beyond that role, together they fill the void below the column. Together they recall a long-ago conversation in Zagreb: *I know we think of the space between the volumes as a negative space, but in some ways it's positive space too, because it separates and creates a tension between the figures that has to be filled creatively, and from all directions.*

The last, sternward section of the deck holds several diagonal shapes of what may be armour-plating tilting upwards towards the bow. The upper part may allude to the wing of the airman. Together, they threaten to dominate the human forms and accentuate the vessel's forward motion.

The stern gunner's right leg extends beyond the ship itself to materially connect with the composite base of the structure. The enormous anchor chain reaches far beyond the water-level, literally anchoring the ship to the shore.

FIGURE 5.3

Diver, detail, Naval Memorial. Source: Con Boekel.

I think she works well both as a sculpture in relation to the whole work, and in her own right.

126   THE LIFE AND WORK OF ANTE DABRO

The triangle's base-line emerges as the bottom of the sculpture itself. That was Dabro's first lesson of his first live model session: *Don't let your model float like an angel suspended in mid air.*

A third unifying element emerges from out of sight from the right-hand side of the column, a wide spiral structure bearing no relation to any actual ship. It disappears out of sight as it ascends, but the angle of its graceful curve is continued exactly by the left arm of one of the straining sailors at the masthead. The human forms reinforcing either the vertical or the diagonal axes show how diligently Dabro worked, consciously or unconsciously, to integrate the column and the deck that might otherwise threaten to work against each other. This measure acts to resolve the centuries-old problem that sculptors must address, of integrating two apparently opposing sculptural masses.

Not one of the fourteen crew members makes eye contact. Unlike the two huge soldiers of the Memorial to the Australian Army opposite who rely intimately on each other, each sailor is intent on their duties, relying on each other to carry out their duty to enable each one to do his or her own. Their disconnected relationship touches Dabro's several two-figure bronzes produced over several decades of women or men who may be standing or sitting close but do not directly relate to each other except through their negative space. A key element in interpreting Dabro's life work is apparent. The sailors reflect the tendency of the outsider to stand back to observe rather than to participate.

Dabro constantly insisted and insists that the Navy Memorial is not a diorama and should never be regarded as such. This is no encapsulated moment of history such as depicted by Felix de Weldon's sculpture of the US Marine Corps War Memorial raising the flag on Iwo Jima. The sailors of Anzac Parade occupy an individual state of being, an 'everytime'. They rely on their ship, the ship relies on them. The crew rely on each other, too, but ultimately each is as solitary as their creator, on this and any warship, not just any warship, but solitary in the whole of life.

The sculpture itself represents no more than an idea of a ship. The anchor chain lies aft, not on the forward bow. The skipper positions himself on the poop, not the bridge, as if master of a sailing clipper. What was once a naval gun is caricatured as a popgun.

Towards the stern, the water pulses as if from a propeller; from the bow, it is supposed to hiss like a ship in motion, yet visually it flows from high amidships as serenely as the cascades of the Trevi Fountain. The two officers fore and aft draw the eye of the viewer as they command and unite the sculpture. Men and machines are one. The brutal bronze armour plating threatens visually

Making Bronze 127

to crush the crew, but it does not. Body parts vanish into the superstructure. Dabro's work is entitled *Men and Ships. Dependence and Interdependence.*

Touching the first conception of the Naval Memorial were doubtless elements of a shared striving towards a distant goal of the Socialist Realism tradition in which Dabro had been raised. There are perhaps echoes of the triangular forms of humanity that crowd onto a tiny raft in Gericault's painting *Raft of the Medusa.* He finds a distant inspiration in Boccioni's 1913 miniature bronze *Development of a Bottle in Space.* Many are the allusions to the Renaissance fountainhead that Dabro imbibed: the triangular/vertical symmetry of Michelangelo's *Madonna of Bruges,* or the horizontal, triagonal and vertical axes of his *Tomb of Lorenzo de Medici* from 1520 to 1524. Someone as deeply versed in the European traditions could not help but be influenced in his initial conception of the crew: the elongated limbs of Michelangelo's *David* carved in anatomical correctness would seem too long if not viewed from below; the long vertical arms of Rodin's *Burghers of Calais* serve to emphasise their state of resigned but despairing grief. The extended arms and hands of Rodin's *The Thinker* allow the figure to stretch, with elbows bent, over the figure's knees while crouching forward in an attitude of deep contemplation. The Naval Memorial, while entirely original in its conception, draws at every moment on a lifetime of immersion in artistic traditions. Five thousand years of the visual imagination of European humankind are embedded in Dabro's artistic repertory as he first sketched out a shape in the sands of Broulee Beach. Like the symbolism everywhere apparent in Renaissance art, so many of the elements of this sculpture carry a double meaning. The central column alludes to a mast *and* an unobtainable golden fleece. The submariners amidships represent the intimate mutual reliance of officers and ratings *and* their solitary inward psyches. The body parts that absorb into the superstructure push away from literal realism *and* speak of how the crew and their ship are one. The upward tilt of the ship is a cresting wave and a propeller of forward motion, mobile in a mobile element. The officer's binoculars are raised to glimpse enemy aircraft *and* the moving margin of an untravelled world. The structure is a ship *and* a depiction of individual and solitary being. The work, in size as well as conception, is as daring as anything conceived by the Florentine masters whom Dabro so admired.

After the unveiling, Dabro wanted to do no more than to get away. He reflects: 'I was unhappy being there. I realise now that I was experiencing withdrawal symptoms, which I often have on finishing a work'. As contra-suggestive as ever, within a few days he rejected the suggested offer of an Order of Australia before flying to the United States and Croatia to find his extended

128   THE LIFE AND WORK OF ANTE DABRO

family elated and the supposedly anti-imperialist press much more excited by his having met the Queen than by the sculpture itself. He waved away the official Mercedes sent to meet him and travelled in the battered Yugo of Vladimir, brother of his first wife Zlatica, to stay with him. Jola was impressed, but it was only Džamonja with whom Dabro was able to hold a serious conversation; but even his old mentor was displeased that while Dabro had met the Queen, he himself had never been invited by Tito to join the official party of any of the openings of his public commissions. Returned to Canberra after six months, Dabro refused to sign the work until the water flowed properly, while the NCDC withheld the final payment until he did so. When he consented at last to do so, his signature was almost invisible.

Reviewing the work, Sasha Grishin wrote that, though he withheld a final judgement until the water element was resolved, he noted some possible inspirational sources like the Socialist Realist Russian sculptor Vera Muchina. Grishin wrote: 'He has arrived at a compromise by combining bulky generalised figurative forms with an essentially abstract constructivist structure. [...] The strength of this work stems from the conflict and tension between the dynamic abstract masses and the bursting figurative elements.' To judge that it was very much better than the public commissions with which Australians were favoured wasn't saying much, continued Grishin, amounting to no more than the occasional bleached Anzac on guard, a dog on the tuckerbox or the welded rusty girders sometimes painted with bright colours. 'But the RAN Memorial shows an enormous development in the thinking and technical skills of this sculptor.'[8]

The historian Will Durant, in relation to the Italian Renaissance, remarked that despotism was a boon to Italian art, whereby a dozen rulers competed with each other in seeking architects, sculptors and painters to adorn their capitals and their memory, and in their rivalry won something far greater than a single sponsor might achieve. This observation well describes the unedifying saga that followed the failure of the NCDC to adequately fund the design and construction of the waters that were supposed to flow from the bow. During one crisis meeting, Dabro was asked how he knew his design would work. 'I designed it on a model in my garden with the hose'. Everyone laughed until the meeting consultant, Robert Woodwood, Australia's premier water-feature architect, cut in: 'That's exactly how I do it myself'. Bureaucratic meddling and obduracy, rather than shortage of funding, in Dabro's view, led to an inconclusive result. To this day, the water flows only from two sources, not three.

Making Bronze 129

Two reflections on the Naval Memorial Tourist Bureau website:

Loved the use of moving water to bring home what our men and women do in Defence of our Nation.

And,

A good place for reflection. Also a beautiful sculpture and water feature. Noisy and peaceful at the same time.

CHAPTER 6

MAKING SCULPTORS

Ožujak, March, the first week of classes. Dabro had trudged through the Australian National University, stopping off for a coffee at the Calypso cafe run by his Croatian-born friend Stipe to reach the art school on the other side of the campus. He was to join the other teachers of the first-year Foundation students at the first life-drawing class of the year. One of his new students was Ed Hayes, who had just completed one year at an art school in Norwich, England. Twenty minutes into the class and Dabro knew that this English lad is both talented and serious:

> Now Ed, you know about Giacometti's nose don't you? His famous sculpture of a human head has a nose about 20 centimetres long. Why? Because that's all he could see when he looked at his model front-on. He had only a two dimensional-view, and he sculpted it with a nose like Pinocchio's because that's exactly what the nose of his model seemed like to him.[1] Maybe he didn't have a model, but he was making a point. We sculptors have to learn to see what's in front of us. Observe, observe, observe. Sculptors who haven't learned to observe will never be much good.

Dabro stands behind him, holding the same view.

> Now where's your light source? Don't draw what other models looked like in Norwich, and don't draw what you remember Susan looking like when you saw her stepping onto the podium. Draw what you can actually see of her from exactly this point. Follow the contours of her face and body. Don't let her float around the room like an angel either, put the podium in, and maybe the window where the light's coming from. Anchor her to the floor. Doesn't look much like her? Don't worry. Some artists are lucky enough to be born with the talent and be good at reproducing a pretty image. It's nice being born with the ability to draw well, but that doesn't tell you anything

132　THE LIFE AND WORK OF ANTE DABRO

except that you are good at drawing. Observe and observe again, then take that visual information to make it your own. You don't know what's behind her, and in fact you don't even know what's on the other side of Susan's face since she's sitting in profile. Don't draw what you think must be on the other side, only what you actually can see.

Okay, you've got on paper what you saw. She's become a form, your form, and now you have to get your form to speak.

Hayes finds himself as obsessed with the human figure as his teacher. 'If I was a painter it would be portraiture', he reflected in 2022. 'I guess it was a way of finding out about myself.' Week after week in 1982 and 1983 he created and re-created the human head or figure in half or quarter size, hoping in the end to make something worth casting.[2]

Meanwhile, Dabro is continuing his appraisal.

I can teach you the principles of drawing and I can teach you perspective in your field of vision. This is one of the most important discoveries that Duccio and Giotto gave us. I was raised in these lessons every day when I was in Art School. Let me show you. But you know that I can't teach you how to create.

Two months later. In the sculpture workshop, Ed Hayes is modelling first in clay on a turntable, then a quick waste-mould in plaster to document progress. Unlike the other students, Ed has been here since 8.30 a.m., modelling a human head. Enter Dabro.

Good morning Ed. I'm glad to see you're working at it already. I do the same. When you enter the studio don't just wait for enthusiasm or inspiration, it may never come. Just start something with your hands. Make anything and use your muscle memory.

Hmm, that's not bad. You don't know what it will become when you've finished? Doesn't matter, I never do either. Keep working with your fingers. Build and reduce. Build and reduce. Sometimes I have no clue of how whatever I'm making will end, sometimes I don't know even when I've finished. Keep working. Every day of your life. Creativity never ends.

Now remember, even in one-to-one model like this one you still need to give the eye spaces to rest. If there are no quiet spaces it will be a bad sculpture. When you start dreaming about the work, that's when you really

Making Sculptors   133

have become a sculptor. What you need all your life is passion and a touch of madness.

Hayes recalled:

> Some of his work I find has a hyper-masculinity or a suggestion of sexual violence that is a bit too strong for me. But I loved the Rodinesque muscular twisting and turning working within the Socialist European tradition. He had that link with Rodin and he could do it. 'Look, making objects is incredibly hard.' What a privilege to work with him.

October 1982. Hayes, Dabro, plus all the teachers and students of the sculpture workshop have gathered to examine Hayes's most recent sculpture. Some students hate these 'crit sessions'. Julie Basset, who had begun learning sculpture in Canberra six years earlier, found the public appraisal of her work 'like standing naked on the plinth'. Hayes more often found the sessions challenging and stimulating, and today it was his turn to present his half-size plaster sculpture. It's two figures, female and male, set half a metre apart. Dabro waited till the others had finished, then began:

> The male figure is solid and strong. The woman doesn't look very feminine – is that what you want? Now what's this accented line going from her nose to her lower chin. Does it have to be there? Does it help to profile the line of the jaw or obscure it?
>
> The two figures are working together sculpturally but to me – continues Dabro – there's not much emotional tension between them. It has to be there or you will only finish up with two statues instead of one sculpture. Did you try to configure them differently when you were modelling them? How are you going to make them relate to each other? Try to turn the head of the woman a little more. Maybe shift them just a fraction closer together. You've got a good balance in the negative space by making one a bit taller than the other without being too literal. They're nicely hinting at symmetry without being symmetrical.
>
> Now let's have a look round the back. It's not working here. You've got to think in three dimensions, or more if you're going to look up or down on your work. This left side is strong because the linear motion right to left that you've established towards the smaller figure is continuing down this side and it more or less carries on behind. But then it fizzles out. Come round here and have a look. You've got to see your work as linear after the eye starts at

134 THE LIFE AND WORK OF ANTE DABRO

the point that you want it to. Make the direction obvious, if you're uncertain. If the rhythm is working it will start well and continue like a piece of music. But as I look from the side there is nowhere for the eye to rest. The journey you started ends nowhere. You've lost the cadence. The music's stopped.

From the front it's working well, Ed. But I don't want to hear about the decline of humanity alluded to in anyone's work, or how this one relates to [George] Grosz's *Private Dining Room*. I can tell you what I think about it and I can tell you what I see, but don't expect me to accept the bullshit. It's the object that talks. Get to work on the issues on the right hand side and you may be ready to cast.

Hayes reflected in 2020:

Ante taught like Ante and he couldn't be anything else even though everyone was trying to get him to be. He was completely immersed in his own projects. Teaching and his work were the same. He didn't read the textbook the day before, he just lived it. What bothered me was that he couldn't allow difference; but I think that he thought that the post-modernists had stolen the name 'sculpture' and then betrayed it.

Throughout his undergraduate course and later, when he returned to complete his MA, Hayes felt elated working with Dabro but somewhat disillusioned with the rest of the school. In Norwich he had found that art was regarded as a respected vocation and that it was hard to get into his college. Canberra students, he thought to be different. They seemed so lackadaisical, not stressed or anxious or pushing themselves to solve any artistic problem. 'No one turned up till ten, then they had a coffee and chatted, then there were some hammering noises and then they just seemed to disappear.'[3] In protest, Dabro tried to shut out anyone who arrived after nine, as did the Head of the Glass Workshop, Klaus Moje; but the school seemed to have no heart. When Dabro was absent from the life classes, they seemed a poor imitation of those at Norwich: 'I got the feeling that it was the drones who were being sent as teachers. They didn't have their hearts in it or seem to know what they were talking about.' Other parts of the Art School seemed to Hayes pretty dismal too. Not everyone found it so. Jay Arthur, a student studying Graphic Investigation with Peter Herel, found the classes intellectually challenging and rewarding. Yet the History of Art classes, Hayes recalled, started with Sidney Nolan. Outside the sculpture workshop, his experiences were 'pretty lightweight'. Dabro, to Hayes, was one of the few standing against the eroding tide. At the crit sessions, 'everyone had

Making Sculptors 135

an opinion but Ante was the only one living the dream'. So flourished a formal three-year relationship with his supervisor, Dabro, that bloomed far beyond his graduation as Master of Creative Arts in 1986.

Coinciding with, but not unrelated to, the school's malaise was the deadly international drift towards artistic de-skilling sweeping the world, by which the viewer might spend longer reading an artist's wordy description than studying the work itself. Three or four art students might paint the same piece simultaneously. Traditions eroded. Less emphasis was placed on life drawing coincided with discussions about whether the History of Art should be removed from the curriculum altogether.

What had gone wrong?

One of the first students of the 1976 rebranded Canberra School of Art was Bruce Sutherland. Seeking a career as an art teacher, he enroled in the four-year Teaching Diploma in Fine Arts. Though a high standard was expected from essays in art history, he found the atmosphere in the Sculpture Department congenial. 'If you wanted help, you asked for it'. Sutherland recalls almost no formal training apart from the life drawing-classes where he found that Dabro 'sometimes cut people off at the ankles': but not Sutherland himself whom Dabro regarded as one of his most promising students. In this laissez-faire student atmosphere, he recalled pursuing his own interest in learning to cast in bronze and resin. In the modern quagmire of high fees and KPIs, the informal atmosphere now seems extraordinary but it suited Sutherland, whose ambition to be 'first in, last out' equalled Hayes's dedication. It was a philosophy of teaching that perhaps best matched the prosperous Australian post-war decades. Klaus Moje, head of the Glass Workshop declared: 'Art is not teachable. The teacher's role was to help the students work out their own artistic direction and become their own best critics.'[4] Between Sutherland and Dabro there developed a mutual respect. He doesn't recall any formal instruction from Dabro (though Dabro himself does) or anyone else; but what he took from Dabro was the way that he embraced the all-consuming life of a sculptor and a determination to keep alive the tradition and techniques of the classical figure.[5]

In 1978, Bruce Sutherland graduated just as the Canberra School of Art was taking a new and decisive direction.

From an international field in 1977, the appointments committee chose Udo Sellbach as Director. It was a bold decision, for Sellbach, trained in Cologne as a printmaker, was now to establish a curriculum loosely based on the Bauhaus of the 1920s in Weimar, Germany. Guided by Bauhaus philosophy, his decisions in the next decade were to affect the staff even more than the students.

136 THE LIFE AND WORK OF ANTE DABRO

Founded by the architect Walter Gropius, the Bauhaus philosophy was intended to 'erode the distinction between artist and everyday life, that is, to unite the divisions between the fine and applied arts [...] Art and the people must form an entity', Gropius wrote.[6] Theoretically, no distinction was to be recognised between artist and craftworker. Leading figures of art practise, each united by a desire to imbue objects of everyday life with an artistic essence, were to teach in workshops based on a mutual relationship more like a medieval guild than the traditional hierarchies followed in other Australian art schools. Students, who might be thought of more as apprentices, were to study a basic art language, Foundation, in their first year through studies in art history, drawing, life classes and three-dimensional work.[7] Into the curriculum thereafter would be introduced specialities more usually associated with trade workshops, leatherwork and furniture, photomedia, textiles and ceramics.

Sellbach proposed an almost mystical comminution of art and craft derived from the Bauhaus stricture that 'Architects, sculptors, painters, we must all return to the crafts'.[8] Sellbach himself held that 'Fine art and craft or design, as categories are irrelevant and misleading for educational purposes'.[9] Philosophically, the notion was anathema to Dabro, and nowhere was the polarity clearer than when the new director asked him to design and oversee a fence around his swimming pool. He refused, as, he said, any true artist must do. 'I don't think he ever liked me from then on.' Dabro's position was: 'Craft glorifies the surface, art glorifies the subject: that's the difference. [...] I used to say that in the Crit. Sessions: "I can't teach you art but I can teach you craft and out came the guns all pointed at me."' Emphasis on decoration through skilful craft might easily drift into narrative. Constantly, he reminded his students and himself to never confuse their sculptures with telling a story. He reminded journalists that the Naval Memorial should be thought of as a sculpture, not a ship. He dismissed the Boer War memorial in Anzac Parade by the sculptor Louis Laumen – an evocative depiction of four bronze horsemen descending a slope – as finely modelled, but, in the end, a diorama.

Many of the staff were at first unconvinced. Jan Brown, Lecturer in Sculpture, recalled: 'Udo [Sellbach] went down like a lump of lead with the staff initially [... but] he insisted on a lot of things that were very good [... and] dreamed of a new Art School. Though everybody said "you haven't got a hope", we got it.'[10] The Gropius principle of the weekly assessment of student work by all workshop staff and students, in Crit Sessions, seemed reasonable. So did learning the basic artistic languages for all Foundation students in the first year: but staff having to learn a second teaching subject? (Dabro chose ceramics, where, predictably, he claimed to have produced in three hours an acceptable piece for which students were allowed a whole term to create.)

Making Sculptors 137

Sellbach's school took fire: in 1977 he employed 38 full- and part-time teachers, a figure never likely to be equalled again. From Tasmania, the prospective sculpture student Julie Basset heard that the corridors of the Canberra School of Art were paved with gold. Enroled, she found the rumour almost to be true. A minivan took the students to a sandstone quarry to choose their own materials! She undertook supervised bronze casting, still most unusual in other schools. Her scholarship allowed three flights home per year. These were Basset's 'days of decadence'.[11] Enroling just as Sellbach arrived, Julie Basset found the atmosphere exciting. She found Dabro most helpful in the life classes in portraying three-dimensional perspective. 'I found him outstanding'. In sculpture, she was drawn more to the large modernist works of Ron Robertson-Swan, the sculpture workshop's first head. Returning to Canberra to complete a master's degree in 1983, she was aware that she would never measure up to Dabro's Beethoven-like insistence that one must dedicate the totality of one's existence to the divine gift that had been vouchsafed her. 'If you were not like that, then you were not a true artist'.[12]

To work side by side with advanced students echoed the medieval guilds where master and apprentice worked side by side and sometimes together. Basset moved to the Woodwork workshop where she believes her elongated creations influenced Jan Brown's bird sculptures now well-known in Canberra. Bruce Sutherland, as a postgraduate sculptor, developed an above-ground gas melt so that lifting the crucible no longer relied on a two-stage manoeuvre with tongs. Dabro approved and regularly used Sutherland's advanced casting techniques.[13]

Following Gropius, Sellbach's plan was to invite practitioners with international reputations to head each department. Dabro, already a staff member, was not asked to apply, possibly because his Canberra address may have seemed too parochial, more probably because within the school, the traditional figurative artist was already regarded as old-fashioned and opposed to post-modernist adventures. Yet he was at first enthusiastic. 'It was a noble idea which I approved very much'. He recognised the 'master-apprentice' workshops as similar to his own postgraduate training with his Croatian teachers. Some of the Sellbach vision he applauded, especially that the instruction was to be given by active practitioners who were also allowed two days a week for their own studies. But he was no artistic friend of Ron Robertson-Swan, an aficionado of the abstract sculptor Anthony Caro who utilised welded scrap metal in large assemblages.

If the Bauhaus was distrusted and then terminated by the Nazis, the bold Sellbach venture was extinguished more prosaically by the Australian Capital Territory becoming self-governing in 1988. In 1978, confronted by the choice,

138 THE LIFE AND WORK OF ANTE DABRO

the wise Territorians had voted to remain shielded by the Federal Government financial umbrella. Enough of democracy! The plan to force the ACT to self-government continued to simmer in the late 1970s, fostering first an unease, then a steady eroding confidence in the school's future just as Hayes was enroling for his first classes. The official historian of the Art School recorded that Sellbach 'saw the writing on the wall: the inevitability of self-government for the ACT with an expected miniscule education budget to replace its Federal counterpart, and the foreseeable amalgamation with other institutions in order to survive. The financial halcyon days of the 1970s were over'.[14] Without the industry support that Gropius had enjoyed, the Canberra School of Art had no chance of independent survival. In 1989, the ACT became self-governing. By then, the Canberra School of Art, as well as the music school, had already been rolled up into the Australian National University.

Just as Dabro was returning from the Naval Memorial construction, budgets and morale collapsed. First a Technical Officer, then Lecturer in sculpture, the ceramicist Nick Stranks understood the worsening stresses on staff, especially those trained in the European Academies. The University's accountants preferred lecture halls of 500 seats to the dozen individually trained students in each of the school's workshops. They demanded a precise mark and grade, not the 'Pass' or 'Fail' of the guild-like enclaves. Stranks recalled:

> Ante came from quite an academic background where the Master's opinion was the only opinion that mattered. [...] Once the marking scheme came in, it had to be much more objective about what is a sixty four (Pass) or a sixty six, (Credit) so you needed to have a scale to mark it against. You had to be able to listen to the other side. Marks had to be competitive compared to other art schools. In the end it changed the type of students who went through the school.

The school's funding formulas demanded Key Performance Indicators of published papers, criteria not at all applicable to works that took two years to complete. The art critic and Professor of Art History Sasha Grishin was asked if he could compress his course of 42 weeks into 14. What he called the 'toughness and integrity' of the Sellbach years dissipated.[15] Within the workshops, students were required to be more verbally literate. The school's focus became more theoretical. Unlike most of the staff, Dabro angrily opposed the merger that was probably always inevitable.

Now, a second thunderhead long rumbling on the horizon was about to break over the school. Arriving first at the school as usual during his

Making Sculptors 139

1983 postgraduate year, Bruce Sutherland noticed an enormous piece of graffiti written on the wall of the sculpture workshop denouncing all its male members as sexist exploiters of women. The sleazy atmosphere that several students, including Hayes, had felt for years had been publicly exposed. Dabro was not named, but the discomfort that several of the female students had felt for some time with his mischievous provocations was about to be united with feminist attacks on the gaze of the male artist on the nude female figure with its implied invitation to other males to enjoy the spectacle. The international uproar, by now a decade old, was about to engulf the Australian National University. As was intended, Dabro took the invective personally. He responded with both hurt and fury. In the declining days of the Sellbach years, the most tumultuous years of his adult life were about to begin.

Several signposts mark the course of the excoriating dissection of male artist and observer that falls upon the female nude. They included Simone de Beauvoir's *The Second Sex* (1949), John Berger's TV series and accompanying book *Ways of Seeing* (1972) and Laura Mulvey's article 'Visual Pleasure and Narrative Cinema' (1975).[16] The argument turned on the premise that any form of artistic reproduction of a woman, particularly a nude woman, is presented to a male gaze that deprives her of social identity and agency while reinforcing the unbalanced power relationship of society. Mulvey argued:

> The image of woman as (passive) raw material for the (active) gaze of man, takes the argument a step further into the structure of representation, adding a further layer demanded by the ideology of the patriarchal order as it is worked out in its favourite cinematic form – illusionist narrative film.[17]

In discussion with the author of this paragraph, Dabro responded, 'This may be true for some, but not me'.

By the 1980s, critics had widened their attack from movie-makers to artists, especially those of the nineteenth century. Gill Saunders, senior print curator at the Victoria and Albert Museum, observed in 1989:

[Matisse] looks at her; her gaze is averted, downcast; her pose is designed to display her body. She is the subject of art, he is the creator who will transform her. Matisse voices the unconscious egotism of man the creator who transcends the imperfections, even the presence of the model. Whether or not the depicted woman was passive, returned the gaze of the viewer, was preoccupied within herself or offered herself to the onlooker, the representation alone was taken as indicator of an intolerable power imbalance.

140   THE LIFE AND WORK OF ANTE DABRO

If the depiction of the female nude is received from less polarised positions today, such was not the case in the Canberra School of Art in the 1980s at the time when Susan Boden-Brown was modelling, Hayes was sculpting, and Sutherland was developing his above-ground crucible. Dabro might dismiss Berger as 'just another Marxist', but the students did not. He found himself derided as old-fashioned even by some staff members. His general response was: 'How blind you are. Can't you see how important this kind of art is to humanity? The women whom I create are not individuals nor even idealised womanhood, but another step in the search for perfected humanity.' The personal criticisms of Dabro became more pointed. His goading of students or staff members in the 1970s seemed, by the mid-1980s to be no longer funny; at best, childish, at worst, insulting and offensive. Graffiti appeared in the women's toilets about several male lecturers around the university, including 'Ante Dabro is a dirty old man'. From his perception of fifteen years earlier that women were 'debasing themselves', it seemed to him now that women were denying their own 'natural sexuality' in asserting themselves. The 1960s incoming tide of female sexual liberation had overwhelmed and disgusted him; now, in the 1980s, the fact that women were speaking out left him equally perplexed, stranded on a beach from which his idealised woman was only perceptible as a Rhine-maiden perched on an outer reef. As the vilifications grew, he felt mystified and humiliated, but unlike most others, he publicly defended himself. 'I have always admired and respected women'. He pondered whether he should enrol in a PhD course to express his distress, 'Bra Burning and Its Artistic Consequences'. No one wanted to supervise the topic. Vicky told him not to be ridiculous.

Hearing of damaging graffiti directed at himself, he burst into Sellbach's office, threatening to sue the school unless the writings about him were removed and discontinued. More than once on the campus, he was heard to shout at his student detractors. At a staff seminar, he became more and more agitated as the female guest lecturer, as it seemed to him, vilified every aspect of masculinity expressed in painting. During the sustained applause, he grimly folded his arms, stood up and walked out. The overt masculinity of rural Dalmatia seemed as impossible to escape as his immersion in the sculptural achievements of the Florentine Renaissance. The entire Dabro universe was cracking. Dabro recalls with some understatement, 'I was not a loved person, they thought me just a nasty sexist'.

In 2023, Dabro pondered the seminar that he had rudely exited. 'On reflection, my thoughts seemed correct at the time. I certainly wouldn't speak out loud now, but I would still walk out. All I wanted was that this issue be properly

Making Sculptors 141

debated'. He concedes that a distrust of modern trends in art paralleled his failure to recognise how Australian society itself was changing. Nick Stranks, Dabro's bronze caster and fellow teacher, reflected:

> He couldn't do now what he did then. It was a different era and he would have a very different time now. [His behaviour] was difficult to see and accept. Sometimes I think it was taken badly because he was trying to be provocative but it just wasn't very tasteful. I grew up being accountable for what I said because you were held accountable, and you either had to meet that model or not be there. A lot of the lecturers at the School had a style of teaching that didn't recognise what was required nor the need for political correctness; Ante fitted in with them.[18]

Ed Hayes observed:

> I was there in the 1990s after he'd been tamed and civilised but I don't think he was as bad as some people made out. The European gentleman, for that's what he was, respected women deep down. There were others who were worse but they hid it, and there was always an atmosphere of sleaziness in the sculpture workshop. Ante liked a blokey chat, yes, but it was always open. He enjoyed pissing people off just to get a rise out of them and got himself into trouble by starting something he couldn't control. He copped the karma of his own actions and his lack of ability to see the consequences of his words. He pissed women off, yes, and by then art was shouting at history trying to reassert some balance. It was very loud and sharp criticism.

Julie Basset had arrived in Canberra, she said, knowing little about feminism, but found several women in their thirties with much life experience to be good role models.

> Ante used to talk about nipples, yes, but he loved the human body. He talked about it a lot and that came through in his work. And I too love the male and female human body. We are a very prudish society and I wish women could take their tops off! The prudish attitudes of the west still make it so difficult for artists. I'm not defending his sexism, but he was charming and sexist simultaneously. He tried to bait people, but he never directed any remarks at me.

The ANU's history of the Canberra School of Art, *The ANU School of Art. A History of the First 65 Years*, skirts evasively around the issue of sexual harassment

142 THE LIFE AND WORK OF ANTE DABRO

in the university, remarking: 'A number of staff from that period have shared stories of unprofessional conduct, and personal behaviour which was quite unacceptable.'[19] The author could have added that overt sexual harassment was not uncommon in any university (or elsewhere) at the time; or that reminiscing former students still recall certain department heads physically pursuing female students around their offices; or that the ditty '"Oh professor, do not touch me" as she slipped between the sheets with nothing on at all', sung to the tune of John Brown's Body, was a well-known number for Orientation Week performances. (The last word of the line was omitted in each verse, until the last 'Oh [...]' was succeeded by the tune alone.)

Dabro remained, and remains, traumatised and mystified by the events of the middle 1980s. In the 1990s, he chose his whimsical sculpture of a man hiding under a piece of fabric, *Now You See Me Now You Don't*, now held in the Canberra Museum and Art Gallery. In an act of private revenge, he juxtaposed this work with an unsuccessful entry for the Australian Service Nurses memorial in Anzac Parade. Here, three angelic nurses hovered over what he had conceived originally as a fountain. Arranged now around the figure, the women became vengeful harpies, sneering at the victim who could do no more than hide himself from their scorn. Dabro presented himself thus as a 1980s artist-as-victim.

A different response might well have been a defence he proposed to the author in 2021:

My models have something in common, and one of these many elements is a sense of mystery. Like most artists, perhaps, I'm not trying to reproduce *this* model, but rather an essence of humanity, not necessarily a figure of beauty but of femaleness. It's true that they're invariably female and young. I've never had older women models, either, except when I was teaching. Of course there's an erotic charge there, yes, but it's not exactly sexual, but there is something of the unknown. As I'm working she [the plaster shape] will begin to talk to me and I'll talk to her. There's a tension that I can't put into words. It's definitely not a desire to sleep with a model, but it's almost like a dream, and when I start I'm taken into a world that's not real. And it's a necessary mystery. One time I needed to work with the sculpture after my model had left. I couldn't get it right, it was just becoming imaginary so I asked Vicky to pose for me. Because I knew her so well, it was hopeless.

Cultural responses to female nudity in public art in these decades were slow but could be resolute. The University of Canberra, accepting his donated *Reclining Figure,* described it as 'a fine example of his ability to render the life, movement

Making Sculptors 143

and vitality of the human figure in bronze'. The university unveiled the figure in 2007. It remained at the University entrance for a decade until, he was informed, a student objected to its nudity, whereupon the authorities removed it from its central location to relocate it safely out of sight in the university Arts Precinct.[20]

Of his Canberra works, Julie Basset finds the Naval Memorial 'breathtaking' and *Resilience* 'so dynamic and powerful and strong', the sculptures of the children and grandchildren 'quite stunning [...] It's a real shame he is currently overlooked. His works are mighty'. She is unrepentant that she likes music, bushwalking and paddling and has recently re-established a studio, but like most of his former students she can feel a little awkward in meeting Dabro again. 'He thinks sculpture has to be your whole world or you're not a true artist. But I don't care!' Sutherland remained a part-time founder and caster. Apart from taking a degree in architecture and building structures on his rural property, he is still the art teacher that he first enroled to be. The spirit of creation has never extinguished: 'What I took from Ante was osmosis'. Dabro's gift to Sutherland that sustained him and continues to sustain him, he says, is 'his powerful spirit'.

In a gesture worthy of Marko Dabro, Ante parried the question directed to him in the 1990s, 'When are you going to retire?', with 'That's for you to find out'. He was content to depart, though, in 2004 from what had been yet again rebranded as the National Institute of the Arts. The Foundation Year, the starting point of the Sellbach vision, was extinguished. In the corridors, Dabro heard the whisper: 'Do we still have to waste time drawing life models?' He found himself forbidden to shut late students out (till the first break). Informally, no one was supposed to fail. Discussions about the value of a graduation piece work were complicated when grades had to be standardised across art schools to accommodate transferring students.[21] The Australian Research Council grudgingly accepted creative arts projects as 'Research', even though the Art School was already totally enmeshed in the university and its administration. Students learnt rapidly the need to explain their works in voice and written word. Dabro remained as unimpressed as he had been a decade earlier: 'If you want to philosophize about your work then enrol in the Art History and Art Theory Major across the road' [at the Australian National University main campus]. He continued his slide-shows open to all students illustrating the history of art but felt that the ground beneath him had dissolved.

As Hayes revolved his memories of what were among the happiest times of his life, the Dabro principles returned to him again and again, as much the postulates of the artist's life as the techniques of execution. He saw him as a

144 THE LIFE AND WORK OF ANTE DABRO

'professor dad'. Like Susan Boden-Brown, he appreciated his physicality and that to be a sculptor was to fully inhabit the life of the creative artist. Hayes compared that to the totalising life of the agrarian peasant. One's whole body and intellect were absorbed in the daily problem-solving of season, planting, weeding, irrigating. Mind and muscle were simultaneously and inextricably engaged. Through all his years as a student, Hayes concluded, Dabro kept the flame burning, teaching him what art could be. 'I've never forgotten it'. Dabro remains one of the biggest influences in Hayes's life. Later Hayes set up studios in Canberra and Sydney but found it hard to work without the stimulation of the Art School. For a time he became depressed in losing a higher meaning in his life as he pondered the 'might-have-beens'. He became a teacher of art for children with special needs but feels embarrassed when Dabro asks him if he's still sculpting. Not that he is impressed by the contemporary scene. Hayes believes that:

> I know when sculpture is happening but you hardly ever see it in Australia. There's still the body memory, but for me sculpture is problem-solving that seems so straightforward but it's so impossible! Even though I'm teaching sculpture rather than practising it, twenty years on I'm still thinking sculpturally, because you can still make progress intellectually even if you haven't got your hands in the clay. So there are some ghosts: every day I look at someone or think of a solution to a sculptural problem.

These students took from him, as the literary critic Lyn McCredden puts it in discussing the works of the Australian poet Les Murray, 'an understanding of human finiteness nesting at the very heart of creative presence and power'.[22] Murray wrote:

> We bring nothing into this world
> except our gradual ability
> to create it, out of all that vanishes
> and all that will outlast us.[23]

That, and a touch of madness.

CHAPTER 7

MAKING COMMISSIONS

Enormous bronzes depicting imaginary people present one set of problems. Life-size renditions of well-known and recognisable individuals present another. Those who commission bronzes of public figures naturally want them to look like the person photographed or the person whom they remember, but to the physical features Dabro imparted his own character appraisal: Alfred Deakin became the severe and cerebral prime minister drawn from photographs and his reading, and John Molony the affable professor of history whom he modelled from life directly in clay. Dabro admired Sir Robert Menzies as an upholder of democratic values, order and stability and for his faith in higher education, so for the headquarters of the Australian Liberal Party he gave the long-serving prime minister a noble brow, a solemn demeanour, squared shoulders: a nouveau-Roman Consul. A bust of Winston Churchill, commissioned by the Churchill Foundation, brought out his mixed emotions. The British, to Dabro, held a centuries-old and irrational mindset against the Croatians. It was a British plane that had bombed his family in the Čavoglave valley. Churchill himself

> was an absolute bastard, a mean character, but determined and arrogant. For him it was perish or survive. He told the truth and I admire him. Blood, toil, tears and sweat. Perish or survive. I wish we had a Churchill now in the west, to resolve our stupidity and weakness.

The most significant of the commissions of individuals was that by the Australian government to commemorate the Bicentenary of the French Revolution. Dabro was to create a bust of Jean-François de Galaup, Comte de La Pérouse, whom King Louis XVI in 1786 had ordered to lead an exploratory expedition around the world. La Perouse stands high in the pantheon of French scientific illuminati and is improbably well-known in Australia because he visited Botany Bay, Sydney, shortly after Governor Arthur Phillip had

FIGURE 7.1

Sir Winston Churchill, c.1993, bronze, 1:1.3 life size. Australian National University: Con Boekel.

I wish we had a Churchill now in the west to resolve our stupidity and weakness.

arrived, charged with establishing the first British settlement. He stayed in Sydney for some six weeks before departing for the Pacific, where his two ships foundered on a reef in the Solomon Islands. He left his name to a Sydney suburb close to where he landed in Botany Bay, now known irreverently to local residents as 'Lapa'.

FIGURE 7.2

Sir Robert Garran, bronze, 1983, 1:1.3 life size; Department of Foreign Affairs and Trade, Canberra. Source: Artist's collection.

I like this work and the Garran family liked it too.

French Ambassador Francois Duzer, having earlier approved the maquette, arrived with his entourage at the Dabro's garden to view the full-size plaster model. Senator Gareth Evans, Minister for Foreign Affairs, presided at the unveiling. His Excellency pronounced it magnificent before indignantly dismissing Dabro's suggestion of a hint of arrogance in the French hero.

Now for the bronze unveiling in Paris. Because of Australia's displeasure with the French over nuclear testing in the Pacific, Senator John Button,

148   THE LIFE AND WORK OF ANTE DABRO

Minister for Trade, was scheduled to unveil the work rather than the prime minister (Hawke later presented a smaller version to the Mayor of Paris, Jacques Chirac, in June 1991). As a guest of the French government, Dabro left Australia for Paris just as the fighting in Croatia was approaching Split. His country seemed to be tearing itself apart; his family was in great danger. From Italy he asked his brother Jole by telephone if he should visit him. Jole, a senior member of the Split militia and a marked man in opposing the Serb advance, warned him that it was far too dangerous. 'Ante, what you hear in the background is shooting.' If he came at all, he warned him, he would have to wear a military uniform. Dabro's Australian minder, intent on getting him to the opening, would have none of that, reminding him that the government, as sponsor, was paying for his ticket. Taking the train across Europe to Paris, Dabro told a guard the reason for his visit. Intrigued and excited, the guard travelled to the opening. When, wondered Dabro, would an Australian train official ever do that? On the night following the unveiling, Senator Button, due to deliver a public address, invited Dabro to attend. There, Button explained to his audience his role as the unveiler of the work. Dabro rose to take the applause. When would an Australian audience ever do that?

Several contemporary portraits reveal La Perouse as round faced, chubby and rather pleased with himself. Dabro's commander is not only that of an aristocrat of the *ancien regime,* but La Perouse the philosopher, commander, botanist, geographer and cartographer.

In the proportion of 1:1.5, the sculpture dominates its location by the Seine in Paris, dwarfing its viewers who must look up at him; but the captain stares resolutely over their heads into the middle distance. This is a work speaking the values of eighteenth-century French civilisation, its respect for learning, for understanding the geographical world, the temptation and joy of jumping into the abyss.

The first major shifts from wood to bronze were Suzanne and a sculpture of two female figures, *Sisters.* This commission followed an open competition by the Queensland government for a work to be placed outside the state Cultural Centre. From a distance, it is obviously the work of the same creator in its preoccupation with the sculptural rhythms that can be imparted to static figures. Neither figure was sculpted from life.

Even though they are sited no more than a metre apart, the larger-than-life female figures hold an emotional relationship. The legs of the seated figure are, like *Suzanne*'s, similarly crossed; her left foot touches the plinth. At first sight, she seems almost identical, but she is not. Unlike *Suzanne*, whose upper body weight is carried by her right arm, this figure leans only slightly to the right,

FIGURE 7.3

La Perouse, bronze, 1989, 1:1.3 life size, Promenade d'Australie, Paris, Source: Artist's collection.

What inspired me in making this work was thinking about the French cultural achievements of the eighteenth century, not just La Perouse himself.

causing it to carry less weight. Her weight distribution, more centred, allows her to place her hand further away from her body, more for balance than support, precisely contacting the corner of the plinth. Dabro discarded an initial placement of her right hand on the knee – it seemed too dominating, the fingers were too busy, he recalled, so now the figure holds her hand between her

150 THE LIFE AND WORK OF ANTE DABRO

thighs. This figure is appreciably younger than both *Suzanne* and her standing sister.

It is said that Michelangelo, annoyed by criticism that his commissioned sculptures sometimes bore little facial resemblance to their subject, replied that in a thousand years no one would know what they looked like anyway: it was the sculpture that mattered. Dabro too followed that principle in non-commissioned works. Very few of his sculptured faces, though never uninteresting, reveal much emotion nor can even be identified in a particular ethnicity. Here the face of the younger, seated sister is unusually expressive. She looks downwards in an expression that is far from content. Accented by the large eyes, the face carries a deep and reflective sadness.

By contrast, her noticeably older sister, standing upright, seems to bear a caring responsibility for both. Clearly, by her face, a close relative, she looks to the left. Her face is calm and clear, less contemplative than her sister's, but watchful, a trifle apprehensive. Her elongated right arm crossing her breast and her right hand held behind her signifies that at this moment she is stationary. Although Dabro is no longer content with the sculpture, it is *Sisters* to whom young people relate by touching, polishing, standing beside and even sitting on the lap of the seated figure whose knees are kept highly polished by what must be hundreds of admirers.

Sisters depicts not only a physical but an intriguing emotional relationship. Here Dabro seems to be touching a preoccupation of Rodin after 1890, whose subject sometimes only became apparent after its completion. 'Instead of explaining', according to an NGA Catalogue Essay, 'Rodin extends the work's meaning into a world which is no longer that of sculpture but rather one of poetry'.[1]

The plaque reads:

Sisters
Ante Dabro
Croatia b. 1938 arr. Aust 1967

At the unveiling, the Queensland Minister for the Arts enquired unguardedly to which nationality Dabro belonged. Always sensitive to a multiculturalism that emphasised difference at the expense of an Australian identity, Dabro snapped: 'Until you asked me I used to be Australian'. The minister turned his heel. Insulting as the question was, as usual, Dabro's tongue had run ahead of good sense.

While the Australian National University was riven by its long overdue reassessment of its campus sexism, staff ratios and student relationships, a much

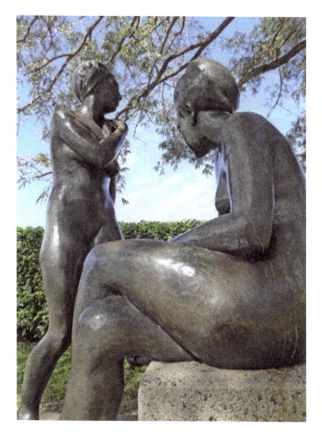

FIGURE 7.4

Sisters, 1975, bronze, 1:1.3 life size, Queensland Cultural Centre, Brisbane.
Source: Author.

I'm happy with the seated figure, but the one standing is a bit stiff and formal.
Maybe I should have made her with both arms hanging down.
That way she would have looked more relaxed.

more deadly civil war was breaking out not 100 kilometres from Dabro's birthplace in Čavoglave.

In the late 1980s, the fragile Republic of Yugoslavia was everywhere disintegrating. Partly in answer to the growing desire of the Croats to leave the Republic, in 1991 the Yugoslavian government declared an enclosed area known as Krajina ('Frontier') long ago created as a buffer state against the Ottoman Empire by the Habsburg Monarchy to separate surrounding Croatia.

FIGURE 7.5

Sisters, detail. Source: Author.

I'd like to meet her again in my dreams.

Naturally, the ethnic and religious profundities of the four-year war, complex as they were, touched Dabro deeply. The disputed area came close to his own immediate homeland – Split, Čavoglave, Knin, the home of the Dabros, the birthplace of Meštrović, the family holdings, Lačina and his own immediate and extended family. The fighting, killing and destruction of civilian property that occurred during this ferociously bitter war, like the changing fortunes of World War II, took place everywhere within the known and so-familiar landscape. Televised news and family phone calls confirmed how close the skirmishes and battles were to his birthplace. Some twenty-five young men of

Making Commissions 153

the district joined and fought in a guerrilla war around the village, an attack repulsed only at the creek he had crossed on the way to midnight Mass in December 1944. Jole became a marked man, telling his brother he might never see him again. At that moment, Dabro was in Rome en route to Paris for the unveiling of La Perouse. At an unofficial dinner, a US official told Dabro: 'You trouble-making Croatians are going to lose'. 'If you think that, Sir, you don't know us'.

Only two years after the uneasy peace was concluded, Dabro returned to his birthplace. On a blazing day of midsummer 1997, the Ministry of Culture organised an escorted tour of the war zone for him and the author. They began at Lipik, once a village of 150 people, now abandoned because of hundreds of anti-personnel mines buried in unknown locations. Fences lay overthrown, front doors gaped. In the town square of the town of Pakrac stood a bronze monument to the suffering of World War II created at the time that Dabro was a student. It depicted a dying soldier in extremis, battle jacket in tatters, head thrown back, ribs protruding horribly, the body arched to breaking point: but now the sculpture and the plinth were pock-marked by shrapnel. Jasenovac, the infamous concentration camp at which an unknown number of Serbs and Četniks perished at the hands of the Ustaše, was desecrated. The ornamental portal was shot in, the flagpole smashed, the garden trampled; huge black-and-white photographs of murdered men and women hung ripped from the walls, machine gun bullets traced across walls and ceilings. At Hvratska Kostanica, 56 villagers in 1995 gathered up their handbags and umbrellas to answer a summons to assemble near the town hall where they were loaded onto trucks, taken to a green rolling meadow just 2 kilometres from the town, and murdered with machine guns. A nephew in the militia, ablaze with wartime passion, related sensational stories from the war. Dabro felt himself an outsider in his own birth country merely by looking on at the carnage:

> I think generations are going to be destroyed and distorted from now on. Lots of kids, you can imagine, without parents. When you look at my nephew, it's not him anymore. He's absent-minded, he talks to himself, shaking. He said to me with a raised voice, 'You know nothing. Nothing!' I tried to have an opinion but he shouted at me: 'You know nothing about it.' Quite angrily. And rightly so.

Dabro felt the anger thrown at him, especially from the refugees, that he was from the West and ought to be doing more to help. With other Croatians, he sent food and relief, but felt angry, useless, ashamed and alone.

154 THE LIFE AND WORK OF ANTE DABRO

As terrible seemed the destruction of modern buildings: bowling alleys, supermarkets, cannon shells fired through barn walls, machine gun bullets stitched across a high suburban wall. Abandoned roofless homes: broken concrete, smashed tile, dead pot plant, garden without nurture, door frames without doors, playroom without toys, kitchen without warmth, table without conversation, bedroom without love. And the tomb of Ivan Meštrović himself: smashed open, the body stolen. It was many years before it was recovered, but the bronze doors have vanished. Dabro could do no more than exclaim 'Vandals!' *This is not my country.*[2]

Shaking with rage at the empty tomb and the destruction of his country, Dabro had never endured such depression. Yet, like so many artists plunged into the crises of private life, Dabro produced in these troubled years some of his most assured and cloudless works.

Foremost among them is *Contemplation* created for the opening of a new staff accommodation wing, the Judith Wright Court at the Australian National University. The formal commissioning looked a little ominous when two or three officials came to visit his studio to ask him not to create anything too controversial – by which they meant, of course, nude females. Dabro replied that he would prefer to create a partially draped figure anyway, since the folds and creases of material offered a more powerful challenge. He consulted the writings of the woman who was in the 1950s perhaps Australia's most admired poet to find her words invoking symbols which, when language faded, left the ache of lost human relations.

> sexual fire,
> > This is the strength that your arm knows,
> > the arc of flesh that is my breast,
> > the precise crystals of our eyes.
> > This is the blood's wild tree that grows
> > the intricate and folded rose.
> the power of place that fastens the unsaid word in the blood
> > Only the rider's heart
> > halts at a sightless shadow, an unsaid word
> > that fastens in the blood of the ancient curse,
> > the fear as old as Cain.

The blood's wild tree. Unsaid words. Sightless shadows.[3]

As a student, alone in Rodin's sculpture garden in Paris, Dabro mentally measured the proportions of his works to their surroundings. 1:1.25 worked

FIGURE 7.6

Contemplation, 2002, bronze, 1:1.3 life size, Judith Wright Court, Australian National University (ANU). Source: Artist's collection.

Her hand suggests that as she pushes down on the column of water, the other column rises. But due to poor maintenance by the ANU, the fountains often do not work properly.

best. Such would be the dimensions of an idealised feminine beauty for the entrance of Judith Wright courtyard. He would not work from life: he wanted this creation to be younger than his usual models, slim, graceful, an essence of womanhood.

The figure of *Contemplation* looks perfectly proportioned, but there is nothing about the figure that is natural to the relaxed pose that she seems to be holding. Her left arm does not reach straight to the fountain, which it might for anatomical convenience, rather, she bends it slightly while the hand itself bends another 30 degrees to the water. Her right foot is turned uncomfortably upwards, yet sculpturally it completes the required visual cadence. The fingers of this hand are the only part of her extremities to be clearly articulated.

The right arm, as elongated as the left arm of Rodin's *Thinker*, forms an almost straight line down the left leg to the heel, which, turning gracefully

FIGURE 7.7

Contemplation, detail: 1:1.5 life size, detail. Source: Con Boekel.

*I've seen people sitting quietly around the pool. That was my intention.
I had Judith Wright's words in mind as I sculpted the figure.*

inward but slightly uncomfortably, forms another visual end point. Yet, this arm is not quite straight, for she pushes her elbow slightly outward, acting to underline the curved circle of her lap. That space, enclosed by a right-angle triangle, is matched by the triangular space enclosed by her right-angled knee across her lap. Her left foot, unlike Suzanne's, is some 30 centimetres above the surface.

Contemplation sits over an irregularly shaped pool designed by the sculptor in which a second fountain rising to the height of the figure's head balances

Making Commissions 157

the work analogously to the smaller figure in the airport's *Introspection*. Concentric wavelets wash towards the human figure; but the disgraceful and disrespectful maintenance by the Australian National University frequently reduces the second fountain to no more than a ripple. Sometimes neither fountain is flowing at all. Yet the work aims at some of those qualities Dabro looked for in Michelangelo. Does the figure return the gaze of the viewer? Is *Contemplation* experiencing an intimate moment or does she share it with us? Is she part of our world or hers? How does she manage to float between wakefulness and sleep, silence and speech, stasis and movement, thought and contemplation?

Sixteenth-century Italian sculptors might well have delighted in this portrait of an idealised femininity: it was no accident that Dabro did not model the work from life. Yet while the work is unmistakably Dabro, there is a hint in this work, not of the French Aristide Maillot or the Italian Marino Marini, whose works he had admired as a student, but of Rodin. For all her apparent tranquility, *Contemplation* is a somewhat unsettling work, whose quality may lie in her slightly oversized head and her intricate headpiece. The figure's head is not only contemplative but seems a little troubled. This is an older, wiser and more experienced face set on an adolescent body. It may be this that halts the heart at the sightless shadow. The created sculpture is serene, but the figure itself is not.

Not more than a hundred metres away stands another Dabro, *Standing Figure*. The ANU's *Sculpture Walk* explains:

> Dabro modelled this work from a model, Karen, which may account for the unusual subtlety and complexity of *Standing Figure*. The girl's stance is meditative and has great stillness, but it is also braced as if with a workman-like readiness for muscular and disciplined action. The artist has said that while ever a living sculpture sings and vibrates in its own language and in its own space, it needs neither explanation nor apologia.[4]

Standing Figure presents precisely the polarity between the idealised femininity of *Contemplation* and this delineation of an actual human form. Karen chose her own pose, which allowed Dabro's interest in human hands, like Rodin's, to explore some real complexity. In her right hand, she holds a small bag, but her left elbow forces the hand downwards in an intriguing curve. Dabro has portrayed her *contrapposto* leaning slightly to the left, sculpturally demonstrable in that a line extending vertically from the nose would touch the plinth not between the feet, but almost at the left toe. The weight transfer is more obvious

FIGURE 7.8

Standing Figure, 1981–1982, bronze, life size, University House, Australian National University, Source: Author.

I like this figure, though I'd prefer that she stood in the native grasses rather than on a pedestal.

Making Commissions 159

from the rear: the right leg is slightly bent and the right shoulder is subtly higher than the left.

The ANU's commentary on the campus sculptures rightly notes the figure's apparent readiness for 'muscular and disciplined action'. Indeed, she bears features that are becoming more prominent in Dabro's later work. She is no idealised beauty but a real woman, one of the very few Dabro works to have pubic hair. Like Meštrović, Marko Dabro and Ante himself, *Standing Figure* is a *vlaj*, the ancient Roman name for the rough outsiders of the Croatian hills, the strong, athletic, determined and hard-working Illyrians.

CHAPTER 8

MAKING BEHEMOTHS

In 2006, the Croatian business group Consolidated Builders ACT commissioned Dabro to create a work that would illuminate the process of immigration to Australia. The sculpture stands in the Central Business District of Canberra, Civic, between City Walk and Benara Street.

A huge and highly burnished diagonal dominates the work from left to right. A woman lies crushed beneath it. Her hands seem to continue to push it away. She lives, but impassively is resigned to the continuing struggle. On the right, a child, perhaps a younger child of the woman and who seems more female than male, crawls upwards. Her face is much more hopeful than those of the other women. The angled planes leave no doubt as to the journey that she must take. Will she ever reach her sister? Is her task to relieve her?

The dominant human feature of the work is the older child in the top centre who shoulders an enormous sarcophagus-shaped burden. Though she is strong and muscular, and her face a little older than her *vlaj*-like body, her back is bowed by the impossibly heavy weight. Her oversized big toe digs into the supporting substance, her right thigh strains with effort. Yet she seems as resigned to her task as is the woman lying crushed beneath her own unsupportable burden and her sister who climbs intently towards her. Symbolically, she is Atlas, the mythical Greek figure who holds up the sky.

The oldest sculpture of Atlas is accepted to be the Farnese Atlas in the Naples Archaeological Museum, dated 150 BCE; but of all the hundreds of sculpted Atlases created since then, none seem to support the burden of the firmament with more equanimity – not even resignation – than this figure.

Visually, the three figures belong together, perhaps as members of a family. They represent three parts of the struggle of emigration: the older woman, crushed but seemingly accepting her destiny, attempts to hold off her inevitable death. An older child, equally uncomplaining, bears a stupendous weight that is the burden of migration or perhaps of merely living. She bears the sky to

161

FIGURE 8.1

Resilience, 2008, bronze, 3.8 x 3.25 x 1.8 m. Source: Con Boekel.

I like this work. It fits into the environment well.

allow her Sisyphus-like younger sister to advance ever to windward, irrespective of the casualties. In her turn, she will lie crushed beneath the cruel diagonal. And another little child will crawl past her vacant space.

The commissioners planned that the work be sited beside their own building. Fortunately, the ACT Chief Minister Jon Stanhope intervened to insist that it be placed centrally in the square as the public monument that Dabro had intended. So now, the viewer walking from the business end of Civic Centre will encounter *Resilience* from the rear and be surprised by a high relief depiction of a couple in a kiss more loving and less passionate than, for example, Rodin's *Eternal Springtime*. Dabro believes it is just as emotionally necessary as it is sculpturally essential, for the work might otherwise be interpreted too pessimistically.

FIGURE 8.2

Resilience, detail. Source: Con Boekel.

Will she ever get there? Metaphorically speaking, no.

Yet there is no violence here, just love and passion. Love is as necessary as the ambition of the crawling child if migration – and life – is to continue.

Physically, emotionally and sculpturally apart stands the male figure. He seems the oldest of the four figures and, perhaps for that reason, the most despairing. He, too, was strong and muscular, but his strength is spent. He gazes down, apparently defeated, clearly an older and more desolate depiction of the kissing man. Is he the patriarch of this suffering family? Physically distanced, he is sorrowful, ready to help yet not quite able to fully participate, not sure what to do next, not even certain why he stands apart from the group of females, his family. Sculpturally, he strongly reinforces the vertical lines of the work; symbolically, he is the Greek chorus offering a melancholy commentary on the emigrating experience. He stands forever outside.

Dabro acknowledges *Resilience* is the most autobiographical of all his sculptures:

FIGURE 8.3

Resilience, detail. Source: Con Boekel.

*The kiss is one of the most important parts of the work.
No migrant will ever succeed without love.*

The standing man? That's me! That's my portrait! I was going into an unknown, always jumping into the abyss. I'm proud of being Croatian even though I left. I'm proud to be a peasant even though I never really accepted being one. That's why I'm an outsider. It was bloody hard when I came here. I wasn't glorifying anything. My language was non-existent. The kiss is the meaning of real love that I found here.

Within my extended family I feel I never was really accepted. It's partly my own fault: I'm a good provider and a good family man – but whatever you stand for I'll be against. Actually I may really agree with you but I won't let you know. I had to do this in philosophy classes in Zagreb, that is to take the opposite view of any class discussion. So within the family I'll argue passionately against their views. I've supported unpopular politicians and

Making Behemoths 165

I don't watch my language. I don't pussyfoot around. So they think I'm a right wing reactionary, but I'm really not that at all.

Very many of the angry exchanges within the family were about local or international politics:

[My extended family] think I'm an extreme right winger and call me 'off the scale', but that's extremely arrogant and shallow. It really hurts me, I'm a very passionate person.

Where was relief? The Cuban writer Gustavo Pérez Firmat could find refuge for his own homeless mind only within himself:

Lección de exilio: el único regreso posible es hacia adentro, no hacia atrás.
[Lesson of exile: the only possible return is inwards, not backwards].[1]

Dabro had no return to the vanished Croatia of the 1950s. His artistic mainspring had never coiled with any conviction in Australia. Nowhere in the Europe of the twenty-first century seemed there a home for this peregrine soul to roost. Progressively disenchanted with Australia, his family disenchanted in him, Ante found himself on many occasions playing dejectedly with the dogs or the grandchildren.

Sculpturally, *Resilience* returns us to the *Naval Memorial*. Without the secondary perpendicular figure of the officer with the binoculars, the sailors beneath the mast would look a little lost. Without the standing male, the central mass – the child's burden – of *Resilience* would become too dominant. The strong perpendiculars of both works stabilise and contain the action within. The diagonal plane that dominates the compositions is softened by the central Trevi-like fountain, and the girder that crushes the woman in *Resilience* is relieved by the woman's oversize outstretched hands.

The sculptor's solitary psyche emerges as strongly as in Anzac Parade. The three female figures of *Resilience*, that is, the three phases of the migrant journey, are bound in a common experience but show no indication that they are even aware of the others' existence. Like the sailors, they embrace and accept their task. They form a family: but like the sailors, none looks at each other. The treasures of life are unobtainable; they must always be out of reach – but the struggle continues. It becomes apparent that the child who climbs upwards will not reach her destination and may not even be aware of what it is.

166 THE LIFE AND WORK OF ANTE DABRO

At some point in the mid-1970s, Ante met Terry Snow, already a successful Canberra builder with a sympathetic and knowledgeable interest in painting.[2] Snow wanted to meet some sculptors from whom he could commission works to expand his collection. In their several ways, both men had prospered individually; Dabro in establishing himself as a protégé of Phillip Bacon Galleries in Brisbane and as a leading figurative artist with a major retrospective in 2000, Snow in dignifying a business empire well-known for its philanthropic and environmental dedication. The meeting of minds solidified in 1998 in Snow's purchase of a 99-year lease of Canberra Airport, including the civilian complex, a large area of unused space and the partly disused Air Force base. In 2002, Snow visited Dabro's studio at home, then at Womboyn 40 kilometres from the airport, and thought it too far away for someone from whom he aimed to commission several major sculptures. Four or five years later, Snow had prepared the former RAAF Fire Station at the airport as Dabro's on-site studio. By 2008, he was established in what was then described as the only airport in the world possessing its own resident sculptor. It was an amicable and fruitful relationship; but while Lorenzo de Medici and Pope Julius II never let Michelangelo forget who was in charge, neither did Snow.

Dabro could scarcely fathom his newfound artistic freedom. Snow might ask him to do more than 'fill this space'. Dabro would present two or three ideas, then a maquette; once approved, the work began without haggling. Snow commissioned a cast of *Suzanne* to be placed by an ornamental pool in the Brindabella Business Park, adjacent to the airport, which he owned. During the decade, *Suzanne* was re-created, her legs dangling over a recently constructed pool. Another re-casting was *Contemplation*, now installed complete with properly maintained fountains, in the building housing the Office of Homeland Security – which he owned. Snow asked for a large and interesting work to be installed in his home at Bawley Point. The several prototypes became *Mother and Child*. At the Fairbairn studio, Snow might enter the studio to point to a sculpture he liked: 'Can you cast ten of that one for me to give to my friends or associates'.

At no point was there a discussion about a fee, nor whether the plinth was to be concrete or marble, nor whether it would be kept burnished, nor whether the fountain pumps would be maintained. That could be taken for granted.

Snow was aware that he had come to Ante's artistic rescue after several unsuccessful tenders for national commissions. He wanted to help him, no great favour because he loved the work of this first decade of their relationship. He found his resident sculptor 'a bit bolshy, outspoken, a bit of a male

Making Behemoths 167

chauvinist, having a European conviction of himself as invincible and not one to change his views on anything'. Yet he recognised in him those same qualities of the practical hard-working *vlaj* that he valued in himself. The first commissions especially he found 'really attractive'. The two men found a mutually respectful relationship. Snow recalled: 'He was pretty fragile at one stage, not really thinking about other people or their views. I knew which buttons to push. But don't mention Yugoslavia'.[3] In return, Dabro respected the acumen of a businessman, the earthiness of a builder and the appreciation of a patron of the arts:

> He loved my work and we had a lovely rapport. I respected him, he was honest and fair, and if he didn't like something he'd tell me. He didn't like my rough angles and would even come to the studio, picking up a tool and pretend to soften them up. I'd tell him to go away. He was like a *vlaj*, there was no nonsense about him. I respect him very much and he was a godsend to the ACT and I defended him against a lot of critics many times.

Dabro's next essay in the two-figure form was for the main interior concourse of the Canberra Airport. He named it *Introspection*, relating that:

> When I was asked to create a work for the departure lounge, immediately I knew it had to be of the right scale to blend in with the people passing through, waiting for planes, and to be very much part of the life going on around them.

In fact, its position had been decided only after a serious discussion with Snow:

> Terry asked me to do something in a thoroughfare. I said: 'no, my sculptures won't work there. If it goes in a passageway it will be just a decoration. It'll have to be in the lounge or upstairs.' So Terry moved it there.

The work is indeed part of the diurnal life of the passengers: the knees and shoulders of both figures are foundry-bright, polished by the hands of hundreds of travellers daily seeking more than a visual connection with the intriguing sculpture. When the terminal is crowded, the figures appear unexpectedly convivial, sitting among the crowd as the passengers check the flight information or their phones. When the area is empty, their presence is gallery-like. At first glance, the two figures seem to be conversing, or as Dabro puts it, 'they

FIGURE 8.4

Introspection, 2013, bronze, 1:1.3, Canberra Airport. Source: Con Boekel.

*I had the problem of relating the two figures to each other
and at the same time relating them to the crowd of passengers.*

are in a state where conversation may not be taking place, but where speech is possible'. It is an inviting notion.

Just as anxious airline passengers may sit awkwardly to command many angles of vision, the commission seemed a consummate opportunity for Dabro to extend his explorations of the twisted human torso. A close examination reveals a number of sculptural liberties. While the right-hand figure (viewed from this angle) is life-size, the dominant figure on the left is much larger, at

Making Behemoths 169

least 1:1.25. With her huge raised left thigh, she is particularly oversized below the waist. No concession is made to her left leg that rests on the right; it merely occupies a small scoop just above the knee.

The figure is almost as contorted as Michelangelo's 1504 famous study of naked soldiers at the Battle of Cascina. Indeed, like that sculptor's *David*, the larger figure here would look very odd if she could be, as it were, induced to lie down flat. Yet viewed from the front at a distance of a couple of metres, both figures look to be of similar dimensions. The two heads, in fact, are precisely the same size.

Introspection, rather more than *Sisters*, is an investigation of the relationship between large forms. Fingers and toes are no more than alluded to. The enigmatic faces of both figures carry no particular emotion; rather, the triangular shape of the larger figure's face is more than a little reminiscent of Dabro's *The Bureaucrat* of 1990, itself an allusion to the comic-sinister masks of Venetian tradition. Dabro wishes the viewer to follow the form of the bodies first, the faces later.

Between the figures, and unlike *Sisters*, there is little hint of an emotional relationship. Yet, they need each other sculpturally: the larger figure would be rather awkwardly marooned, without a *raison d'etre*, if she were not balanced by the smaller figure to whom she visually relates.

The space between the base of the spinal column and right shoulder blade of the smaller figure traces an elegant lineament that bears little relation to human anatomy: a prominent vertebra like *Suzannne's* would detract from the sweeping semi-circle that Dabro has created here.

The necks of both figures have been subtly lengthened to allow each head to turn at a full 90 degrees from the chest. Despite its innocent title, *Introspection* is a radical departure from conventional commissioned sculptures of the human form, but such is the artist's skill that the distortions seem to be no more than necessary to present an artistic reality. *Introspection* is a remarkable tour-de-force whose anatomical interventions are concealed within the calm exteriors of the two figures.[4]

The two figures of *Introspection* inside the airport seem, from some angles of vision, to be placed too far apart for a strong emotional association; yet several plaster versions of the same work existing in the studio are set much closer together for convenience and instantly relate to each other as two women. In their present configuration, the figures communicate with each other less readily than *Sisters* outside the Brisbane Art Gallery. It is one of the few instances in Dabro's work where the need for sculptural balance outweighs the

FIGURE 8.5

Introspection, detail. Source: Con Boekel.

Making Behemoths 171

FIGURE 8.6

Dancer 2, 1980s, bronze, 39 x 26 x 18 cm. Source: Private collection.

*I love this work in its original position. She has a teasing balance.
We wonder, 'Will she fall over?'*

172 THE LIFE AND WORK OF ANTE DABRO

human need to emotionally relate. Whether the figures relate to each other or not, the passengers relate to the figures. Nick Stranks, who cast the work, comments:

> At the airport there are always people looking at these works and sitting on these works and touching areas of skin. That's the lovely thing about bronze, the more people are allowed to handle it, the better it looks. And bronze doesn't normally attract vandals. I can't recall any of Ante's works being vandalised.

In 2001, Dabro became acquainted with an ANU academic visitor, the French Nobel Prize–winning physicist, Pierre-Jules de Gennes. With Degas' dancing ballerinas perhaps in his mind, Dabro created a dancing figure some 30 centimetres in height that de Gennes placed in a window box in his home overlooking the Luxembourg Garden in Paris. In the Canberra studio, Snow noticed the plaster maquette of the same figure. 'I want that'.

The work's destination was a public square in Snow's latest enterprise, the Brindabella Business Park, one of whose buildings won a five-star rating from the Green Building Council of Australia. Today, with some leafy groves, a child-care centre, medical facilities and cafes, it is becoming a high-tech but artistically reassuring suburb.

How would the work speak to its *plein-aire* surroundings ten times larger than its original interior placement? Dabro devoted an entire interview with the author to discuss the position and relative size of his exterior works.

> I'm always aware and concerned with the surroundings for my sculptures. Sculpture has to have a space where visually it is comfortable in its surroundings and is talking to its surroundings. *Suzanne* is a bit lonely where she is, I never imagined her in such a wide and empty space. On the other hand, my sculptures have lungs, they have to breathe and need air around them. I learned that from Rodin. There's a front and back and around.

Light, reflected surfaces and the height of adjacent buildings and trees all dictate the position, even the size of every work. For a breezeway designed for his home 'Eagle's Eye' on his south coast estate, Snow commissioned a work on the theme of mother and child. Dabro obliged with the colossal *Mother and Child*, nearly three metres in height, of a woman swinging aloft her baby boy at the very top of the arc, the split second before the child's giggling descent.

FIGURE 8.7

Dancer 2, 2005, 1: 1.5, life size, plaster, artist's studio, artist's collection.
Source: Con Boekel.

This is one of the best angles to see this scaled-up version.

Mother and Child rejoiced in its surroundings at the Eagle's Eye, but installations at the airport were more problematic, not least because the precinct was incomplete. By 2012, Dabro was no longer content with the position of *Suzanne*: since her installation in 2005, tall buildings had grown around her until the work looked rather distant and forlorn, especially when viewed from the leafy and attractive lunch area of Brindabella Park.

174   THE LIFE AND WORK OF ANTE DABRO

Dancer's position was set, but not her proportions, which must now be enlarged from a work of half a metre. If *Dancer* was to satisfy the eye in the proposed space, her proportions would be critical.

The work of some ten times the size of the original, its balance, weight and mounting needed major recalculation. Scaling up a work from a one-piece pour to a dozen large sections is very likely to lose detail. Raising the observer's viewpoint from eye level to an upward gaze will foreshorten its perspective. Standing at the site, Dabro calculated that in relationship to the surrounding buildings, *Dancer* would have to be 3 metres tall, an enormous technical challenge for such a top-heavy structure. Silicon bronze, the strongest of alloys, would need the support of a concealed steel rod for a figure of nearly a tonne balancing on the point of one foot: even Degas' bronze ballerina *Développé en avant* (1909) has her foot flat on the ground. The allotted site would funnel and whirl the Canberra south-westerlies around the confined space. Snow insisted that *Dancer* be sited in a pool of imperceptibly flowing water that would demand engineering at microscopic tolerances. Privately, Dabro and Stranks wondered whether the enormous work, so finely balanced, might not snap or topple over.

Like the twin figures in the airport's *Introspection,* this work reveals Dabro's continued preoccupation with the most external aspects of the human form. As he chipped at the full-sized plaster model, he pondered three possible visual starting points for *Dancer:* her right foot, her head and left toe.

> When I'm starting on a new work the head and face will come last. It can be almost ignored when I start. You have to see the whole body as one, you work as a whole. Ideally when the work is complete, the viewer will start at the toes, follow up the body to the head, then down again.

Following the same phases of creation, the eye tracks the largest shapes to the smallest. The cadences of head and foot are held in the figure's C-curve by the piled hair at one end and the right foot at the other, while the mass of the arched back balances the tremendous leverage of the extended leg. *Dancer*'s head balances her larger-than-life thigh. Come closer: the detailing of the figure's torso is less distinct. It is not even immediately clear where the top of the tutu – if that is what it is – falls. Unlike Degas's ballerinas, nothing outside the body itself is allowed to distract the eye, for the right arm tightly holds down her garment, and the left is absorbed into the thigh itself. Of the body extremities, only the big toe of the right foot can be identified. One or two right-hand fingers hold down the skirt. Only at the end of the viewing cycle, as in so many Dabro works, does the artist allow the viewer to alight on her face, somewhat concealed in the downward tilt of her neck. A smaller plaster maquette in the studio holds no face at all.

Dancer's parallels to other Dabro works relate both to the energetic solidity of *Standing Figure* at University House, and the idealised femininity of *Contemplation* in Judith Wright court. *Dancer* may be thought to be held as in a snapshot of a sweeping pirouette, but she is not; she balances motionless on one foot, rather improbably without a hint of tension or concentration. That's how Dabro conceives her: 'In another moment she would collapse or have to get up'. Indeed, if Degas inadvertently revealed his feelings towards his suffering subjects, so does *Dancer* whisper the psyche of her own creator. Majestically, she balances on her toe; yet there is still that certain earthiness about her that grows more characteristic of Dabro's sculptured women after 2000. *Dancer*'s face is as composed as *Suzanne*'s, yet she is as strong as a *vlaj*. Not only is the work a further exploration of the idealised female form, it also exemplifies the qualities of Dabro's *actual* perceived woman: graceful and strong, dignified and tranquil, hard-working and stoic; she carries within her both the inner stillness of a Michelangelo and a hint of the Dalmatian *vlaj*.

The poet W. B. Yeats pondered the association between the created work and the impulse of the first imaginative leap. The blossoms of the chestnut tree flowed back through its branches into the roots, the creative fount of every being and every work of art:

O chestnut tree, great rooted blossomer,
Are you the leaf, the blossom or the bole?
O body swayed to music, O brightening glance,
How can we know the dancer from the dance?[5]

Dancer is both idea and execution, both flower and essence of the dance itself.

Brian Kennedy, retiring director of the National Gallery of Australia, unveiled *Dancer* in June 2005. Snow and Dabro, he remarked, were two remarkable men who had become soulmates. 'Both men assiduously reject fashion, despise hypocrisy and lack of candour'. Dabro he recognised as 'without doubt one of, if not the, foremost standard bearers in Australia for the figurative bronze sculpture tradition'. His work was 'as uncompromising and as identifiable as [Snow's] – always the mark of a strong artist'. The Canberra Airport digest *The Hub* reported: 'More than three metres high, *Dancer* is the work of renowned Croatian sculptor, Ante Dabro, and portrays a female poised in a position that almost defies gravity.'[6]

176   THE LIFE AND WORK OF ANTE DABRO

In 2000, a visit by an exchange student from Kyoto Seika University began cultural interactions with the ANU's Institute of the Arts, from which Dabro benefitted enormously. He took his first trip to the ancient royal and artistic capital of Japan, Kyoto, in 2001. He loved the politeness of everyday people. He began learning Japanese. In the city, he slept in a former palace reserved for Westerners. He staged an exhibition of smaller works and sold more than half. During a four-months Visiting Professorship, he gave a series of lectures that caused a commotion by urging that the students return to their own cultural roots.

> In the west we seek God vertically, while your traditions are centred on the horizontal [...] I respect and love your culture: stick to it, don't follow the worst of western fashion in art, don't keep copying the worst art of the contemporary decadent west when your own traditions are so strong.

Even the very concept of an artistic exhibition, he explained, was Western.[7] Unexpectedly, he found himself almost overcome by spiritual forces in the Kinkaju-ji temple. On the sacred mountain of Mt Kurama, north of Kyoto, he told the students to go ahead while he entered its ancient shrine. 'I stopped quite still, my hair on end. It was a very spiritual moment'. Like an Aboriginal visitor to new country, he appealed to the land spirits; mentally, he besought them: *I come from a faraway land. I come in friendship. I'm not here to harm you.* Though Japanese three-dimensional sculpture seemed unsophisticated, he was entranced by *ikibana* and its sensibility of aesthetics. 'I liked the masks, the folds and the crispness of the Kabuki art-form costumes'. Through his several visits, he absorbed the ancient traditions of the formal and arranged garden landscape peopled by nature spirits. He loved the household and nature gods, which answered the animistic preferences in his own innermost spiritual life. Most of all, he imbibed the formal geometric gardens whose waters moved so slowly and subtly that it was hard to tell if the surface was moving at all. He compared the soaring cathedrals of his birthland to the equality of elements within a Japanese garden. Each one held a precise relationship to other trees, bushes, ornaments, water features or objects of the space. Above all, he appreciated the philosophy of Zen, the desired state of calm attentiveness from which the creative urge flows, the roots, not the blossoms, where action is guided more by intuition than conscious effort. It seemed a guiding principle for every artist. As the Australian poet David Campbell puts it:

Making Behemoths 177

Matter would take fire without
the channelling restraints of thought
That lock wild arbours up in stone
to lend his concepts flesh and bone.[8]

It was in 2006, during this period, while Dabro was fully absorbing the subtleties of Japanese garden architecture, that Terry Snow called him to his office. A formal avenue would shortly be constructed in a central area of Brindabella Park. A long rectangular garden would define a central approach of two parallel walkways divided by a narrow watercourse leading up to a wide raised precinct from which a sculpture or sculptures would be raised. At each end of the avenue, a small fountain. Snow wanted the sculpture to complete the logic of the grand entrance, which, since the walkways already contained water, would also need to incorporate water in some way. The new work was to be placed at the end of the walkways on a wide and raised upper precinct. Dabro would need to consult the architect Alistair Swain in augmenting this Japanese-style garden that was already well in its planning. For the first time in his artistic career, Dabro's sculptures were to be but two discrete elements within other complex dimensions: a Japanese garden of two separate levels containing two parallel walkways, two fountains, a water feature, tall trees, low bushes and an ornamental pool in a long, narrow avenue ending in a broad T. Ideally, all elements of the garden would relate to each other equally and from all points. No feature would command the space. Simultaneously, his two sculptures would have to be small enough not to dominate the walkway, but large enough not to be overwhelmed by the surrounding buildings. Was it possible artistically? What Japanese garden containing nothing higher than shrubs of half a metre would ever be asked to contain a man-made object two metres tall?

Dabro, Snow and Swain agreed that, given the proportions of the avenue, two sculptured objects would be required. To Dabro, they must, of course, be two human figures.

The first issues were where the sculptures would be placed and their relationship not just to each other, but to the other equal elements in the design. Owner, architect and sculptor all placed them at the southern end of the staircase leading up from the walkway immediately visible to a pedestrian entering from the avenue. Placement and size therefore were critical. Spaced too near, they would not close the endpoint of the avenue; too far, they would be invisible from below and cease to relate to each other sculpturally or in terms of their humanity.

FIGURE 8.8

Avenue Bathers, 2007, 1:1.3 life size, Brindabella Business Park, Canberra.
Source: Con Boekel.

The figures look right from this angle, but from the top, they are too far apart and don't relate to each other properly. They become decorations.

For the figures, Dabro has chosen the configuration used in Brisbane of one bending figure and one standing, both at 1.5 life size. They stand on rocky mounds enclosed by an oval pool a few centimetres deep, set on black tiles. The still and unruffled water strikingly throws back the surrounding trees. The taller figure, modelled on a sketch of Snow's daughter, stands upright holding a towel over her shoulders. The second bather, not modelled from life, dries her right foot held on her knee while balancing on her left. This foot turns slightly and subtly outward not to physically balance the work itself (which, reinforced by a stainless steel rod inserted through foot and leg, doesn't need balancing) but for the bather to balance herself: almost all her weight is carried on the right side of her body.

Her body forms a C-shape tighter than *Dancer's* while the taller figure, standing erect, positions herself evenly balanced on her two separated legs. Perhaps because she looks straight ahead, her face is more finely modelled than the bending figure's face. Her body language asserts something of 'Don't

Making Behemoths 179

mess with me', but in her slightly distracted facial expression there is a touch of *Suzanne* and *Contemplation*.

That the torso of this taller figure seems unusually distended indicates the pressure Dabro felt to accommodate the complex demands of the entire space. Unsurprisingly, he is unhappy with the placement.

> I would prefer them closer, because at some point they stop relating to each other. I don't know why I allowed them to be where there were, perhaps there were some geographical issues; but if they were closer they wouldn't work looking from the bottom. The far end of the avenue is the best angle to view them from, because from there they definitely work together.

The answer perhaps is that there can be no full resolution, and that every element in the design has had to compromise.

In 2008, Terry Snow's stepson and airport manager, Stephen Byron, had a large piazza to fill outside building 25 in the Business Park for which he was directly responsible. He sought from Dabro a large, energetic work that would reflect and encourage the busy social gatherings that he envisaged. One stand-alone work, he judged, would be sufficient.

Without preliminary drawings, Ante constructed in wax several versions of his proposal: the massive *Genesis*, the extension of the loving kiss of *Resilience*, depicting the moment of passion, the origin of the human species. *Genesis* was to be a logical synthesis of the work of a sculptor who saw the sexual act as *fons et origo* of art as well as life. Sculpturally, *Genesis* was to resolve the tension between two separate figures springing from the same source, which in an abstracted form he had explored 35 years before.

Byron was delighted with the wax maquette and asked Dabro to begin at once. Snow, of course, needed to be consulted, and perhaps was less enthusiastic both for the contrast between the hard and rounded surfaces, and for the explicit subject. The contract, however, was Byron's call. All that was necessary in the decisive business practices of the airport was for Snow to stamp 'OK' on the sketches.

Few are the depictions in classical art or sculpture of the actual sexual union between man and woman, and none bears the persona of their creator with more certainty than *Genesis*. As usual for Dabro, it was the sculptural issues that first demanded resolution. He explained:

> [*Genesis*] is not a narrative, these are sculptural issues. A good sculpture is a visual symphony. Words are unnecessary, and if you are visually literate

180 THE LIFE AND WORK OF ANTE DABRO

enough it will touch you. If you're not it should still touch everyone, though at different levels. If it doesn't speak for itself it's no good. Matter and spirit are one.

Matisse and Picasso are among the twentieth-century sculptors who simplified the body and delighted in the flat planar surfaces that accentuate the direction that the eye should follow. The work Dabro planned – with wax, not pencil – would explore the same commingling of line and plane, the hard and soft surfaces that had first entered his sculptures of his daughters Jessica and Sarah in the late 1970s. The straight surfaces at the base of *Genesis* would act as resting points for the eye. He explained: 'If it was all smooth surfaces, the eye would go there and back away. Hard surfaces tell you things on your journey round the work'. If the work was a symphony, then the hard planes and angular changes of directions should act as cadences or movements. This work, *Genesis*, would pivot on the central moment of human life: the moment of conception, but distant philosophically from both Courbet's *L'origine du monde* and Rodin's *The Kiss*. As modelling began, Snow preferred the more classical rounded forms of his earlier work. He came once to the studio, picked up a stone and made to rub off some of the hard angles on the plaster model. 'Leave me alone, Terry'.

The Governor-General Quentin Bryce unveiled the work on 2 June 2009. The publicity hand-out revealed Dabro's intentions: '[Genesis is a] Symphony of forms and echoes the beginning of time. I sensed the site called for a composition of two. I wanted to create something where the harmony of shapes creates unity'.

The 'harmony of shapes' of *Genesis* is created by a pattern in a figure-of-eight that uses the elbows both as visual cadences and to change the direction of the eye. The man's vertebra, twisted towards the top, follows vertically as it follows the direction of the muscles, acting to stabilise the upward thrust of the work.

Beginning from the man's left heel (at the bottom left of the work) the eye follows the curves up the man's torso, flattens to an arc as his right arm touches his head, follows down to the sharpest cadence of the work at the woman's elbow, descends past her head to sculpturally unite with her curving right arm, mirroring the man's right arm diagonally opposed, down across the box-like plane surface, to the woman's left foot. The visual journey of both the eye and the geometric figure are together complete.[9]

Sculpturally, Dabro is now unsatisfied with the work, believing that the two figures fuse too closely. Another smaller cast version of *Genesis,* created later, places the upper torsos much further apart.

FIGURE 8.9

Genesis, 2009, bronze, 1:1.3, life size, Brindabella Business Park.
Source: Con Boekel.

I hope this will be one of the works for which I'll be best remembered.

At this point, a sculptural analysis becomes one with the humanistic interpretation. Dabro reasons that the world moves to the rhythms of two opposing forces, yin and yang, man and woman. 'Biologically we are different and coming together we create a spark'. The two figures of *Genesis* are more than sexually united. Both are in orgasm, for what is depicted is the moment of male

FIGURE 8.10

Genesis, 2009, bronze, half-size and remodelled. Source: Artist's collection.

This version, where the figures are further apart, works better as a sculpture.

ejaculation. The woman's hand tightly holds the man's thigh, yet their upper bodies arch away from each other. In sculpting the woman, Dabro now wonders to what extent he had in mind Bernini's 1652 mannerist sculpture of *The Ecstasy of St Theresa*, who described her union with God as:

> In his [an angel's] hands I saw a great golden spear, and at the iron tip there appeared to be a point of fire. This he plunged into my heart several times […] and left me utterly consumed by the great love of God. The pain was so severe that it made me utter several moans. The sweetness caused by this

Making Behemoths 183

intense pain is so extreme that one cannot possibly wish it to cease, nor is one's soul then content with anything but God.[10]

The women in Bernini's and Dabro's sculptures both push back in orgasmic ecstasy. Both male and female of *Genesis* have their eyes closed. The man arches his head and pulls his massive upper body away from her. His hands do not touch his partner but entwine convulsively in his own hair; his right arm seems almost to be pulling his head away from her. Dabro comments:

> The two figures don't look at each other. The act of sex is violent, but the feelings and the experiences are different. Her pleasure is not your pleasure and my pleasure is not her pleasure. Woman does it differently. Woman has an internal orgasm and probably is far more powerful.

Discussing the relationship between the two lovers, Dabro, like most artists, responds: 'You've put me on the spot. I never think about these things except in terms of their resolution. I don't see it'. And as usual, any interpretation of the work in human rather than artistic terms leaves much ambiguity. The withdrawn bodies and the away-turned faces may signify, like Dabro's interpretation of *Introspection*, that speech and sight may be equally superfluous in a deep human contact. No emotions of love or passion could be stronger than in the moment of sexual orgasm: but the turned faces may equally signify that even the most intimate moments in a person's life are solitary. These lovers, like the sailors of Anzac Parade, share a common destiny as fellow humans; they share life's experiences; they respect and may love each other – but each at every moment is utterly alone.

Genesis in Dabro's estimation is his best work. It is unmistakably mature Dabro in style. Its proportions are massive but speak perfectly to their surroundings. Its energy is as powerful as the writhing *Laocöon and His Sons*; its emotions bubble from every centimetre of the skin. Ultimately it answers Dabro's consuming psychic and artistic absorption in male and female difference. 'Biologically we are different and coming together we create a spark'. It is his first mature work in which the subjects are not peaceful, contemplative, serene or accept their fate. For the first time since the 1970s (the time of *Diagonal Direction*) Dabro depicts a moment of violence. It should come as no surprise that the violence is a moment of sexual passion.

Fifty-four years after arriving in Australia, filled with promise and hope, Dabro received a major disappointment.

FIGURE 8.11

Flight, plaster, 2010, 70 x 33 x 30 cm, Stephen Byron collection.
Source: Unknown photographer.

I'm still in mourning for him.

After *Genesis,* plans began for an even larger work to be situated inside the entrance concourse of the Canberra airport. Following a request by Snow, Dabro created *Flight*. A young man balanced on one foot, wings spread, poised at the moment of leaving earth. At 4 metres it would dwarf the passengers. To Snow it must have seemed a return to the style of the younger Dabro. He

Making Behemoths 185

approved the preliminary work; yet abruptly the project was cancelled without explanation. A metallic feather of the same height, created by another artist, was erected in its place. Dabro, though unused to verbally expressing such a private emotion, exclaimed: 'It almost broke my heart. It almost destroyed me but I had to get up again'. Privately he protested:

> Yes, there are about ten Dabros at the airport already and now the airport management wanted a contemporary sculpture. But I wonder how much people can relate to a piece of rock rather than to humanity. A feather may symbolise flight, yes, but it doesn't trigger an emotion. All works must be related to we humans. You can't force it to pass on its message. Or maybe its message is not even there.

The abrupt termination of the work-in-progress may not have been much of a mystery. Airport manager Stephen Byron stated: 'It simply cost too much'. In conversation with Byron, I remarked,

> Ante told me it nearly broke his heart.

Byron replied:

> All artists work better with a broken heart. But I believe that Ante has one or two great works still left in him.[11]

Given the nearly three-year Covid-induced virtual absence of domestic passengers as well as the forced closure of the newly constructed international departure hall of the airport, a financial constraint on *Flight* by the management was understandable. Yet, against the enormous plate glass sheet looking to the runways, the bronze figurative sculpture would have been unforgettable. The 4-metre currently unnamed and unattributed metallic feather which now commands the space, and another large but grotesque work outside the main entrance, are in no sense memorable. Had Snow and Byron at this critical moment of construction lost their nerve? It was unfortunate that the logic of a figurative sculpture-inspired airport precinct had been abandoned at the airport's most symbolic point.

CHAPTER 9

MAKING WAY

Following the rejection of *Flight*, Dabro's disappointment deepened. He conceded the right of Snow to think, 'I have ten Dabros here, that's enough for one person', but he privately nursed his distress at the absence of any provenance of *Introspection* inside the Homeland Security headquarters in the Business Park, and he objected to the signage on *Dancer* that read 'Property of Terry Snow'. A dread of what he identified as political correctness seemed to lower over his creations. He wondered if *Mother and Child* could ever be exhibited publicly given that the naked child was a boy. At times he returned to sculpting the figure of Karl Marx addressing his sycophantic followers. It's a powerful work indicating his contempt for the what he sometimes called the 'loony left' but his intention is to smash it. 'I was too angry when I made it and works done in anger never make good sculptures'.

In interviews, his mind revolved around many of his preoccupations that disturbed him, the spoken voice of convictions once built upon rock that had become quicksand:

> Are we losing our freedom? No, we've already lost it. Rapists? Cut their balls off, but the ABC portrays all men as if we all are rapists. Just acknowledge the difference between men and women. Boys and girls are born different. The extreme left won't recognise anything different between them. #Metoo will pass or all of us men will be dinosaurs. And another thing. Why bang on about Aborigines all the time? One of my students once asked me, 'Mr Dabro, is there anything worth looking at in Australia beside Aboriginal art?' Placing it at the peak of Australia's artistic achievement does no good service to them or us. But I have to hope. If you don't have hope, what's the point of living?

188   THE LIFE AND WORK OF ANTE DABRO

Following the defeat of Donald Trump in the US elections of 2020, Dabro tweeted sarcastically that North Korea should be invited to supervise the USA's next election. An avalanche of hate and abusive messages forced him to close the account. It seemed a vindication of his long-held conviction that the radical left was dominating public discussion. If only they could understand what it was like to live under Socialism! In truth, many of the Australian themes most urgently debated, from climate change and 'The Voice' (the right of an Aboriginal elected body to provide formal advice to the national parliament), to less crucial issues like whether to call one's spouse 'partner' or 'wife' and the compulsory wearing of masks against Covid, had little or nothing to do with the traditional left/right political spectrum. It was a long tradition: conservatives and progressives had dragged social questions like these into left- or right-wing ideological conflict for more than a century, but Dabro would not be persuaded. Like many migrants, he lamented the decline of Australian society from the ground-zero at which he had arrived in 1967. After the election of Rudd, he had refused to vote.

> All my good memories are clouded now. I loved this country so much, but it didn't take me long to start doubting. Until Howard I voted, and I did so thoughtfully because I can't stand the club mentality. Now my family call me an extreme right-winger, but if I am one, why did I vote for Hawke for years? And Rudd. I can't celebrate this democracy, because it's no longer that, and it's getting worse and worse. At least in North Korea I would know what I could or couldn't do. I'm anti-priests and imams. I'm a believer but only in the original religion, I only go into church when the priests aren't there.

> Can't we see what we're doing? I hate the politicians. Acknowledge the difference between men and women. Abolish those wishy-washy Arts Grants committees that just subsidise what is trendy. Wake up Australia, otherwise we're doomed.

Dabro despaired at the artistic decline of both the necessary skill and spiritual force that had once driven the graphic arts of the world. 'The modern decorative fashion is impersonal and devoid of humanity and spirituality – are they dirty words?'

Dabro's malaise had many wellsprings. Today's Split is thronged with tourists. A double-lane carriageway towards Šibenik roars past Čavoglave, the site of Marko's workshop on the river and St Ilija on the hill. Virtually nobody of Dabro's generation remains alive. Croatian art, after his most recent visit in

FIGURE 9.1

Unnamed Figure, 2017, plaster, 405 x 20 x 10cm, artist's studio.
Source: Con Boekel.

The world doesn't understand me.

2022, seemed to him to be generally uninteresting. The monstrosities of what seemed to him the 'neo-nothingness' of the Venice Biennale seemed to him worse than ever. His distress at the political repression of his youth and the 1990s destruction in Krajina had become directed, to the irritation of his family, at what he saw as the radical left personified by the Australian Broadcasting Corporation, feminism and Indigenous demands. Most of the bluster, of course, concealed what was actually a solitary and rather apprehensive personality

190 THE LIFE AND WORK OF ANTE DABRO

that eluded outsiders. So the thoughtful, highly informed and measured discussions about sculptural principles and the history of European art that I, as biographer, enjoyed with him, were lost to almost everyone else. He had never quite understood that the cause of the opprobrium directed at him at the Canberra School of Art in the 1980s that had brought so much trouble on himself and despair to several directors, derived not from anger at his artistic creations but from his supposedly jocular banter and deeply insulting remarks. While such attitudes had been tolerated in the 1970s, in the 1980s there was no forgiveness. The mood of that generation of young people was taking no prisoners. Radical students demanded not only the outing of sexism but espoused a form of anti-intellectualism that assumed the right to set one's own exams (even mark them) and to create new courses such as Maoism. Decades later Dabro protested: 'I'm not a follower of trends. Why can't we debate these issues? If they just shut me down they're not intellectuals but pseudo-intellectuals. If we all agree on everything then one of us is not thinking'.

The changes went far beyond intellectual debate. Any art teacher past middle age might find themselves sidelined. In any case, by 2000 the discipline of life drawing was struggling to survive. Art History, if it was taught at all, needed to encompass Indigenous, Performance, Feminist and political standpoints. The teacher – no longer in any sense a Maestro – might find students expecting as much attention to be given to advanced 3D modelling as to carving. They expected that their written explanations of their work be taken seriously. Health and safety structures tightly governed the use of acid, fibreglass, timber and bronze dust. Graduating, the would-be professional artist would find foundries fewer and more expensive. Even the future of the solitary sculptor of large public commissions was endangered: a large consortium might already employ its own architects, landscapers, designers, engineers, lawyers, even a sculptor before tendering for a major work.[1]

One of the most succinct opinions of how critical judgement had become distorted, in which Dabro was in full agreement, was a judgement on the winning portrait of the Australian Archibald Portrait Prize of 2022. The chief art critic of the conservative *Australian* newspaper, Christopher Allen, ridiculed the awarding of the winning entry:

Alas, they [the Trustees] couldn't bring themselves to award the Archibald prize to the best picture when there was the irresistible temptation of a work by a black artist whose subject was a black woman. As a bonus they got a reference to the Lismore floods. Progressive signalling and compassion. It seems the trustees simply couldn't bear to select an artist who happened to be male and white.[2]

Making Way 191

Though Allen's judgement seemed rather ill-tempered, and whatever the massive injustices of the past committed against minority groups, older practitioners like Dabro might well find themselves taken less seriously. In 2022, the Tate Modern's Exhibition entitled 'Australian Art 1993' contained, without explanation, nothing except the productions of Indigenous artists.

After a 2022 research trip, fresh commissions in South Korea and Croatia seemed possible. Yet, Dabro remained unpredictable.

So many artists from Tintoretto to Keith Looby alienated their supporters and patrons by uninterest or worse, and Dabro admits that at times he has been his own worst enemy. His abrupt rejection of the Queensland Arts Minister's insulting question at the opening of *Sisters* illustrated his worsening unpredictability on public occasions, until even his advocates discussed whether it was wise to invite him to deliver a public lecture. Even a set speech might produce an outrageous remark during question time. He carried the weight of the ageing artist who floats culturally detached from international artistic currents, in which the pain of an intellect adrift can be as harsh as the physical estrangement. In his poem 'On the Term of Exile' Bertolt Brecht bitterly observed the plight of the exile who can never again find peace. The old and new countries will become such homogenous mush that a physical return will be pointless:

> No need to drive a nail into the wall
> To hang your hat on;
> When you come in, just drop it on the chair
> No guest has sat on.
>
> Don't worry about watering the flowers—
> In fact, don't plant them.
> You will have gone back home before they bloom,
> And who will want them?
>
> If mastering the language is too hard,
> Only be patient;
> The telegram imploring your return
> Won't need translation.
>
> Remember, when the ceiling sheds itself
> In flakes of plaster,
> The wall that keeps you out is crumbling too,
> As fast or faster.[3]

192   THE LIFE AND WORK OF ANTE DABRO

Forty years after Laura Mulvey's attack on the male gaze of feature-filmmakers had set the industry ablaze, perhaps the sharpest criticism that could be levelled at Dabro's sculptures of female nudes was that he had created them at all. To stand aside from the front line was to accept that many female artists were not as troubled by the female nude as the critics. The British sculptor Barbara Hepworth 'hated male or female work' and thought that 'the only equilibrium seems to be the fusion of strength and tenderness'.[4] Australian sculptor Rosemary Madigan became best known for her carved female torsos, of which she created several during her career. Mary Beard, an eminent historian and producer of the BBC series *Shock of the Nude*, volunteered to be painted nude. She quite enjoyed the experience and 'didn't mind being leered at'.[5]

Even such notorious exponents of the 'male gaze' as the nineteenth-century painter Pierre-Auguste Renoir, who had taken 'such presumptuous, slavering joy in looking at naked women' in 2020, had his female defenders. The editor of *Symposium*, Peter Tracinsci, asserted that 'political messaging about race and gender, indeed the whole contemporary ideology of "identity politics" was now becoming the dominant standard for judging art'.[6]

> Pleasure, once celebrated, now sets off alarm bells. It must mean kitsch, or misogyny, or bourgeois blandness, or – even worse – that we are not serious viewers of art.[7]

The Shakespearean scholar Marylin Simon observed:

> Renoir's nudes are the evidence of a tirelessly hopeful soul struggling against the dingy reality of the modern world, with its modern industry and its modern warfare, that turns all human flesh into disposable objects, without joy or humanity.[8]

It was in August 1968 that Robin Wallace-Crabbe noted that Dabro, while an accomplished sculptor, had not yet become Dabro. Forty years later, it was clear that he had fulfilled the potential that his teacher Antun Augustinčić had invested in him in the 1960s, a figurative modeller in a world of abstract sculpture. He has lost count of his works sold, while his skill in three-dimensional portraiture has attracted dozens of commissions.

Of the achievement of a lifetime's work, opinions differ. Phillip Bacon remained a constant admirer, while Sasha Grishin judged Dabro's best years to be the risky, expressive and challenging works of the 1970s. The period with Snow, to Grishin, marked a retreat because his patron demanded a more

Making Way 193

traditional and classically beautiful style that misdirected Dabro's development.[9] Nick Stranks, bronze-caster, sculptor and Dabro's close associate, reflected:

> I think in some ways Ante's softened. Since his grandchildren were born I've seen a new sensitivity. It is really nice to see these warm studies, they're really beautiful and sensitive works. In a lot of ways I enjoy some of Ante's smaller works. They're some of his smaller studies in wax, only a couple of inches long, figurative and abstract at the same time, really lovely gestural pieces. He's got an amazing collection of works, an incredible body of work that represents a serious amount of enquiry. He's made a significant contribution to Canberra where he has been quietly working in his studio. He hasn't gone out to the public with exhibitions, and he hasn't had to.

Ed Hayes asked why anyone should call Dabro a dinosaur. No successful artist ever needed an annual re-invention: 'If that's what your best stuff is, just keep doing it'. Hayes judged the Naval Memorial to be a perfect example of the best of multicultural Australia [that is, the intermingling of several artistic traditions] of the 1970s and 1980s. People would admire it for the next thousand years. 'That's if we don't get invaded'.

By 1980, Dabro had acquired an unmistakable style. Two decades later, he had freed himself from Rodin; even Michelangelo had become more of an orbiting planet than a guiding star. He never apologised for his devotion to the Renaissance; now, *Dancer* and *Genesis* had broken free from the sculptural contours of old Italy. Dabro had indeed become Dabro.

If his students missed his philosophy, then they carried another gift: the osmosis of a passionate artist. Add the tools of Dabro's sculptural language: the ability to size a work to its surroundings, his sense of sculptural rhythm, the potential of negative space, the power of a visual memory, the virtue of intense perception, the strength of a deep artistic tradition, the sheer craftsmanship that flows from a decade of strict instruction, the endless subtlety in imagining the human form, the way that sculpture, like music, can take the viewer on an emotional as well as physical journey that returns the eye to where it began. Even now, these qualities are hovering above the echoing floor of a concrete maintenance shed beside a noisy Canberra runway.

February 2023. Dabro has arrived at the usual time at his new studio, a huge converted RAAF workshop, set aside for his use by Terry Snow and Stephen Byron. It is draughty and dusty. Dabro prefers the intimacy of the cramped fire station that formed his first studio, but in time this structure will

194 THE LIFE AND WORK OF ANTE DABRO

have a ceiling that will resonate less after the last, huge sculptures like the *Return of Homo Sapiens* arrive from storage. Whatever its defects, it is the current and possibly the permanent repository for the extant productions of a working life. Today, tomahawk, spatula, penknife, chisel, scissors and rasp are lining up to give life to a very odd configuration of sticks wrapped in hessian. He'll put plaster on it tomorrow and see what, if anything, emerges.

The largest casts of *Mother and Child, Genesis* and *The Bathers* first seize the eye of the visitor. In a corner, lurk the tiny waxes: horses, a crucifix, an original cast of *Dancer,* two Churchills in conversation, dozens of the human shapes in dozens of contorted poses that Stranks so admired. On a huge table stand dozens of objects rescued from the dusty floor: a plaster pregnant woman, a heroic forearm and fist clutching with difficulty a rectangular block. Karl Marx is still surrounded by his sycophantic admirers. The artist himself has impaled himself on a long pole through the stomach, like an Egyptian tomb-robber. A female figure has four legs but no arms. On a desk, a drawing pad is covered with human figures. Here's an ecstatic wax horse whose tail has fallen off, a nude Terry Snow, a baby perched on its mother's shoulder, loving busts of three of the grandchildren and an intriguing female head. Each of the hundreds of wax or plaster figures in the studio has been born from the emotion of the moment, or the week. Or out of the life force that for fathomless generations has driven men and women towards each other. Lying on the edge of the table is an energetic plaster sculpture of three figures crouching hunched together in a conspiratorial whisper. Their heads abut in a hairy tangle.

I remark:

This is a very strong work.
Yes, they're my threesome.
Has it been cast?
Oh yes. And sold.
Who to?
I've no idea.
Is this nearest figure male or female?
I've no idea.

'I kept the flame alive.' Dabro's mantras that he repeats more often these days are not those of an artist who despaired of the value of art or the impossibility of reproducing the human form. This is not the grief of Goya's old age, but a glimpse of seven decades of serious enquiry, a lifetime's passionate response to

FIGURE 9.2

Luca, Evey and Max, plaster, 2009–2015, .5 life size. Source: Con Boekel.

Three of my grandchildren, Luca, Evey and Max. I love them all dearly.

the summer as well as the winter of human life.[10] Disillusionment and anger unite with joy, curiosity, love, heroism and beauty to drive the complex emotions that bear the artist every day to the airport studio.

After this last studio visit, Dabro's biographer Read and photographer Boekel departed.

Conversation over some maintenance issue drifts through the industrial windows and metal walls and fades. There's no more sound than a pencil moving on the drawing pad. Crouched at the desk a little like Dürer's engraving of *St Jerome in His Study*, Dabro yet again invokes a dialogue with Michelangelo. His mind rehearses his most recent visit to Florence in July 2022. Two hundred metres from his hotel to the bridge that crosses the Arno, then it's a straight line to Santa Croce and Michelangelo's tomb. The mystical exchange begins, as usual, with a respectful greeting. As he ages, Dabro is more preoccupied than ever with how in the long ages his work will be measured.

Dabro: Good morning Maestro.

Michelangelo: Hello again. I'm here, as usual, not far from my Bandini Pietà. I'm always close to my children. Yes, young feller, I know who you are. You're that *vlaj* from across the water in Dalmatia. I remember your great great great great great grandfather. People have told me what an inspiring place it was for young artists to grow up in Split. Diocletian's Palace. I hope you made the most of it. Are you still carving?

Dabro: These days I find that plaster is more subtle in just working with my chisel. You and I know that the greatest art is figurative and the greatest figurative art is the human form.

Michelangelo: We've dreamed all our pieces again and again and they have become us.

There's a nobility as well as the essence of humanity that is always just out of our reach. Even mine.

Dabro: In 2023 and in Australia, people think I'm a dinosaur. I've got used to it and am almost proud of it. Did they think you were old fashioned?

Michelangelo: No no. And I wasn't, either. I was just a grumpy old man who was quite happy to work all night with only a candle and not talk to anybody and forget to eat. People mostly kept away from me because I was full of opinions that everybody got tired of.

Dabro: I can understand that. It's like that in my family.

Michelangelo: What sort of work do you do?

Dabro: Bronze. Plaster cast to bronze. Big and small human figures. You worked with men, I work mostly with women. But we're all equal, we're all humans. I just hope that my life's work has been good enough.

Michelangelo: We're all humans, boy. And to tell you the truth, I was never so good with nude females. Now I hope you have some sense of restraint. Styles come and go. Stay true to yourself and don't get pushed into new fashions by the Pope or whoever is paying for your work. Now, is there anything in particular you want to ask me?

Dabro: Well Maestro, you said you've seen the shades of many departed artists who slide past you on their way to the underworld. Well – Where are you then?

Michelangelo: I'm in the special place reserved for great artists.

Dabro: Will I be there too?

Michelangelo: Ah well that's an interesting question. I know the answer. And you don't. You'll have to wait a few hundred years before you find out.

In the mean time, just remember this: Life is very short and art is very long.[11]

FIGURE 9.3

Ante Dabro, 2023, Studio. Source: Con Boekel.

Ante Dabro was five years old when, in May 1943, the Australian poet Douglas Stewart was fishing on the Cowan Creek, near Sydney. It was full tide, and midnight. The moon, he wrote in his poem *Rock Carving*, lit 'a thousand candles upon the water'.[12] The ebb tide set; and as the line grew slack and the boat tugged at the anchor, there fell upon Stewart a sombre moment of reflection, not that of the solitary muse but the loneliness of the outcast. Where would the mind make camp, Stewart pondered, in an empty pattern of human life as cold and inhuman as the tide? Was there no relief from the certainty that all things must pass?

Stewart's torch caught the contours of a centuries-old Aboriginal rock carving.

FIGURE 9.4

Dabro in his new studio, Canberra Airport, 2023. Source: Con Boekel.

The act of creation to me is no different than breathing.

Shine the torch on the rock; we are not the first
Alone and lost in this world of water and stone.

There on the rock was a carving of a kangaroo. In the shaft of light, the poet felt the touch of spiritual connection with his long-dead fellow artist. 'Fishermen both, and carvers both, old man!' Stewart the wordsmith knew that the mark made by either European pen or Aboriginal chisel might well be lost to wind and weather. Yet the genius of the poet or sculptor might survive to assuage that desolation of the mind's last understanding that life is finite. The imaginative response followed. Look for it on the page or the stave, the dancefloor and the canvas, the rockface and the ritual; and the sculpture in *bihacit, mulika*, wood, marble, alabaster, bronze, plaster or stone.

The passion and the offence, the prejudice and the trauma will pass, but the creations of artists remain to still the midnight sea that swirls in the very blood of human existence.

That is the gift of the artist from them to us and from us to them.

Who can do more than that?

NOTES

Introduction: Making a Mark in Stone

1. Martin Edmond, 'Review *Australian Art: A History*, by Sasha Grishin', *Sydney Review of Books*, 29 July 2014, https://sydneyreviewofbooks.com/review/australian-art-history-sasha-grishin/.
2. Peter Haynes, Curator statement on *Now You See Me, Now You Don't*, Canberra Museum and Gallery, 2003, http://www.cmag.com.au/collection/items/now-you-see-me-now-you-don-t/detail.
3. Sigmund Freud, 'The Moses of Michelangelo', in *The Standard Edition of the Complete Psychological Works of Sigmund Freud*, ed. James Strachey et al. (London: Hogarth Press, 1913–14), vol. XIII, 209–38 (230).
4. National Gallery of Australia, *Rodin, Sculpture and Drawings* (Canberra: NGA, 2000), 43–44.
5. Anne Wagner, 'Miss Hepworth's Stone is a Mother', in *Sculpture and Psychoanalysis*, ed. Brandon Taylor (Leeds: Ashgate, 2006), 71–94.
6. William Turner, *The Fighting Temeraire*, Wikipedia, 25 February 2023, https://en.wikipedia.org/wiki/The_Fighting_Temeraire.
7. Lin Onus, *Firing the Humpy*, 1990, National Museum of Australia, https://collectionsearch.nma.gov.au.
8. Bertolt Brecht, 'On the Term of Exile', translated by Adam Kirsch, reproduced by permission of the translator, The Poetry Foundation, June 2011, https://www.poetryfoundation.org/poetrymagazine/poems/54759/on-the-term-of-exile.
9. Anthonis Mor, *Mary Tudor, Queen of England* (1554), Museo del Prado, https://www.museodelprado.es/en/the-collection/art-work/mary-tudor-queen-of-england/aef6ebc4-081a-44e6-974d-6c24aef95fc4?searchid=51f46267-5307-2cdf-8927-33be1244a4a8.
10. 'Bulls of Guisando', Wikipedia, 20 October 2022, https://en.wikipedia.org/wiki/Bulls_of_Guisando.
11. '*The Deposition* (Michelangelo)', Wikipedia, 21 February 2023, https://en.wikipedia.org/wiki/The_Deposition_(Michelangelo).

CHAPTER 1: Making the Outsider

1. Adapted from 'January 1938', Wikipedia, 28 February 2023, https://en.wikipedia.org/wiki/January_1938.
2. Paul Trathern, *The Florentines* (London: Pegasus, 2019), 46.
3. Wordsworth, *The Prelude*, Book ll (441–46), The Poetry Foundation, accessed 26 March 2023, https://www.poetryfoundation.org/poems/45543/the-prelude-book-2-school-time-continued.
4. Granville Crawford, quoted in Peter Read, *Returning to Nothing* (Melbourne: Cambridge University Press, 1996), 54.
5. Sharon Zukin, *Beyond Marx and Tito. Theory and Practice in Jugoslav Socialism* (Euston: Cambridge University Press, 1975), 75.
6. Melissa K. Bokovoy, 'Collectivisation in Yugoslavia. Rethinking Regional and National Interests', in *The Collectivization of Agriculture in Communist Eastern Europe*, ed. Constantin Lordachi and Arnd Bauerkämper, 251–92 (Budapest: Central European University Press, 2014), 251–92 (251); Constantin Lordachi and Arnd Bauerkämper, *The Collectivisation of Agriculture in Communist Eastern Europe* (Budapest: Central European University Press, 2014), 56.

CHAPTER 2: Making the Artist

1. This had come about through one of his cousins, Šimun, taking a box of smaller *mulika* sculptures to the School Director for assessment.
2. National Gallery of Australia, *Rodin, Sculpture and Drawings* (Canberra: NGA, 2001), 83, 87.
3. *Starohrvatska prosvjeta III*. Serija—Svezak 35 (2008): 123–33 (133).
4. Wordsworth, *The Prelude*, Book ll.
5. Giulio Argan, *Džamonja* (Beograd: Mladost, 1981), 53.
6. Ibid., 60.
7. Catherine Hunter, prod. and dir., *Jeffrey Smart*, documentary, 2022, https://nga.gov.au/on-demand/jeffrey-smart-documentary/.
8. The imagined exchanges that Dabro regularly holds with Michelangelo have been composed by the author, following Dabro's suggestions as to the nature of the conversations.
9. Varchi, *Due Lezzione di M. Benedetto Varchi* (Florence, 1550).
10. Dabro and Zlatika divorced in 1965.
11. 'Relief Sculpture', *Encyclopaedia Britannica*, no date, accessed 25 March 2023, https://www.britannica.com/art/sculpture/Relief-sculpture.
12. Alfred Lord Tennyson, 'Ulysses' (1833 ll. 19–21), The Poetry Foundation, September 2018, https://www.poetryfoundation.org/poems/45392/ulysses.
13. Joseph Conrad, *The Shadow Line. A Confession* (1916), The Project Gutenberg, 9 September 2016, https://www.gutenberg.org/files/451/451-h/451-h.htm.
14. Joseph Conrad, Preface to *The Nigger of the Narcissus: A Tale of the Forecastle* (1897), The Project Gutenberg, 2 March 2018, https://www.gutenberg.org/files/17731/17731-h/17731-h.htm.

Notes 201

CHAPTER 3: Making the Australian

1. Drawn in part from Nicholas Brown, *A History of Canberra* (Port Melbourne: Cambridge University Press, 2014).
2. Dabro repeated this story in an article about himself, *The Canberra Times*, 14 January 2023.
3. Interview, Lola del Mar, Canberra, April 2022.
4. Ken Scarlett, *Australian Sculptors* (Melbourne: Nelson, 1980) xix.
5. Brenda Neill, *The Boyds. A Family Biography* (Carlton: Miegunyah Press, 2002), 354–56.
6. A. D. Hope, 'Australia', in *Australian Poetry*, ed. R. G. Haworth (Sydney: Angus and Robertson, 1945), 21–22.
7. Bernard Smith, *The Death of the Artist as Hero* (Carlton: Melbourne University Press, 1988), 181, 189.
8. Deborah Edwards, '20th Century Australian Art: Abstraction in the 1950s and '60s'. Sydney, Art Gallery of NSW, no date, accessed 25 March 2023, https://www.artgallery.nsw.gov.au/artsets/liohiq/slideshow.
9. See also the National Gallery of Australia Catalogue, *The Antipodeans: Challenge and Response in Australian Art 1955–1965* (Canberra: NGA, 1988), 42–43 (Manifesto), 194–216.
10. *The Canberra Times*, 13 August 1968.
11. *The Canberra Times*, 25 September 1968.
12. 'John Olsen', in Barry Pearce, *Australian Art in the Art Gallery of New South Wales* (Sydney: Art Gallery of New South Wales, 2000), 249–50.
13. Les Murray, 'Louvres', in *Les Murray: Collected Poems* (Melbourne: William Heinemann, 1994), 241.
14. Rosemary Madigan interviewed by James Gleeson, 1 January 1979, National Gallery of Australia, John Gleeson Oral History Collection, https://nga.gov.au/on-demand/rosemary-madigan-interview/.
15. Interview Tony Stuart-Smith, 11 September 2022.
16. In 1969 Dabro, now in Canberra, in error contracted a proxy marriage conducted in Zagreb. Both partners soon realised the mistake and mutually dissolved the contract.
17. Michael Agostino, *The ANU School of Art. A History of the First 65 Years* (Canberra: ANU Press, 2010), provides a guide to staffing in these decades, available online at: https://press-files.anu.edu.au/downloads/press/n1667/pdf/book.pdf.
18. David Brook, *The Sydney Morning Herald*, 25 June 1969.
19. Interview, Tony Stuart-Smith, 11 September 2022.
20. Dabro later confronted Brook with the fact that he had never heard of Klippel at the time. Brook apologised to him personally and in print.
21. *The Sun*, 25 June 1969.
22. Peter Haynes, curator, *Humanscapes*, Exhibition Catalogue, Canberra, March 2004.
23. Paul Klee, 'Exact Experiments in the Realm of Art' (1928), Art History Project, accessed 25 March 2023, https://arthistoryproject.com/artists/paul-klee/exact-experiments-in-the-realm-of-art/.

202 *Notes*

24. James Gleeson, comment on Klippel's *Op 329* and *714*, in *Robert Klippel* (Kensington: Bay Books, 1983); Rosemary Madigan interviewed by Deborah Edwards, 9 June 1994, Balmain, Sydney; Barry Pearce et al., *Australian Art in the Art Gallery of New South Wales* (Sydney: AGNSW, 2000), 274, 222.
25. Anon, 'Magna Carta Design Competition. Statement of Design', 1 November 1999.
26. 'Magna Carta Place', Australian Government/National Capital Authority, Canberra, no date, accessed 20 March 2023, https://www.nca.gov.au/attractions/magna-carta-place.
27. Art in America. 'Aught Culture: The Exhibitions that Defined the 2000s and Pointed the Way to the Present', 8 December 2020, https://www.artnews.com/list/art-in-america/features/the-exhibitions-that-defined-the-2000s-1234578321/.
28. Daniel Thomas, *Recent Past. Writing Australian Art* (Sydney: Art Gallery of NSW, 2020), 95.
29. *The Canberra Times*, 2 February 1977, Maloney quoted by Edna Boling.
30. Virginia Ironside, 'We Paid the Price for Free Love. The Flipside of the Sexual Revolution', *The Daily Mail*, 19 January 2011, https://www.dailymail.co.uk/home/you/article-1346813/The-flip-1960s-sexual-revolution-We-paid-price-free-love.html.
31. Anne Summers, *Damned Whores and God's Police: The Colonisation of Women in Australia* (Ringwood: Penguin, 1975).
32. *Diagonal Direction*, in Peter Haynes, *Ante Dabro and the Aesthetics of Ambiguity, Survey Exhibition 1968–1999* (Canberra: Arts ACT, 1999), 5.
33. *The Canberra Times*, 9 June 1970.
34. *The Canberra Times*, 24 April 1979.
35. *The Canberra Times*, 15 November 1980.
36. *The Canberra Times*, 26 November 1977.
37. Sasha Grishin, *The Canberra Times*, 15 November 1980.
38. Catalogues and pricelist kindly supplied by Phillip Bacon Galleries.
39. Dabro Family Video, Lonerock Productions, 2000.
40. David Malouf, *An Imaginary Life* (Sydney: Vintage, 1999), 13.

CHAPTER 4: Making the Human Form

1. For the discussion of the experience of working with Dabro, and of being an artist's model generally, I am grateful to Susan Boden-Brown, interview, 13 October 2021.

CHAPTER 5: Making Bronze

1. Drawn from Derek Parker, *Cellini. Artist, Genius, Fugitive* (Sutton: Phoenix Mill, 2003), 192–95.
2. Homer, *The Odyssey*, Book 5, The Literature Page, accessed 25 March 2023, http://www.literaturepage.com/read/theodyssey-83.html.
3. 'National Memorial to the Royal Australian Navy'. Royal Australian Navy, accessed 25 March 2023, https://www.navy.gov.au/customs-and-traditions/national-memorial-royal-australian-navy.

Notes 203

4. *Encyclopaedia Britannica* defines *ciment fondu as* 'a cement most widely used by sculptors [...] which is extremely hard and quick setting.'
5. Dabro particularly thanks the team of highly skilled welders and his water engineer: 'They were marvellous.'
6. *The Canberra Times*, 24 February 1986.
7. Tennyson, 'Ulysses'.
8. Sasha Grishin, *The Canberra Times*, 9 May 1986.

CHAPTER 6: Making Sculptors

1. In his 1947 sculpture *Le Nez*, Giacometti 'saw himself as a realist, attempting the "impossible" project of representing the appearance of things as he saw them, in a manner acknowledging that our comprehension of the perceived world is never fixed but constantly subject to change'; Alberto Giacometti, 'Alberto Giacometti: [brochure] The Museum of Modern Art, October 11, 2021–January 8, 2022', https://www.moma.org/documents/moma_catalogue _165_300204588.pdf.
2. Ed Hayes, interview, 8 December 2022.
3. Ibid.
4. Quoted in Nola Anderson, *Glass: The Life and Art of Klaus Moje* (Kensington: Newsouth, 2021), 82.
5. Bruce Sutherland, interview, 10 January 2023.
6. Walter Gropius cited in 'History of the Bauhaus', Getty Research Institute, no date, accessed 24 March 2023, https://www.getty.edu/research/exhibitions _events/exhibitions/bauhaus/new_artist/history/.
7. Anderson, *Glass*, 83.
8. Walter Gropius, 'Bauhaus Manifesto 1919', Gropius House, no date, accessed 24 March 2023, https://gropius.house/location/bauhaus-manifesto/.
9. 'Canberra School of Art, Accreditation Submission', 1977 cited in Agostino, *The ANU School of Art*, 28.
10. Jan Brown, interview, cited in Agostino, *The ANU School of Art*, 26.
11. Interview, Julie Bassett, 18 November 2021.
12. Interview, Julie Basset, October 2022; Bruce Sutherland, pers. com., 16 January 2022.
13. Ibid.
14. Agostino, *The ANU School of Art*, 43.
15. Interview, Sascha Grishin, January 2023.
16. Simone de Beauvoir, *The Second Sex*, trans. H. M. Parshley (London: Jonathan Cape, 1953 [1949]); John Berger, *Ways of Seeing*, TV series, BBC Two, 1972, and *Ways of Seeing* (Harmondsworth: Penguin, 1972); and Laura Mulvey, 'Visual Pleasure and Narrative Cinema' (1975), in *Film Theory and Criticism: Introductory Readings*, ed. Leo Braudy and Marshall Cohen (New York: Oxford University Press, 1985), 833–44.
17. Mulvey, 'Visual Pleasure', 843.
18. Nick Stranks, interview, 25 October 2022.
19. Agostino, *The ANU School of Art*, 35.
20. Ante Dabro, *Reclining Figure* (University of Canberra), no date, accessed 26 March 2023, https://studentvip.com.au/uc/main/maps/139418.
21. Nick Stranks, interview, 25 October 2022.

204 *Notes*

22. Lyn McCredden, 'In His Last Poems, Les Murray Offers a Gentle, Gracious Bow of Farewell, and Just a Few Barbs', *The Conversation*, 28 February 2022, https://theconversation.com/in-his-last-poems-les-murray-offers-a-gentle-gracious-bow-of-farewell-and-just-a-few-barbs-176535.
23. Les Murray, 'Continuous Creation', cited in McCredden, 'In His Last Poems'.

CHAPTER 7: Making Commissions

1. National Gallery of Australia, *Rodin, Sculpture and Drawings*, 43–44.
2. See also, P. Read, 'Fantasy on One Note', in *Writing History. Imagination and Narrative*, ed, A. Curthoys and A. McGrath (Monash University: Monash Publications in History, 2000), 40–44.
3. Judith Wright, 'Woman to Man', Lyrik Line, no date, accessed 26 March 2023, https://www.lyrikline.org/en/poems/woman-man-1239; and 'Bora Ring', Poetry Nook, no date, accessed 26 March 2023, https://www.poetrynook.com/poem/bora-ring.
4. 'Karen', no. 14 in 'ANU Sculpture Walk', brochure, Australian National University, Canberra, December 2010, https://services.anu.edu.au/files/guidance/Sculpture-Walk-Brochure_0.pdf.

CHAPTER 8: Making Behemoths

1. Gustavo Pérez Firmat, *Cincuenta lecciones de exilio y desexilio* (Miami: Ediciones Universal, 2000), 51.
2. The information in this section is drawn from an interview with Terry Snow, 11 November 2121.
3. Interview, Terry Snow, 11 November 2121.
4. Megan Doherty, 'Public Art the Private Sector's Gift with Soul', *The Age*, 25 May 2013, https://www.theage.com.au/national/act/public-art-the-private-sectors-gift-with-soul-20130524-2k7e4.html.
5. 'Among School Children', in *Yeats's Poems*, ed. A. Norman Jeffares (London: Macmillan/Papermac, 1989), 325.
6. 'Dancing in the Park!', *The Hub*, Issue 28, June 2005.
7. Dabro, lecture notes.
8. David Campbell, 'The Heart of the Matter' and 'The Red Page', *The Bulletin*, 1 January 1958.
9. The face of Dabro's Australian Terrier 'Chico' appears on the base of *Genesis*.
10. Gian Lorenzo Bernini, *The Ecstasy of Saint Theresa* (1652), Artble, no date, accessed 27 March 2023, https://www.artble.com/artists/gian_lorenzo_bernini/sculpture/the_ecstasy_of_saint_theresa.
11. Interview, Stephen Byron, 6 May 2022.

CHAPTER 9: Making Way

1. Drawn from Nick Stranks, interview, 25 October 2022.
2. Christopher Allen, '"Political Gesture": The Art of Cruelty', *The Australian*, 14–15 May 2022.
3. Brecht, 'On the Term of Exile'.
4. Gregory Day, 'Review *Barbara Hepworth: Art and Life* by Eleanor Clayton', *Australian Book Review* (October 2021): 64.
5. *Mary Beard's Shock of the Nude*. TV series, BBC Two, 2020.
6. Peter Tracinski, commenting on an article on Renoir by Peter Schjeldahl. Tracinski, 'Renoir is Cancelled: Identity Politics Didacticism is Taking Over the Art World', *The Bulwark*, 28 October 2019; Peter Schjeldahl, 'Renoir's Problem Nudes', *The New Yorker*, 19 August 2019, https://www.newyorker.com/magazine/2019/08/26/renoirs-problem-nudes.
7. Martha Lucy, writing for the Clark Art Institute's exhibition catalogue for the exhibition, 'Renoir: The Body, The Senses', cited in Lydia Figes, 'Revered or Reviled: Do We Still Like Renoir?' Art UK, 2 December 2019, https://artuk.org/discover/stories/revered-or-reviled-do-we-still-like-renoir.
8. Marilyn Simon, 'In Praise of Renoir's Male Gaze', *Quilette*, 10 September 2019, https://quillette.com/2019/09/10/in-praise-of-renoirs-male-gaze/.
9. Phillip Bacon and Sasha Grishin, phone discussions.
10. Robert Hughes, *Goya* (Milsons Point: Vintage, 2003), 379.
11. Conversation written by the author at Dabro's request.
12. Douglas Stewart, 'Rock Carving', *The Bulletin* 64, no. 3302 (26 May 1943): 2.

WORKS CONSULTED

Agostino, Michael. *The ANU School of Art. A History of the First 65 Years.* Canberra: ANU Press, 2010. https://press-files.anu.edu.au/downloads/press/n1667/pdf/book.pdf.

Allen, Christopher. '"Political Gesture": The Art of Cruelty', *The Australian*, 14–15 May 2022.

Anderson, Nola. *Glass: The Life and Art of Klaus Moje.* Kensington: Newsouth, 2021.

Anon. 'Magna Carta Design Competition. Statement of Design', 1 November 1999.

Argan, Giuilo. *Džamonja.* Beograd: Mladost, 1981.

Art in America. 'Aught Culture: The Exhibitions that Defined the 2000s and Pointed the Way to the Present', 8 December 2020. https://www.artnews.com/list/art-in-america/features/the-exhibitions-that-defined-the-2000s-1234578321/.

'Australian National University Sculpture Walk', brochure, ANU, Canberra, December 2010. https://services.anu.edu.au/files/guidance/Sculpture-Walk-Brochure_0.pdf.

Berger, John. *Ways of Seeing.* Television series, BBC Two, 1972.

Berger, John. *Ways of Seeing.* Harmondsworth: Penguin, 1972.

Bernini, Gian Lorenzo. *The Ecstasy of Saint Theresa* (1652), Artble, no date, accessed 27 March 2023. https://www.artble.com/artists/gian_lorenzo_bernini/sculpture/the_ecstasy_of_saint_theresa.

Bokovoy, Melissa K. 'Collectivisation in Yugoslavia. Rethinking Regional and National Interests'. In *The Collectivization of Agriculture in Communist Eastern Europe*, edited by Constantin Lordachi and Arnd Bauerkämper, 251–92. Budapest: Central European University Press, 2014.

Brecht, Bertolt. 'On the Term of Exile', translated by Adam Kirsch. The Poetry Foundation, June 2011. https://www.poetryfoundation.org/poetrymagazine/poems/54759/on-the-term-of-exile.

Brown, Nicholas. *A History of Canberra.* Port Melbourne: Cambridge University Press, 2014.

'Bulls of Guisando'. Wikipedia, 20 October 2022. https://en.wikipedia.org/wiki/Bulls_of_Guisando.

Campbell, David. 'The Heart of the Matter', 'The Red Page', *Bulletin*, 1 January 1958.

Canberra School of Art, Accreditation Submission, 1977.

'Ciment Fondu'. Encyclopaedia Britannica, no date, accessed 25 March 2023. https://www.britannica.com/technology/ciment-fondu.

208 *Works Consulted*

Clayton, Eleanor. *Barbara Hepworth: Art and Life*. London: Thames and Hudson, 2021.

Conrad, Joseph. *The Nigger of the Narcissus: A Tale of the Forecastle* (1897). The Project Gutenberg, 2 March 2018. https://www.gutenberg.org/files/17731/17731-h/17731-h.htm.

Conrad, Joseph. *The Shadow Line. A Confession* (1916). The Project Gutenberg, 9 September 2016. https://www.gutenberg.org/files/451/451-h/451-h.htm.

Dabro, Ante. *Reclining Figure* (University of Canberra), no date, accessed 26 March 2023. https://studentvip.com.au/uc/main/maps/139418.

Dabro Family Video. Lonerock Productions, 2000.

'Dancing in the Park!' *The Hub* 28, June 2005.

Day, Gregory. Review *Barbara Hepworth: Art and Life* by Eleanor Clayton. *Australian Book Review* (October 2021): 64.

de Beauvoir, Simone. *The Second Sex*, translated by H. M. Parshley. London: Jonathan Cape, 1953 (1949).

'*The Deposition* (Michelangelo)'. Wikipedia, 21 February 2023. https://en.wikipedia.org/wiki/The_Deposition_(Michelangelo).

Doherty, Megan. 'Public Art the Private Sector's Gift with Soul', *The Age*, 25 May 2013. https://www.theage.com.au/national/act/public-art-the-private-sectors-gift-with-soul-20130524-2k7e4.html.

Edmond, Martin. 'Review *Australian Art: A History*, by Sasha Grishin', *Sydney Review of Books*, 29 July 2014. https://sydneyreviewofbooks.com/review/australian-art-history-sasha-grishin/.

Edwards, Deborah, '20th Century Australian Art: Abstraction in the 1950s and '60s'. Sydney, Art Gallery of NSW, no date, accessed 25 March 2023. https://www.artgallery.nsw.gov.au/artsets/liohiq/slideshow.

Figes, Lydia. 'Revered or Reviled: Do We Still Like Renoir?' Art UK, 2 December 2019. https://artuk.org/discover/stories/revered-or-reviled-do-we-still-like-renoir.

Freud, Sigmund. 'The Moses of Michelangelo'. In *The Standard Edition of the Complete Psychological Works of Sigmund Freud*, edited by James Strachey et al., vol. XIII, 209–38. London: Hogarth Press, 1913–14.

Giacometti, Alberto. 'Alberto Giacometti: [brochure] The Museum of Modern Art, October 11, 2021–January 8, 2022'. https://www.moma.org/documents/moma_catalogue_165_300204588.pdf.

Gleeson, James. *Robert Klippel*. Kensington: Bay Books, 1983.

Gropius, Walter. 'Bauhaus Manifesto 1919'. Gropius House, no date, accessed 24 March 2023. https://gropius.house/location/bauhaus-manifesto/.

Haynes, Peter. *Ante Dabro and the Aesthetics of Ambiguity, Survey Exhibition 1968–1999*. Canberra: Arts ACT, 1999.

Haynes, Peter, Curator. *Humanscapes*, Exhibition Catalogue, Canberra, March 2004.

Haynes, Peter. Curator statement on *Now You See Me, Now You Don't*, Canberra Museum and Gallery, 2003. http://www.cmag.com.au/collection/items/now-you-see-me-now-you-don-t/detail.

'History of the Bauhaus'. Getty Research Institute, no date, accessed 24 March 2023. https://www.getty.edu/research/exhibitions_events/exhibitions/bauhaus/new_artist/history/.

Works Consulted

209

Homer. *The Odyssey*, Book 5. The Literature Page, accessed 25 March 2023. http://www.literaturepage.com/read/theodyssey-83.html.

Hope, A. D. 'Australia'. In *Australian Poetry*, edited by R. G. Howarth, 21–22. Sydney: Angus and Robertson, 1945.

Hughes, Robert. *Goya*. Milsons Point: Vintage, 2003.

Hunter, Catherine, prod. and dir. Jeffrey Smart, documentary, 2022. https://nga.gov.au/on-demand/jeffrey-smart-documentary/.

Ironside, Virginia. 'We Paid the Price for Free Love. The Flipside of the Sexual Revolution', *The Daily Mail*, 19 January 2011. https://www.dailymail.co.uk/home/you/article-1346813/The-flip-1960s-sexual-revolution-We-paid-price-free-love.html.

'January 1938'. Wikipedia, 28 February 2023. https://en.wikipedia.org/wiki/January_1938.

Klee, Paul. 'Exact Experiments in the Realm of Art' (1928). Art History Project, accessed 25 March 2023. https://arthistoryproject.com/artists/paul-klee/exact-experiments-in-the-realm-of-art/.

Lordachi, Constantin and Arnd Bauerkämper, eds. *The Collectivisation of Agriculture in Communist Eastern Europe*. Budapest: Central European University Press, 2014.

Lovelace, Richard. 'To Lucasta, Going to the Wars'. Poetry Foundation, 2023. https://www.poetryfoundation.org/poems/44658/to-lucasta-going-to-the-wars.

Madigan, Rosemary, interviewed by Deborah Edwards, 9 June 1994. Balmain, Sydney, NSW.

Madigan, Rosemary, interviewed by James Gleeson, 1 January 1979. National Gallery of Australia, John Gleeson Oral History Collection. https://nga.gov.au/on-demand/rosemary-madigan-interview/.

'Magna Carta Place [Design Brief]'. Australian Government/National Capital Authority, Canberra, no date, accessed 20 March 2023. https://www.nca.gov.au/attractions/magna-carta-place.

Malouf, David. *An Imaginary Life*. Sydney: Vintage, 1999.

Mary Beard's Shock of the Nude. Television series, BBC Two, 2020.

McCredden, Lyn, 'In His Last Poems, Les Murray Offers a Gentle, Gracious Bow of Farewell, and Just a Few Barbs', *The Conversation*, 28 February 2022. https://theconversation.com/in-his-last-poems-les-murray-offers-a-gentle-gracious-bow-of-farewell-and-just-a-few-barbs-176535.

McInerney, Rebecca. 'The Male Gaze', Art History Perspectives, 2 April 2021. https://www.arthistoryperspectives.com/posts/themalegaze.

Mor, Anthonis. *Mary Tudor, Queen of England*, 1554. Museo del Prado. https://www.museodelprado.es/en/the-collection/art-work/mary-tudor-queen-of-england/aef6ebc4-081a-44e6-974d-6c24aef95fc4?searchid=51f46267-5307-2cdf-8927-33be1244a4a8.

Mulvey, Laura. 'Visual Pleasure and Narrative Cinema' (1975). In *Film Theory and Criticism: Introductory Readings*, edited by Leo Braudy and Marshall Cohen, 833–44. New York: Oxford University Press, 1999.

Murray, Les. *Continuous Creation: Last Poems*. Melbourne: Black Inc, 2022.

Murray, Les. *Les Murray: Collected Poems*. Melbourne: William Heinemann, 1994.

210 *Works Consulted*

National Gallery of Australia. *The Antipodeans: Challenge and Response in Australian Art 1955–1965.* Canberra: NGA, 1988.

National Gallery of Australia. *Rodin, Sculpture and Drawings.* Canberra: NGA, 2001.

'National Memorial to the Royal Australian Navy'. Royal Australian Navy, accessed 25 March 2023. https://www.navy.gov.au/customs-and-traditions/national-memorial-royal-australian-navy.

Neill, Brenda. *The Boyds. A Family Biography.* Carlton: Miegunyah Press, 2002.

Onus, Lin. *Firing the Humpy,* 1990. National Museum of Australia. https://collectionsearch.nma.gov.au.

Parker, Derek. *Cellini. Artist, Genius, Fugitive.* Sutton: Phoenix Mill, 2003.

Pearce, Barry. 'John Olsen'. In *Australian Art in the Art Gallery of New South Wales,* 249–50. Sydney: Art Gallery of New South Wales, 2000.

Pearce, Barry, et al. *Australian Art in the Art Gallery of New South Wales.* Sydney: Art Gallery of New South Wales, 2000.

Pérez Firmat, Gustavo. *Cincuenta lecciones de exilio y desexilio.* Miami: Ediciones Universal, 2000.

Read, Peter. *Returning to Nothing.* Melbourne: Cambridge University Press, 1996.

'Relief Sculpture'. *Encyclopaedia Britannica,* no date, accessed 25 March 2023. https://www.britannica.com/art/sculpture/Relief-sculpture.

Saunders, Gill. *The Nude.* London: Harper and Rowe, 1989.

Scarlett, Ken. *Australian Sculptors.* Melbourne: Nelson, 1980.

Schjeldahl, Peter. 'Renoir's Problem Nudes', *The New Yorker,* 19 August 2019. https://www.newyorker.com/magazine/2019/08/26/renoirs-problem-nudes.

Simon, Marilyn. 'In Praise of Renoir's Male Gaze', *Quilette,* 10 September 2019. https://quillette.com/2019/09/10/in-praise-of-renoirs-male-gaze/.

Smith, Bernard. *The Death of the Artist as Hero.* Carlton: Melbourne University Press, 1988.

Starohrvatska prosvjeta III. Serija—Svezak 35, 2008.

Stewart, Douglas. 'Rock Carving', *The Bulletin* 64, no. 3302 (26 May 1943): 2.

Summers, Anne. *Damned Whores and God's Police: The Colonisation of Women in Australia.* Ringwood: Penguin, 1975.

Tennyson, Alfred Lord. 'Ulysses' (1833). The Poetry Foundation, September 2018. https://www.poetryfoundation.org/poems/45392/ulysses.

Thomas, Daniel. *Recent Past. Writing Australian Art.* Sydney: Art Gallery of NSW, 2020.

Tracinski, Peter. 'Renoir is Cancelled: Identity Politics Didacticism is Taking over the Art World', *The Bulwark,* 28 October 2019. https://www.thebulwark.com/renoir-is-canceled/.

Trathern, Paul. *The Florentines.* London: Pegasus, 2019.

Turner, William. *The Fighting Temeraire.* Wikipedia, 25 February 2023. https://en.wikipedia.org/wiki/The_Fighting_Temeraire.

Varchi, Benedetto. *Due Lezzione di M. Benedetto Varchi.* Florence, 1550.

Wagner, Anne. 'Miss Hepworth's Stone is a Mother'. In *Sculpture and Psychoanalysis,* edited by Brandon Taylor, 71–94. Leeds: Ashgate, 2006.

Wordsworth, William. *The Prelude,* Book ll. The Poetry Foundation, no date, accessed 26 March 2023. https://www.poetryfoundation.org/poems/45543/the-prelude-book-2-school-time-continued.

Works Consulted   211

Wright, Judith. 'Bora Ring', Poetry Nook, no date, accessed 26 March 2023. https://www.poetrynook.com/poem/bora-ring.

Wright, Judith, 'Poetry and Universities' [1963]. In *Judith Wright: Selected Writings*, edited by Georgina Arnott, 51–59. Collingwood: La Trobe University Press, 2022.

Wright, Judith. 'Woman to Man'. Lyrik Line, no date, accessed 26 March 2023. https://www.lyrikline.org/en/poems/woman-man-1239.

Yeats, W. B. *Yeats's Poems*, edited by A. Norman Jeffares. London: Macmillan/Papermac, 1989.

Zukin, Sharon. *Beyond Marx and Tito. Theory and Practice in Yugoslav Socialism*. Euston: Cambridge University Press, 1975.

Interviews and discussions

Bacon, Phillip, phone discussions.

Basset, Julie, interview, 18 November 2021, October 2022.

Boden-Brown, Susan, interview, 13 October 2021.

Byron, Stephen, interview, 6 May 2022.

Dabro, Ante, interviews and discussions.

Del Mar, Lola, interview, April 2022.

Grishin, Sasha, interview, January 2023, and phone discussions.

Hayes, Ed, interview, 8 December 2022.

Snow, Terry, interview, 11 November 2021.

Stranks, Nick, interview, 25 October 2022.

Stuart-Smith, Tony, interview, 11 September 2022.

Sutherland, Bruce, interview, 10 January 2023.

INDEX

aboriginal culture 70–71
abstract expressionism 66
Academy of Fine Arts, Zagreb 40,
   48–49
air-raids 15
Alessi, Galeazzo 34
Alfred Deakin (Dabro work) 145
Allen, Christopher 190
Antipodean Manifesto 65–66
Anzac Parade, Canberra 112
Architecture, Roman 30
Architecture, Romanesque 31, 33, 56
Arthur, Jay 135
Augustinčić, Antun 7, 37, 48, 54–57
Australian Metalworkers Union 118
Australian Sculpture Gallery 79
Avenue Bathers (Dabro work) 177–79

Bacon, Phillip 79, 98, 100, 166
Badnjak, Christmas festival 13
Basset, Julie 134, 143, 149, 153, 158
Beaumont, Admiral 116
bergen (bird) 18
Beuys, Joseph 67, 71
Bihać 55
Blake, William 3
Boden-Brown, Susan 102–4, 108
Boško, Dabro 12
Boyd, Guy 63
Brecht, Bertolt 7, 199
Brindabella Business Park 104
bronze casting 109–11
Brook, David 70, 77
Brown, Jan 66, 68, 83, 137
The Bureaucrat (Dabro work) 169

Butler, Doreen 72, 92
Butler, Peter 76, 92, 135
Butterfly (Dabro work) 68
Button, John 147–48
Buvina 7, 20
Byron, Stephen 179, 185–86

Campbell, David 177
Canberra Airport 106
Canberra city 60–63
Canberra School of Art 66
Caro, Anthony 137
Cassab, Judy 3
casting techniques 109–12
Čavoglave 9, 11, 16, 187
Cellini 43, 109–11
ceramic Shell Casting 111
Četnik 18
Cezanne 29
Charnwood 80
Chiaroscuro technique 100
Ciment fondu technique 115
Commonwealth Aircraft Factory,
   Melbourne 118
Communist Party, Yugoslav 48, 118
Conrad, Joseph 58, 59
Contemplation (Dabro work) 154–57
Contrapunto technique 104
Corregio 34
Cossington-Smith, Margaret 64
Cowley, Brian 77
craft, opposed to Art 135
Crawford, Granville 18
Croatian civil war 151–54
Crucifix (Dabro work) 87

213

214 *Index*

Dabro, Anna 26
Dabro, Ante, opinions on art 1, 45, 47, 48, 94, 98, 102, 114, 142, 172, 174, 183, 185; opinions on life 4, 10, 82, 95, 145, 153, 187, 188; opinions on teaching, 130, *passim*
Dabro, Boško 12, 15
Dabro, Darinka 15
Dabro, Jessica 95
Dabro, Jole 15
Dabro, Maria 9, 14, 22
Dabro, Marko 12–13, 17–18, 21–22, 27, 32, 53
Dabro, Sarah 95
Dabro, Vicky 72–76, 84, 89, 111
Dalmatinac, Yuraj 34
Dancer I (Dabro work) 107
Dancer II (Dabro work) 2, 172–76
David, Michelangelo sculpture 43
De Chirico, Georgio 28
De Gruen, Geoffrey 94
Deakin High School 76
Degas, Edgar 28
Del Mar, Lola 63
Della Francesca, Piero 44–45
Desert landscapes 69
Development of a Bottle in Space 127
Diagonal Direction (Dabro work) 3, 92–93
Dickens, Charles 27
Diocletian 41
Diocletian's palace 41
Donatello 106
donkeys 13, 15
Drniš 10, 18
Duccio 132
Durer, Albrecht 195
Džamonja, Dušan 39–50

Edmond, Martin 3–4
Exhibition, Dabro's first 67–69

Fascists 11–12
Female nude 3, 7–8, 18, 24, 139–41
Figurative sculpture 2, 55, 64–65
Flight (Dabro work) 184–85
Florence 1, 43
Freud, Sigmund 4

Gardens, Japanese 176–77
Gascoigne, Rosalie 69, 70
Genesis (Dabro work) 2, 184–85
Giacometti 131
Giotto 16
Gleeson, James 77
Gleghorn, Tom 68
Gorky, Arshile 43
Gormley, Anthony 80
Grgur Ninsky (St Gregory of Nin) 37–39
Grishin, Sasha 94–95, 128, 192
Gropius, Walter 135–36
Guggenheim, Peggy 43
Gynaecologist (Dabro work) 92

hands, in Dabro sculptures 95–96, 157
Hannaford, Robert 71
Hawke, Robert 82, 115, 123
Hayes, Ed 130–34, 139, 141–44, 193
Haynes, Peter 92, 100
Hepworth, Barbara 5
Her Majesty Queen Elizabeth II, 115, 121–22
Herel, Peter 134
Hermann Noack Foundry, Berlin 112
Hope, Alec 64
Hughes, Robert 63
Humanscape VIII (Dabro work) 78

Ikibana 176
Introspection (Dabro work) 100, 165–70
Ironside, Virginia 87–88

John Molony (Dabro Work) 145

Kandinski, Wassily 28
Kennedy, Brian 3, 175
King and Queen (Dabro work) 72
Klee, Paul 28
Klippel, Robert 77, 80
Knin 16
Komon, Rudy 98
Kršinić, Franjo 50
Kuba, Zlatika 50
Kulaks 22, 39, 52
Kyoto 176

Index

La Perouse (Dabro work) 145–46, 149
Lačina 9, 15
Laumen, Louis 136
Luca, Evey and Max (Dabro work) 195
Lumb, Frank 76
Lyneham, Paul 81

Madigan Rosemary 8, 71, 80
Magna Carta (Dabro work) 27, 83–85
Mahood, Marguerite 70
Maillol, Aristide 54
male gaze 100–101
Maloney, Father 85–87
Malouf, David 100
Marx, Karl 1, 27, 58, 187
Mestrovič, Auguste 7, 36–38, 41–43
Michelangelo 1–2, 8, 29, 41–46, 87, 95, 170, 193, 197–98
models 101
Moje, Klaus 134, 135
Moore, Henry 42, 43
Moses, sculpture 29
Mother and child (Dabro work) 1, 5, 188
Muchina, Vera 128
Mulika 11
Mulvey, Laura 139
Murray, Les 69, 144
Murray-Harvey, Nigel 94
Muslims 18
Mussolini 11

Narikača (Dabro work) 55
Naval Memorial, (Dabro work), 8, 123, *passim*, 165
Niall, Brenda 63
Nikoleski, Vlasa 111
Non-finito technique 100
Now You See Now You Don't (Dabro work) 100

Observing the Masses (Dabro work) 86
Olsen, John 69
Onus, Lin 6

Partisans, Croatian 10, 12–16
Pérez Firmat, Gustavo 165
Pialligo 116

Pietá, Bandini 8
Pollock, Jackson 112
Polykleitis 29

Queanbeyan 66

Radovan 7, 30
Raft of the Medusa 127
Rauschenberg, Robert 64
Reclining Figure (Dabro work) 142
Refugees, Croatian 90–91
Relief, sculptural technique 55
Renaissance, Italian 1, 2, 8, 26, 34, 58, 113
Renoir, Pierre Auguste 192
Resilience (Dabro work) 34, 161–65
The Return of Homo Sapiens (Dabro work) 82
Robertson-Swan, Ron 137
Rodin, Auguste 2, 4, 29, 34, 36–37, 54, 78
Rothko, Mark 64

Salina (Solin) 25, 31
Saunders, Gill 139
Scarlett, Ken 63
School of Applied Art, Split 22, 27
Scribe (Dabro work) 98–100
Selembrije, Jakov 34
Sellbach, Udo, 115, 135, *passim*
Serbia 18
Sex 20
Šibernik 24
Simon, Marylin 192
Sir Robert Garran (Dabro work) 145, 147
Sir Robert Menzies (Dabro work) 145
Sir Winston Churchill (Dabro work) 145
Sisters (Dabro work) 7
Smart, Jeffrey 44–45
Smith, Bernard 65–66
Social Realism 2
Socialist education 35
Solander Gallery 97
Spilt 15, 25–29
St Augustine (Dabro work) 85–86
St Augustine, Farrer Church 85–87

216   *Index*

St Domitius (Cathedral) 29, 30
St Elija, Church 13, 21
Stalin 28
Standing Figure (Dabro work) 157–59
Stewart, Douglas 197–98
Stranks, Nick 138, 197
Stuart-Smith, Tony 72, 76
student life, Split 35–36
student life, Zagreb 36–37, 47–48, 50–54
studio (new) 193–97
Studio (old) 1
Survey Exhibition, 1968–1999 100
Sutherland, Bruce 135, 137, 139, 140, 143
Suzanne (Dabro work) 104–8
Suzanne in the Studio (Dabro work) 106
Swain, Alistair 177

Tennyson, Alfred 58
Terry Snow 166–67, 180
The Thinker 127
Thomas, Daniel 85
Titian 34
Tito 12
Turner, William 6

Unnamed Figure (Dabro work, new studio) 189
Unnamed Figure (Dabro work) 72
Ustase 10

Van Gogh, Vincent 28
Varchi, Benedetto 50
Vassilieff, Danila 63
Venice Bienale 43
vlaj (Croatian peasantry) 2, 26, 27, 159, 175
Voss, Vladimir 33

Wagner, Anne 5
Wallace-Crabbe, Robin 68
Whitlam, Gough 81–82
wolves 16, 20–21
Woodwood, Robert 128
Wordsworth, William 18, 20, 34
World War 2, 7, 10
Wright, Judith 154–57

Yeats, W. B. 175
Yugoslavia 19–22
Yugoslavia army 49, 54–56

Zakaravić, Bratko 116
Zola, Emile 27

Printed in the USA
CPSIA information can be obtained
at www.ICGtesting.com
JSHW012313031123
51440JS00001B/1